RETHINKING THEORY AND HISTO

CASS SERIES: COLD WAR HISTORY
Series Editor: Odd Arne Westad
ISSN: 1471-3829

In the new history of the Cold War that has been forming since 1989, many of the established truths about the international conflict that shaped the latter half of the twentieth century have come up for revision. The present series is an attempt to make available interpretations and materials that will help further the development of this new history, and it will concentrate in particular on publishing expositions of key historical issues and critical surveys of newly available sources.

RETHINKING THEORY AND HISTORY IN THE COLD WAR
The State, Military Power and Social Revolution

RICHARD SAULL

Richmond College, the American International University in London

With a foreword by Fred Halliday

FRANK CASS
LONDON • PORTLAND, OR

First published in 2001 in Great Britain by
FRANK CASS PUBLISHERS
Crown House, 47 Chase Side
Southgate, London N14 5BP

and in the United States of America by
FRANK CASS PUBLISHERS
c/o ISBS, 5824 N.E. Hassalo Street
Portland, Oregon, 97213-3644

Website: www.frankcass.com

British Library Cataloguing in Publication Data

Saull, Richard
Rethinking theory and history in the Cold War: the state,
military power and social revolution. – (Cass series. Cold
War history; no. 2)
1. Cold War   2. International relations
I. Title
327'.09045

ISBN 0-7146-5189-3 (cloth)
ISBN 0-7146-8226-8 (paper)
ISSN 1471-3829

Library of Congress Cataloging-in-Publication Data

Saull, Richard, 1969–
Rethinking theory and history in the Cold War: the state, military
power and social revolution / Richard Saull; with a foreword by Fred
Halliday.
    p. cm. – (Cass series–Cold War history, ISSN 1471-3829; 2)
Includes bibliographical references and index.
ISBN 0-7146-5189-3 (cloth)   0-7146-8226-8 (paper)
1. Cold war–Historiography. 2. United States–Foreign
relations–Soviet Union. 3. Soviet Union–Foreign relations–United
States. 4. World politics–1945–   5. Cold war–Social
aspects–United States. 6. Cold war–Social aspects–Soviet Union. 7.
Military history, Modern–20th century.   I. Title. II. Series.
  D849 .S2355 2001
  327.73047'09'045–dc21

                                                        2001028287

Typeset in 10.5/12pt Times New Roman by Vitaset, Paddock Wood, Kent
Printed in Great Britain by
MPG Books Ltd, Bodmin, Cornwall

Dedicated to the memory of my mother,
Jane Irene Saull (1942–87)

Contents

PART II: HISTORY

Foreword

Richard Saull's work is a vivid example of how, with the conclusion of the Cold War, analysis of this momentous four decades of international conflict becomes more challenging, even as it takes up issues that were debated during the Cold War itself. The end of the Cold War and the dissolution of the USSR in 1991, combined with the opening of large quantities of Soviet archives and publication of other materials, have provided a new, creative, vantage point from which to assess the Cold War in general, and its impact on particular regions of the world. Not only do we have a historical ending, and verdict, on that process, with the collapse of the Soviet bloc and all that was associated with it, but we also have a mass of new documentary, interview and memoir material from which to address the analysis of the 40-year conflict. Little wonder, perhaps, that, in the words of the American historian John Lewis Gaddis 'We Now Know' about the Cold War in a way that was not possible before.[1]

There are, however, important reasons for questioning such a claim if simply stated, not only because there are many things that we still do not know, but also because there are quite a few things that, prior to 1991, we already did know. In the first place, we hardly need reminding that historical distance does not resolve analytic questions: the very abundance of documentary material and the verdict of history do not, alone, resolve major historical issues, be they the origins of the First or Second World War or the causes of the Russian Revolution. There will, when every archive and memoir is available, be plenty of room for analytic and political dispute on the events of these four decades. Secondly, we should be careful about how much has, in fact, been released and about its historical balance. While the American and Western systems are comparatively more open in general, there is plenty that is kept secret on their side, and the process of disclosure this time around has been even more selective: masses of Soviet material have been released, but in a haphazard and often fragmented manner. Research on Soviet materials relating to Afghanistan, for example, has identified areas where a mass of, often trivial, documentation is available, while material on key periods and decisions is not.[2] Those involved in researching the Cold War based on Soviet materials have encountered many difficulties in this regard. Thirdly, we must beware the temptation to proclaim as 'new' that which was well argued, if on the basis of less

evidence, before 1991. The Cold War, including its Third World dimensions, was much debated while that conflict was still in progress, debate
classically falling into an 'orthodox' and a 'revisionist' camp. The shift of
perspective after 1991 has not resolved this issue one way or another: on
some specific questions, for example, the invasion of South Korea in
June 1950, evidence has confirmed an 'orthodox' position, but on others,
for example, the role of ideology in Soviet foreign policy-making, or the
degree of control exercised by Moscow over Third World allies, it has been
the 'revisionists' who would appear to have been vindicated. Those of us
who, in the 1970s and 1980s, argued for both these latter propositions, not
least in regard to the Middle East, would feel vindicated by some of what
has subsequently become more proven.[3]

These questions of analysis are, however, secondary to the much broader
issue of interpretation which any straightforward 'We Now Know' approach
may confuse. For beyond the history of what occurred, there are, as Saull
demonstrates, broader analytic questions that, in the aftermath of the Cold
War as during it, remain in dispute and which documentary materials
alone cannot resolve. Four of these are of particular interest.

What Was the Cold War 'About'?

The Cold War was a multi-dimensional conflict, in the Third World as elsewhere. It involved, most evidently, a strategic and military competition,
which took the form of the nuclear and conventional arms races, and of
competition for influence in spheres of control and, outside of Europe
where the boundaries were clear, in disputed areas. The Middle East, for
example, was certainly an arena for military competition, directly and
through rivals, and it prompted several of the nuclear crises of the Cold
War. But the Cold War had other dimensions: a competition over
economic models, between Western capitalism and Soviet planning, and
at the same time an ideological conflict, about the character of the state,
involving first colonialism and then the character of independent states.
For example, the influence of the USSR could be seen in the ways in which
states that otherwise differentiated themselves from the Soviet system
nonetheless replicated aspects of the Soviet state model (party structure in
the case of Arab Ba'thism in Syria and Iraq, five-year plans in the case of
Kuwait and Saudi Arabia, state social engineering in South Korea and
Singapore).

Conversely, the influence of the Western, particularly US, life-style was
felt even in countries that were aligned with the USSR. Personalities also
mattered in this most structuralist of conflicts: one of the classic early
accounts of the Cold War in the Middle East, Mohamed Heikal's *The
Sphinx and the Commissar* is as much about Nasser and Khrushchev as

about global strategic rivalry. Mao, Sukarno, Ho, Nehru and Castro are all figures of this epoch. Different histories will follow from different analysis of what was at stake in the Cold War, as will different analyses of the legacy of the Cold War.

Determinants of International Policy

One of the central issues in dispute in the Cold War, as in retrospect, is that of the factors determining the strategic policies of great powers, be they the USA, USSR, Britain, France or China. In the Cold War itself this was explained by the respective states in terms of their own justifications – security, the support of allies etc. Several of the most important statements of US strategic doctrine were formulated in regard to the Third World – Truman Doctrine, Eisenhower Doctrine, Kennedy Doctrine, Nixon Doctrine, Carter Doctrine and, with regard to Afghanistan, Reagan Doctrine. On the Soviet side, each of its major formulations of Third World policy, from the 'Non-Capitalist Road' to 'New Thinking', shaped subsequent policy. The colonial powers had their own doctrines, but these were less to do with the Cold War more with the extension of strategic (in the British case) and territorial (in the French case) interests. China's policy was determined as much by rivalry with the USSR as by anything else. 'Revisionist' analyses tended to draw attention to the role of corporate interests, on the US side, and to the inner weaknesses of ideology, on the Soviet side. Here the opening of archives has provided much new, relevant, material.[4]

Regional Actors and External Powers

During the Cold War it often appeared as if in the Third World the external powers were the dominant actors, if not the sole ones. The polemics of both sides suggested that those acting in disputed regions, such as the Middle East, East Asia or Africa were under the control of the external powers: hence the language of 'clients', 'agents', 'mercenaries', 'proxies' not to mention 'running dogs', 'lackeys' and 'puppets' of one side or the other. Interstate conflicts and wars within states were cast in Cold War terms. Yet this was, even at the time, far from being the case. Local states often acted independently, if as they sought to draw their strategic patrons into conflict on their side. External states repeatedly found themselves at odds with Third World allies. Two obvious examples where caution is in order: in the Arab–Israeli conflict, the relation of states and 'non-state' actors (the Zionist movement before 1948, the PLO from 1964) to strategic patrons was far less uni-dimensional than polemic suggested; Iran after

1979, but also in some measure before, was an autonomous actor. The same applies equally to communist allies of the USSR – China, Vietnam, North Korea, Cuba. Against this will be set the cases where external actors did, directly or more probably indirectly, shape events through coups. Yet here caution would still be in order; even where a clear case of external intervention is evident, as in Iran in 1953 or Chile in 1973, the success requires a domestic ally. It is precisely the lack of such an ally which has bedevilled attempts to oust Saddam Hussein since 1990. Where, for example, this leaves analysis of successive Turkish, African or Latin American coups, all blamed on the United States by their opponents at the time, is an open question.

Variant Histories: Political, Social Economic

The diversity of factors underlying the rivalry of external powers is replicated in the complexity of the Cold War *within* states and societies. Conventionally, the history of the Cold War is a history of states, be they global or regional: a focus on military, especially nuclear, rivalry reinforces this. But there is another history of Cold War that, as Saull argues, pays greater attention, in terms of causation and in terms of long-term impact, to the role of social forces. These would include mass movements of a nationalist, communist and Islamist kind, and also the ways in which the Cold War shaped, but was also shaped by, movements of class structure, of ideology and of revolutionary upheaval within states. In the Middle East, Latin America and East Asia, the role of these forces tended to be underplayed during the Cold War, not least because each was presented by its opponents as under the control of external powers. But the briefest of analysis of the Third World during the Cold War can identify a contrary perspective, moments at which it was upheaval within society that led to change. The Cold War was as much a process of social revolution as it was of nuclear rivalry and crisis. Equally it was the development of class and attitude that shaped the longer-run impact of the Cold War, be it in the consolidation of new statist elites or shifts in ideology from secular to more religious ideologies within the Middle East, or the long-run erosion of confidence among the Soviet elite. A study of this, for this region or any other, would involve looking at the Cold War from below, and from the point of view of state formation, class structure and political culture. The social history of the Cold War invites further attention. It would include a discussion of ideology and political vocabulary, as well as a study of literature.

Wide-ranging as discussion of these issues was before the end of the Cold War, it is now in the aftermath that a more extensive discussion becomes possible. If Marxism was mistaken in the specific way it sought to place the Cold War in its socioeconomic context, its insistence on the socioeconomic dimension retains its central validity. Richard Saull's analysis is a rebuttal to any simple reduction of the Cold War to its military or strategic dimensions, even as it opens up the debate on how the political, ideological and social dimensions of the conflict can be integrated with them.

Fred Halliday
London School of Economics
January 2001

NOTES

1 John Lewis Gaddis, *We Now Know: Rethinking Cold War History* (Oxford: Clarendon Press, 1997).
2 Fred Halliday, 'From "Second Mongolia" to "Bleeding Wound": Soviet Decision Making in Afghanistan', *Review of International Studies* (October 1999).
3 Fred Halliday, *Soviet Policy in the Age of Crisis* (Washington: IPS, 1979), reissued as *Threat from the East?* (London: Penguin, 1981).
4 The work of the historian John Kent has, for the British dimension, showed how important strategic colonial interests were, as distinct from Cold War concerns. John Kent, *British Imperial Strategy and the Origins of the Cold War 1944–49* (Leicester: Leicester University Press, 1993); 'Informal Empire and the Defence of the Middle East', in Roy Bridges (ed.), *Imperialism, Decolonization and Africa* (London: Macmillan, 2000).

Series Editor's Preface

Over the past half century, historians and political scientists have developed a long and honourable tradition of speaking past each other in their respective studies of the Cold War. For most historians, the Cold War conflict was about crises and coups, presidents and dictators, strategies and weapons. For most International Relations (IR) specialists, it was about systems, alliances, power and deterrence. Historians, with a few exceptions, tended to deal with the specific; IR people, however, wanted to see the general and comparative. Even when practitioners from the two disciplines reached roughly the same conclusions, tradition prevented them from reaching out across the professional divide and embracing.

The new history of the Cold War has begun to change this pattern, although only gradually and tentatively. The massive amounts of new evidence available from both sides of the former East–West divide have forced both historians and IR specialists to simultaneously re-evaluate their previous conclusions, and in that process they have sometimes sought help from each other. In a few cases they have even sought further afield, and helped stimulate interactions with sociologists and anthropologists on Cold War-related topics. Some of the necessary re-examination of the epoch can now be said – in terms of disciplines – to be transcending those often artificial boundaries that the Cold War concepts of social science imposed. The first volume in this series is an indication of the stirrings created through processes of intellectual cross-fertilization.

The second volume – Richard Saull's present book – is very much inspired by these processes. The intention of the volume is to submit a critique of the Realist-dominated IR approach to Cold War studies, which stipulates that the Cold War was primarily about power and 'national interests' and thereby a continuation – in conceptual terms – of international politics as constituted in Europe since the mid-seventeenth century. On the contrary, Saull claims, the Cold War should be seen as a unique and specific period defined primarily by the conflict between two opposing social systems that emerged with the creation of the Soviet Union in 1917. It is this historical and sociological framework that Saull insists that his IR colleagues take seriously, because if they do not, he asserts, their theories will always lack concrete explanatory power.

This challenge from a Marxist-inspired historical sociology is something from which Cold War studies stands to benefit. In terms of explanations, one of the main weaknesses of the field – across disciplines – has been an inability to link ideologies and state interests, political rivalries and strategic conflict, domestic systems and international roles. What Saull offers here is an attempt to define the Cold War through establishing the domestic social constitutions of the main protagonists and how these, in different ways, contributed to the militarization and interventionism that characterized the epoch. While acknowledging that there is much we do not know and do not understand about the framework of the conflict, especially at the international level, Saull wants to push the field in the direction of asking broader questions, in the hope of getting more comprehensive answers.

Saull's approach is particularly useful for understanding the internationalization and the gradual transformation of the Cold War conflict. Both, according to Saull, have their roots in the social changes that took place globally and within the superpowers themselves in the latter half of the twentieth century. Externally, the challenge came primarily from revolutionary sociopolitical shifts outside Europe. Domestically, it came from the failure of the Soviet state, mainly because of its authoritarianism, to prevent a re-privatization of the economy and other forms of social interaction.

At the core of Saull's analysis is a willingness to address the key questions of social and ideological *differences* between the contending states during the Cold War. This approach must be welcomed whether one agrees with his conclusions or not. There has so far been surprisingly few overall attempts at constituting these differences as the conflict's chief *raison d'être*, and it is to be hoped that Saull's contribution will stimulate a new preoccupation with such issues within IR, international history and beyond.

Odd Arne Westad
London School of Economics

Acknowledgements

This work was originally submitted as a PhD thesis in the Department of International Relations at the London School of Economics. I would like to record my gratitude for the financial support that I received during the completion of my PhD, in particular, my thanks to the LSE's STICERD scholarship, without which I would not have been able to complete my research. I owe a great debt of thanks to the department, both staff and fellow students, for providing an intellectual environment that was both stimulating and supportive. In particular I would like to thank those students and staff who participated in the 'Modernity and International Relations' research seminar and the 'Historical Materialism and International Relations' research seminar. It was in these forums where many of the issues and ideas that came to form the basis of this book were discussed. I would also like to thank my doctoral examiners, Justin Rosenberg and Mick Cox, for the critical comments and suggestions that they made during the *viva*. My greatest debt of thanks, however, must go to my supervisor, Fred Halliday, who has not only been a unique figure within British International Relations, challenging dominant orthodoxies, but was also an excellent source of advice and guidance during the writing of the thesis. It goes without saying that none of the above is responsible for the text, and any errors in the book are mine alone.

1

Introduction: What Was the Cold War?

The Cold War as a focus of intellectual enquiry has occupied a rather unusual position within the discipline of International Relations (IR). Although recognized as a distinct period in world history,[1] its theorization, at least in terms of traditional theories, did not recognize it as such. The acceptance of the transformation of world politics that the Second World War and its end produced did not manifest itself in the form of a reconstitution of traditional IR theory. Rather, IR theory sought to downplay the uniqueness of the Cold War, instead subsuming it within a broader history of great power conflict, or limiting it to a discussion of strategic (nuclear) rivalry.

Moreover, even with the intellectual and political excitement sparked by the collapse of the Soviet bloc after 1989, most of the debates surrounding the end of the Cold War did not seek to redraw the theoretical assumptions that had guided the study of the Cold War.[2] This anomaly – the lack of a general theoretical and historical recognition of the Cold War – is the principal concern of this book. The guiding assumption is that reflection on the Cold War within the discipline of IR, particularly after the end of the Cold War, has not fully addressed its historical uniqueness and sociological specificity. The central claim, then, to be outlined in the following chapters is that the Cold War reflected a unique period in the history of international relations that began in 1917 with the emergence of the Soviet Union, a state born of social revolution and constituted by a new form of politics and international relations.

The basic challenge that this book puts forward is founded on a number of issues that tend to characterize existing understandings of the Cold War. The first of these relates to the temporal definition of the Cold War, in particular, the generalization that it began after the Second World War, indeed, that it was a product of the war. This approach tends to overlook any linkage between the Soviet Union of 1917–45 and the USSR after 1945. The problem with this is that not only does it exaggerate the significance of the postwar conjuncture, but it also ignores any continuity in Soviet *and* American international relations, that became *more manifest* after 1945. While the changes produced by the Second World War were important, did they define the origins of the Cold War, or were they a repetition of the *nature* of the relations between the USSR and the major capitalist powers that had existed since 1917?

The orthodox temporal focus on the 1945–89 period also has a major inconsistency in that the end of the Cold War was marked, most fundamentally, by the dissolution of the Soviet bloc as a set of social and political relations. It was more than a series of strategic agreements, but a domestic as well as an international event for the Soviet bloc. What this highlights is that the orthodox temporal definition of the Cold War is founded on a core substantive understanding, one that relates to the external military–strategic preponderance of the superpowers after 1945. Yet, if the end of the Cold War was signified by the collapse of a social system, does not this weaken the traditional understanding of the origins of the Cold War that tends to ignore or downplay the significance of the domestic characteristics of its major protagonists?

The second feature found in the dominant tendencies of the IR literature on the Cold War is the distinction between the explanatory power of ideology and traditional state interest, particularly in the 'foreign policy' of the USSR. This continues to pervade discussions of the Cold War,[3] and although it illuminates the real tensions within the international relations of the superpowers, it does so at the expense of artificially isolating and abstracting one from the other.

This methodological framework has dominated the research programmes of IR, yet it rests on a dubious assumption that we can always separate ideology as a basis for political action from state interest. By treating ideas and interests as separate sources of explanation we end up simplifying them and overlooking their essential interconnectedness. Thus, the ideology of the USSR was realized within the structures and institutions of the Communist Party-state as much as the 'ideology' of liberal-democratic capitalism was 'actualized' within the social and political relations of American capitalism. The ideology of Marxism-Leninism was present within the structures of the Soviet Party-state; indeed, it was this fact that distinguished the Soviet Union from Western capitalist states. By seeking to identify whether it was ideology or interest that motivated one course of action over another, there is an inclination to assume that decisions can be made in a social and political vacuum rather than acknowledge the fact that ideology is *always* a factor in political action, and yet it cannot be autonomous or separate from the structures and agents within which it exists. To take the separation of ideology from state interest to its logical extreme would suggest that ideology explains everything or nothing, and that either state behaviour is always ideological or always based on its opposite, state 'interest'.

The third tendency within Cold War literature in many respects follows on from the previous point about the artificial separation of ideology and interest, in the inclination to view the Cold War through the prism of strategic-nuclear conflict, and either to ignore other forms of political conflict or to reduce them to issues of domestic politics that did not, ultimately, interfere with the strategic patterns of superpower behaviour. This predisposition is most clearly stated in the 'long peace' thesis, that states that the absence of war between the superpowers was the defining feature of the Cold War.

Such a perspective has been a subject of critical attack from Marxists in particular. I am in agreement with this critique, however; even within much of the Marxist literature on the Cold War there is a proclivity either to reduce the Cold War to the conflicts within American imperialism, thus marginalizing the importance of the Soviet Union to conflict in the Third World, or to assert that Soviet activity in world politics was largely a question of domestic political considerations. There is, then, a space in Cold War literature that goes beyond a focus on the superpower bilateral 'strategic' relationship, yet can explain wider international conflict without reducing it to responses to American imperialism and recognizes the fact that the Soviet Union was a major protagonist in world politics. Moreover, there is also the need to link the currency of military power, particularly nuclear weapons, with other forms of political action and conflict. In this sense, not only was strategic conflict related to other forms of conflict derived from social relations, but the sources of much of that conflict, that came to dominate the Cold War, were located within states.

This leads me to my fourth and final area of critical focus, exposed most visibly by the nature of the end of the Cold War, the linkages between domestic and international politics in the Cold War. The end of the Cold War, and the fact that it was brought about by the implosion of the sociopolitical system of the Soviet bloc, seems to suggest that there was a clear linkage between the external behaviour of the USSR and its internal social constitution. What this suggests – and this relates to all of the preceding points – is not only that the domestic nature of the Soviet Union was of crucial significance in the Cold War, but that because of its domestic nature it was affected by international developments in distinct ways different from those affecting other types of state. The conclusive impact the Cold War had on the USSR and the Soviet bloc that was different from the effect of the Cold War on the Western capitalist states was due then to the manner in which the USSR related to other states and the international system. What ultimately mattered was the domestic nature of the USSR, and how it was socially constituted.

The objective of this book is to outline an alternative understanding of the Cold War, one that focuses on how the social constitution of the major states involved in it was the determining factor for the outbreak, developments in, and end of the Cold War. The Cold War, then, was a product of how differently constituted states related to the international system, and, because of the way they were internally organized, this necessarily led to international conflict.

The main assumption that guides the argument that follows is that, rather than looking at the state as a separate and autonomous agent acting according to a generalized logic of behaviour, based on similar currencies of activity, we should see the state in more historical and sociological terms that can identify its historical specificity and its wider social relationships. Simply put, the argument of this book is one of historical sociology, and, in particular, one that draws on the Marxist tradition.[4] Therefore, terms such as 'state' and 'military power' convey something, but they need to be interrogated to illuminate their essential characteristics that reflect their social and historical uniqueness.

This book seeks to do this in three interrelated ways. First, by analyzing what we mean by the state and politics in the Cold War we can identify the defining features of states, based on their domestic social constitution, which determined how they related to the international system. Secondly, by examining how far the domestic politics of the major states involved in the Cold War were defined by coercive–militarized relations, we can see why the Cold War had the militarized character that it did, rather than seeing international military conflict as the outcome of the timeless operation of the balance of power. Thirdly, it seeks to identify the social processes that produced the changes and conflicts that provided the dynamic of the Cold War. Through this we should be able to see how and why the Cold War came to dominate world politics and go beyond the superpower bilateral relationship, and see the linkages between (revolutionary) domestic sociopolitical change and issues of strategic conflict.

The organization of the book reflects the three conceptual issues discussed here. Part I consists of Chapters 3, 4 and 5, which are devoted to the state in the Cold War, military power and strategic conflict and social revolution. This more general and theoretical discussion is followed by Part II, which will seek to 'concretize' the preceding discussion by focusing on the historical cases of superpower responses to the Cuban and Vietnamese revolutions. These revolutions are 'paradigmatic' of the Cold War in that they reflected the social challenges to the international capitalist order that derived from the conflicts that were a consequence of the ways in which they were incorporated into the capitalist world market. In this sense they form part of a continuum with the Bolshevik Revolution of 1917, yet they are more important in that they provided the 'battlegrounds' of the shifting fronts of the Cold War as each superpower responded to revolutionary change, which provided a means of international expansion for the USSR and a threat to the international order of American power. Moreover, they reflected, in the relationship between domestic change and international relations, the shifting impact of the *political* currencies of political, economic and military power. Finally, the conclusion will summarize the argument and address how the theoretical argument outlined can explain the end of the Cold War.

Chapter 2 provides a brief survey of the literature on the Cold War of the main 'schools' of IR, which provides the critical foundations for the chapters that follow.

NOTES

1 Generally accepted as 1947–89, that is, from the Truman Doctrine to the collapse of the Soviet bloc, and also indicated by the acceptance into the IR lexicon of 'post-Cold War' studies in security and so forth.
2 A typical example is R. Ned Lebow and T. Risse-Kappen (eds), *International Relations Theory and the End of the Cold War* (New York: Columbia University Press, 1995).
3 Mark Kramer's otherwise excellent historical analysis of the Cold War in 'Ideology and the Cold War', *Review of International Studies*, 25, 4 (October 1999), pp. 539–76, continues to work within a conceptual framework that separates ideology from state interest, and seems to end up frustrating his general conclusions about the nature of the Cold War.
4 Thus I identify myself with a developing Marxist-inspired IR literature reflected in the work of J. Rosenberg, *The Empire of Civil Society: A Critique of the Realist Theory of International Relations* (London: Verso, 1994); S. Bromley, *Rethinking Middle East Politics: State Formation and Development* (Cambridge: Polity Press, 1994); F. Halliday, *Revolution and World Politics: The Rise and Fall of the Sixth Great Power* (London: Macmillan, 1999).

2

The Cold War and International Relations Theory

The aim of this chapter is to provide a survey of literature drawn from both theoretical and historical sources that have sought to provide IR with an understanding of the Cold War and, in particular, to point out what each theoretical tradition suggests is defining and most important about it. Through such a survey the foundations will be laid of the subsequent chapters, where the principal conceptual issues mentioned in the introduction will be interrogated and reconceptualized.

The survey has been organized into three broad theoretical traditions: Realism, Ideas-Based approaches or Pluralism, and Historical Materialism. With respect to Realism this chapter draws upon those scholars associated with 'historical' or 'power-politics' approaches, and in particular those who have engaged at both a theoretical and an empirical level with the Cold War. This needs to be emphasized because of the breadth of the Realist canon, and also because much Realist scholarship has *not* explicitly focused on the Cold War as a subject or period for investigation. Because of this neglect at the level of general Realist scholarship, the comments are confined to those diplomatic historians and theorists who have *explicitly* and *singularly* focused on the Cold War. This being the case, this literature survey will outline and criticize the main conceptual arguments provided by these scholars, which in Part I will be related to wider Realist positions.

The examination of Pluralist/Ideas-Based approaches addresses those scholars who have sought to locate the state within a wider context than Realism, based on ideas and norms. These scholars have questioned the utility of understanding the Cold War through conventional notions of power, and instead have stressed alternative, non-state, currencies of international relations.

The final conceptual grouping is distinguished by their focus on the domestic–international relationship as being determined primarily by the 'state–economy' relationship within the dominant states of the Cold War. These scholars, then, have directly engaged with Marxist categories such as capitalism and class, and in doing so have sought to understand the Cold War from a wider historical–social perspective.

Realism and the Cold War

The corpus of Realist scholarship that has analysed the Cold War, either directly or indirectly, is huge, and well beyond any exegesis in this section.[1] This being the case I will limit my analysis to those scholars who have sought to develop general Realist methodological and theoretical assumptions directly through studying the Cold War. In this endeavour I will address the work of George Kennan,[2] Henry Kissinger,[3] and John Lewis Gaddis.[4] This will obviously limit the scope of my project and the power of its critique. However, in many respects such a strategy exposes, arguably, the most important flaw in Realist analyses of the Cold War: that although Realism has sought to understand and offer a theory of the Cold War, the basic premise of its understanding is that the Cold War was *not* historically unique. The Cold War, rather, reflected in general terms the ongoing logic of inter-state conflict derived from the anarchical constitutive nature of the international system, and the 'power maximization' policies of states. What *does* matter for Realists was the form of that conflict, particularly its strategic-nuclear manifestation, and how the transformation of military power conditioned traditional inter-state relations.[5] This issue obviously provided a justification for a focus on the superpowers and the military currency of their competitive relationship,[6] but as a specific historical or conceptual category, the Cold War did not provoke a plethora of specialist texts devoted to its understanding. Instead the Cold War was either subsumed within a broader history of great power conflict, or limited to a discussion of strategic (nuclear) rivalry. If ideology or other non-state issues came to the surface they were discussed in terms of internal relations and sources of internal political legitimacy or rhetoric. The internal arena and its 'empirical clutter', then, did not, ultimately, matter.

The focus of Realist analysis of the Cold War is fixed on the political relations between states, principally the relationship between the United States and the Soviet Union, otherwise known as 'bipolarity', for Realists *the* regulating relationship of the Cold War and postwar world politics. This concern explains the Realist argument over the origins of the Cold War and the relationship, based upon military competition, between the superpowers and the blocs they led.[7] The Cold War began with the end of the Second World War, which produced a geopolitical situation of two states being militarily preponderant over their rivals. It was this that provided a starting point for the evolution of the Cold War that saw the dominance of the arms race and military competition as the main currency in the superpower relationship.

With a prioritizing of state-to-state relations between the superpowers as providing the conceptual framework through which to view the Cold War, Realists have focused on the foreign policies of the Soviet Union and the United States. Thus the postwar policy of 'Containment', which reflected a US concern to prevent any one state from being able to challenge its designs for the postwar international order, was the main prism through which to understand the United States. Similarly, the USSR also acted according to traditional conceptions of state interest,[8] with its anxiety over continental encirclement and fear of attack through Eastern Europe.[9] Thus, the differences between the superpowers were not derived from their domestic or ideological complexion, but rather from the different external challenges they faced to realize their foreign policy objectives. Although the different domestic political systems of each superpower were not ignored by Realists,[10] the fact that the United States was capitalist and the Soviet Union communist was not considered to be the reason for the development of conflict after 1945. After all, such differences had not been enough to produce conflict before 1945. Indeed, such internal differences had failed to prevent an alliance emerging between them in 1941–45.

The concepts that Realists have identified shed some light on our understanding of the Cold War. The focus on states, as the principal movers in the Cold War in its origins and development, is difficult to dispute. Even in terms of the end of the Cold War Realists have a point in emphasizing the central importance of the state. The transformation of Soviet foreign policy under Mikhail Gorbachev, especially the ditching of the Brezhnev Doctrine, provided one of the principal external stimuli to the internal changes in Eastern Europe in 1989. The emphasis on security and military competition is also important. Indeed, the role of military conflict – the 'ups and downs' most marked in official Soviet triumphalism in the apparent shift in the 'correlation of forces' during the 1970s – was extremely important in setting the international scene of later developments in the Cold War. Military competition and the economic cost of that competition and its consequences are pertinent to any understanding of the Cold War. Finally, the claim that one side won the Cold War needs to be taken seriously, even if it tends to be limited to Realist concerns with security and military power.[11]

However, these conceptual insights in themselves, though valuable, are rather one-sided and only provide a partial understanding of what Realism purports to explain. As Halliday has remarked, Kennan's nuanced and prescient understanding of the USSR as outlined in 'Sources of Soviet Conduct', that is *suggestive* of a more sociological grasp of the Cold War, is not realized in Kennan or in Realism's theory of the Cold War.[12] Although Kennan wanted to identify the *internal* sources of Stalin's actions in Eastern Europe, because these were not recognized as invoking a new and different *form* of international relations, his analysis has been unable to appreciate fully the relationship between the constitution of internal politics and foreign policy. Kennan argued that although the Soviet Union was a brutal dictatorship dominated by a 'messianic Bolshevism', in practice it was cautious and behaved like any other great power.[13] He did not see any particular expression of Soviet revolutionary internationalism in the actual conduct of Soviet foreign policy, rather great power opportunism. Indeed, ideology was primarily a domestic issue whereby the Soviet leadership manipulated a perceived external military threat to defend its repressive authoritarian domestic politics.

While Kennan was certainly right in identifying this aspect of Soviet ideology and the relationship between domestic and international, he was only partly right, because he fails to explore fully the nature of the Soviet *and* US politics, and instead concentrates solely on the state and military–political relations. Although Kennan advocated the successful 'expansion' of American values through force of example,[14] he did not fully distinguish the specific nature of the United States as a capitalist state and, in particular, the relationship between 'military containment' and the reproduction of a specific kind of internal and international politics. This was equally the case with the Soviet Union, where Kennan failed to recognize the distinctive form of military power *vis-à-vis* the United States. Kennan's conceptualization of the internal–ideological and international relationship fails to bridge the gap between the internal nature of the state and how this conditions the form of international relations. Although he recognizes internal differences he does not transplant these differences to different international relations, and in this sense remains trapped within the traditional Realist ontology of the state.

The issue of the relationship between the nature of domestic state–society relations and international relations is also to be found in Kennan's understanding of the end of the Cold War. In this case the end of the Cold War was not only about the end of the USSR's international challenge to American power, but was also paralleled by dramatic domestic sociopolitical transformation. The problem, then, for the Realist analyses of Kennan and others is how to explain this type of domestic–international change without resorting to issues of non-state sources of political change located in domestic politics to explain it. If the motivation behind Gorbachev's 'new thinking' was internally derived, then an explanation of the end of the Cold War would need to address the issue of how far domestic factors conditioned external behaviour rather than, as Realism tends to assert, that foreign policy is largely a product of external factors.[15]

The incompleteness of making the external relations of the state a focus for the Cold War relationship is matched by considering the impact of military power and military conflict separately from the broader concerns of each state and social system. Much has been made of this with the assertion that the Reagan arms build-up of the early 1980s had the effect of forcing Gorbachev to redefine radically Soviet foreign policy, thus ending the Cold War.[16] However, if this argument is taken seriously we still need to discuss why military competition (and not war) had the impact it did, and the *way* it affected the USSR and not the United States. Surely this is an issue of the constitution of the domestic state–society relationship, whereby the domestic nature of the Soviet state ensured that it would be much more sensitive to external military pressures than the United States because of the way it was internally organized and the role of military power (its material production and function) in domestic politics. Thus, military competition was not only an international issue, but also had a profound impact on the nature of each side's domestic politics. This was apparent more in the USSR than in the United States, which suggests that the arms race and military competition need to be located in domestic politics as much as in international politics, rather than in only the latter, as Realists tend to argue.

Even when Realists recognize the role of ideology in the Cold War, as Gaddis has done with respect to explaining Stalin's policy toward Eastern Europe after 1945,[17] although this might seem a welcome revelation for a Realist thinker, it does not overcome the continued methodological framework that is based on separating what are seen as distinct conceptual and empirical categories. Rather than seeing how ideology helps to reproduce a specific kind of politics, tangled up with other domestic social structures and relations, which in turn are directly related to the nature of political rule and the form of the state, Gaddis and Kennan end up decoupling ideology, seeing it as a factor that may or may not affect foreign policy. Ideology is treated as something autonomous that can be 'picked off the explanatory shelf' at certain conjunctures alongside national interest. Thus, in this respect, although Gaddis's recognition is important, it does not help us to understand more clearly the complex nature of the Soviet Union and its international relations, because the Soviet Union's *use* of ideology showed it in many respects to be similar to other states (including the United States) in the way in which they were 'ideological'.

Realist theories of the Cold War have argued that the agents of the Cold War were states, the currency of relations was military–strategic, and the goal(s) were power-maximization. They have, then, tended to prioritize formal state-to-state relations, particularly in terms of military competition and conflict. Such an approach highlights a significant aspect of the Cold War. However, Realists have also largely avoided a discussion of the way in which each superpower was domestically constituted and the impact of this on the international political–military conflict, which would show how security concerns and the expansion of international power may be realized in different ways derived from the domestic organization of politics in the state–society relationship. Thus, rather than, as Realists suggest, seeing the Cold War as a repetition of the cycle of strategic conflict based on the 'geopolitically determined' anarchic structure of the international system, we should see the international relations of the Cold War as *contingent* on the domestic nature of each state in question. In particular, what conditions the projection of international power, whether in a military or economic form, will not only depend on the geopolitical context but also on the domestic constitution of that power, and whether it rests on anything other than coercive–military power.

Pluralist and Ideas-Based Approaches to the Cold War

With the end of the Cold War Pluralist approaches have provided the main theoretical challenges to Realist and conservative arguments that US military dominance in the form of the Reagan arms build-up won the Cold War, or accelerated Soviet decline.[18] There are a number of themes that are associated with this approach to the Cold War, which include: a concern to move beyond discussion of the permanence of the military antagonism between the superpowers and focus on the changing nature of that relationship; the need to address developments in world politics, most notably the emergence of former colonies as independent sovereign states that provided a rival political agenda removed from superpower conflict; a focus on alternative forms of power and influence in international relations, most notably the growth of rival ('multipolar') sources of economic power that challenged American and Soviet postwar dominance; the role of misperception in determining foreign policy responses of each superpower;[19] and locating importance in internal political change based around shifting political coalitions and processes, and its consequent impact on the utility of the Cold War for each side.

Pluralist and Ideas-Based approaches see the Cold War as evolving out of the dynamic of domestic political change that was not reducible to the superpowers. Their proponents emphasize that, especially after the death of Stalin in 1952, the Cold War relationship itself, as much as what they consider to be wider global developments, began to change. World politics was not reducible to the Cold War, rather it developed separately from the broader changes of world politics characterized by decolonization and the growth of an international capitalist economy.[20] These developments were not directly related to the 'Cold War System' as some Pluralists termed the superpower relationship, and ended up threatening the dominance of this relationship and the political actors involved. Indeed, by the 1960s the Cold War was becoming a source of weakness for the superpowers, with both confronting difficulties in their respective economies and political systems. This was partially recognized by both sets of elites with the détente of the early 1970s, a recognition that marked a watershed in superpower relations with a recognition of areas of mutual interest that did not conform to the ideological 'straitjacket' of each side's world view. However, it was to take the *rapprochement* guided by Gorbachev and by Reagan/Bush that formalized a recognition of a relationship based on a degree of interdependence.[21]

There are a number of issues that emerge from such an understanding of the history of the Cold War, which relate to Pluralist conceptions of the Cold War. In the appreciation above, the Cold War relationship between the superpowers and their 'blocs' is based upon power maximization or dominance within each respective sphere of influence. Yet within Pluralist approaches to world politics in general there is a consideration of social–economic change, the emergence of other sources of economic power and multipolarity that are removed and separate from developments within the Cold War relationship. However, the marginalizing of the social–economic determinants of the Cold War is curious when they appear to be central to the understanding of developments in world politics. By narrowly concentrating on political power as a way of understanding the Cold War, especially the removal of the Cold War from developments in world politics, Pluralists end up simplifying the Cold War and misreading developments in world politics, particularly in the Third World. In failing to point out the link between US involvement in world politics and the triumph of capitalism, Pluralist theory is guilty of a major oversight. It recognizes that international capitalism proved to be more successful in terms of adoption in the Third World, but does not tell us why it was, and why the state-centred model failed:

> The ideological attraction of the Soviet system, which gained some prestige as a result of the Second World War and some adherents among newly independent Third World countries, waned over the period. By contrast, Western culture and economic methods proved eminently exportable and adaptable to local conditions in many parts of the world.[22]

Although correct in recognizing the long-term failure of the 'Soviet model' in the Third World, this statement does not in itself adequately explain why, or the reasons for the 'success' of capitalism. Neither of these outcomes was inevitable. It was the actions of states, nations and classes that produced them, and the policies and actions of the United States and the Soviet Union were prominent. To talk about the successful expansion and consolidation of capitalist social relations in the Third World without addressing the role of American and Soviet power is a major oversight. Consequently, Pluralist theory fails to draw the strands together that link the Cold War conflict with a broader world politics. Indeed, if one looks more closely at the history of the Cold War it seems quite evident that the dynamic and momentum of the Cold War was propelled by crises primarily in the Third World derived from socioeconomic change and the defining influence of the superpowers on many of these developments.

Pluralist theory does, however, go beyond Realism in its understanding of the Cold War through its theory of change, a theory that provides an explanation for the evolution of Cold War politics between the super-powers. This is based upon an analysis of the relationship between developments in domestic politics and the orientation of foreign policy. In identifying what they label internal *constitutive* norms and values of political systems Pluralists have sought to offer a distinct appreciation of the Cold War and its end. This concentration on internal political values *contra* the Realist fixation with the 'security dilemma' is used to explain the changes initiated by Gorbachev, which led to a US–Soviet under-standing that occurred in a security environment that had not radically altered. Capabilities remained the same, but the norms and rationale that dictated the logic of these capabilities had shifted.[23]

Pluralist and Ideas-Based theories, by looking at the security relation-ship, principally the end of the 'bipolar' security system in Europe established by two mutually hostile security blocs, seek to highlight the problem for Realists of putting forward the impact of external (Western) pressure as a device that can explain Gorbachev's change in foreign policy orientation and domestic change. For example, external change accom-panied internal political changes, and with the failure of the August 1991 coup and the subsequent outlawing of the Communist Party of the Soviet Union (CPSU), foreign policy changes took on a qualitatively new orientation. That is, only after *internal* change in the norms and values that determined political outlook[24] did Gorbachev and the elite decide to remove the structural power position of the Communist Party from Soviet society.[25] For Pluralists it was not the external pressure of one side and the capitulation of the other that *caused* the changes of 1987 onwards; change was mutual – it occurred in both Moscow and Washington – and this explains the peculiar end to the Cold War. It was a recognition of the mutual interests in the avoidance of war, and the need to seek unilateral advantage and escape from the conditioning of either side's postwar national security policies that allowed for the accommodation manifest in the events after 1989:

> because the US and the Soviet Union repudiated the notion of IR as a self-help system and changed the rules by which they operated, they transformed their relationship and, by extension, the character of the international system.[26]

The underlying ontological premise of such an analysis and under-standing is that the Cold War was about the separation of the Soviet bloc through Stalinism based on a different set of constitutive political norms which determined international behaviour. Whereas American invitations to the Soviet Union and the countries of Eastern Europe were spurned and used as an ideological device after 1945, under Gorbachev, because of the crisis of political legitimacy of communist regimes, American offers of membership of multilateral institutions and of economic and financial assistance were welcomed in the late 1980s.[27] The Cold War began and could only continue with the reproduction of different internal political norms represented by Stalinism and American liberalism after the Second World War. It was Gorbachev's initiatives in the 1980s that transformed the relations within and between the blocs and American responsiveness that ended the Cold War.[28]

With the 'mellowing' of superpower relations manifested in détente, the changes from 1989 onwards are seen as part of an historical continuum, which had been blocked by Soviet actions in 1956 in Hungary and 1968 in Czechoslovakia. The changes derived from the political legitimation crisis of communism, which was evident with developments in civil society in Eastern Europe epitomized by the growth of Solidarnosč and Charter '77. These developments saw a relaxation of domestic politics and the end of the Brezhnev Doctrine that fundamentally altered the relations within each socialist state, and was to alter the relations within the bloc formations, especially the Warsaw Pact. Once this was evident the West encouraged reform and supported Gorbachev, and in doing so the postwar political and security divide in Europe was overcome.[29]

We can see that what were the central features of the Cold War for these theorists amounted to the domestic political constitutive norms and values of each bloc, and the role of individual political actors in dealing with the structural–security constraints of the Cold War. The actions of the West, containment, had a role in initiating the Cold War, but the actions of the West, indeed, what the West was, also helped to create the environment that allowed for Gorbachev's reforms.[30]

Pluralist and ideas-based analyses provide a rich source of explanation for Gorbachev's 'New Thinking' in Soviet foreign policy, but it is far too narrow in locating the source of change, what that change meant and the actors involved to give us a full theory of the Cold War, and thus, adequately explain its end. The change in formal political norms is only half the story, and with post-Cold War developments it is evident that socioeconomic transformation is as much a product and cause of the events of 1989 and after as the spread of liberal democracy. In this sense, the end of the Cold War was not a compromise between East and West, nor a quid pro quo to establish a mutual understanding, but the collapse of one sociopolitical system that needed coercive–military power to maintain itself and its replacement by another – liberal-democratic capitalism – that did not. That collapse, moreover, was not just a consequence of decisions taken by two sets of political elites, but was also consequent on a mass mobilization and 'revolutionary' popular protest that were not controlled, initially, by elites. Finally, the events of the late 1980s need to be seen in the context of the failure of the global revolutionary alternative to capitalism and how that failure was influenced by the successful military containment of the USSR and other revolutionary states by the West. The success of the West lay not only at the level of human rights and democracy, but also in the use of force and military power in Europe and the Third World that served to put a very high and dangerous price on Soviet attempts at international expansion.

Historical Materialist Approaches to the Cold War

Scholarship from within the Marxist tradition has provided a rich and varied analysis of the Cold War. What has distinguished these scholars from their intellectual peers has been their attempt to transcend the ontological status of the state, and in a number of different ways examine the social *totality* that encompasses the political in the fabric of a particular set of social relations. This assumption provides one of the most important conceptual differences from traditional IR, and regarding the Cold War it suggests that it was about something more than great power conflict or the socialization of a revolutionary state by 'political learning'. It suggests that the Cold War was, in one form or another, a form of *class conflict*, and in identifying class and social conflict as being constitutive features of the Cold War, Marxist-informed theories provide a conceptual break by locating the axis of postwar world history in the state–society relationship.

Broadly speaking, Marxist-informed theory locates social conflict either *within*[31] the social space of each social system that contested the Cold War – liberal democratic capitalism and communist-revolutionary states – or actually *between*[32] the two social systems. In the case of the former the Cold War was seen as an external manifestation of the class contradictions and conflict within each bloc. In other words the Cold War was a form of externalized class conflict whereby international relations or the Cold War was used to legitimize the internal forms of social organization.[33] In the case of the latter, the focus on the internal was inverted (though not ignored), and instead sought to address what was seen as genuine social conflict at the international level. Capitalism had its own internal contradictions, as significant as some of the internal conflicts within the socialist bloc. Nevertheless there were two distinct social systems, which had little in common and, indeed, were different and antagonistic. The Cold War was the expression of that social conflict waged globally between different social forms that ultimately sought to represent different classes.[34]

With respect to Soviet theory,[35] the internal dynamic that determined Soviet international relations during the Cold War was the 'transition to socialism' under the guidance of the CPSU. The internal goals of material-productive development conditioned the notion of 'peaceful coexistence' and also détente, particularly when such relations facilitated Soviet material development objectives. International relations were also determined by the theory of capitalist crisis[36] and the expectation of long-term capitalist

economic decline. Soviet conceptualization reflected the outcome of officially sanctioned debates within the Party-state, with conceptual development directly tied to political developments in the Cold War. Because of
the lack of a fully self-reflective critical stance within Soviet theory,
although one can find a number of useful concepts, for example the notion
of the 'correlation of forces' to encompass something wider than the
military-based 'balance of power', it is difficult to disentangle theory from
official Soviet positions. Thus, Soviet approaches will not be addressed
directly in this chapter or the book as a whole, but rather indirectly through
the analysis of Soviet policy itself, which, arguably, provides the best focus
for critical attention on Soviet theory.

What follows is an overview of the conceptual issues that a number of
(Western) Marxist-informed approaches use to understand the Cold War.
One conceptual issue that Historical Materialism raises which has been
identified with the work of Michael Cox concerns the nature and development of international capitalism with respect to the postwar political and
economic settlement under American hegemony, and the role the Soviet
Union played in this development. According to Cox, the end of the
Second World War provided particularly favourable circumstances for the
imposition of an American-dominated international capitalist order with
American political and material dominance combined with the *appearance*
of a Soviet threat. Thus, instead of challenging capitalism, as it did in 1917,
the Soviet Union actually facilitated its reinvigoration and dominance in
the postwar era.[37]

The Cold War, then, was not a genuine international conflict between
the United States and the Soviet Union, but primarily a relationship that
facilitated each side in its attempts to realize its goals within its own sphere
of influence; for the United States, this was dominance of the postwar
capitalist order and for the USSR the internal security of the rule of the
CPSU. The presence of the other, particularly its appearance as a political–
military threat, served to provide an external object to justify internal
political dominance within each bloc: for the USSR the threat to Eastern
Europe of a Germany rearmed by the United States, and for the United
States the revolutionary–military threat to Western Europe and elsewhere
posed by the USSR. Thus, the Cold War served to provide the main
ideological tool, if not interdependence, for the dominance of each ruling
class within each bloc of states – the Stalinist elite in the Soviet bloc and
the American capitalist class in the West. Therefore, the Cold War
displayed the appearance of external political and social conflict between
the United States and the Soviet Union, but its *essence* was the maintenance of the dominant position of each ruling class within each bloc. Thus,
it was concerned with stability and the maintenance of the postwar status
quo. The Cold War ended because neither the United States nor the USSR
could maintain the system as it had evolved from 1947. To end the Cold

War was as much a need for the American ruling class as it was for the Soviet one.[38]

Cox's account of the Cold War, then, focuses on conflict *within* each bloc over the appearance of external conflict *between* each bloc. The dynamic of this 'conflict' derived from the internal machinations and manipulations of each ruling class and their attempts to maintain domestic/bloc supremacy. Although he sees the internal class conflict as ultimately defining the Cold War this does not lead him to conclude that there was no hostility between the Soviet bloc and the West. As much as the USSR was hostile to capitalism, because Western capitalism threatened the survival of the Party–state ruling class, so the capitalist West was opposed to Soviet socialism because the capitalist West wanted to end the Soviet bloc's removal from the capitalist world economy and its support for radical–nationalist movements in the Third World.

Cox's theory is a sophisticated analysis of how the consequences of the Second World War came to determine the structure of postwar world politics. His conceptualization of the USSR is highly original in that it is critical of both Trotsky and some of his later 'followers' who claimed that the USSR was inherently anti-capitalist, despite being a coercive dictatorship,[39] but is also critical of those Marxists who claimed that the USSR was a 'state capitalist' social formation.[40] Rather, for Cox, the USSR was fundamentally a weak and unstable social form, prone in the long term to internal dissolution because it was not materially strong enough to compete with capitalism, and it was too repressive to offer a genuine political alternative.[41]

However, Cox's theory tends to reduce the foreign policy of the superpowers to domestic political concerns, and through this overstating of the influence of domestic politics, Cox does not fully discuss the international relevance of military power and, in particular, nuclear weapons, to the Cold War. The biggest problem with Cox's theory, however, is that it rests on an unstated assumption that tends to direct Cox's argument, but is an assumption that casts doubts on his theory of the Cold War as a theory of the Cold War and not a theory of something else. It relates to the need to provide a Marxist explanation as to why capitalism was able to restructure after 1945, and thus overcome the 'inherent' tendencies towards military conflict that the episodes of 1914–18 and 1939–45 had shown. The problem with this is that it tends to subsume the Cold War into the restructuring of capitalism after 1945 and the way in which the USSR came largely to facilitate this process rather than contest it. Because of this his theory of the Cold War could be considered to be a little one-sided. And because of this Cox cannot recognize the shift in the geopolitical power of the USSR and the expansion of the Soviet system after 1945 as anything other than a means to consolidate internally the Stalinist regime.

The tension in Cox's work, particularly with respect to his understanding of the USSR, is that if the USSR was *not* some kind of *deus ex machina* that helped to create a new kind of capitalist order between the major capitalist states, based on the removal of inter-state military conflict, then the orthodox Marxist position over the proclivity of capitalist competition to drive states towards war would be undermined. One could argue then that Cox's theory of the Cold War is also an attempt to defend the Marxist theory of capitalist imperialism, which ends up reducing the Cold War to a kind of functionalism.

The other major tension with respect to Cox's understanding of the USSR is his (and others') distinction between the early period of the Soviet state (up until the early 1920s) and the period after the rise of Stalin. In the early period the USSR is seen as a genuinely revolutionary state committed to international socialist revolution, while in the later period it was no longer so committed, and henceforth was preoccupied with internal political survival. If this is to be believed then the USSR was more of an international threat to capitalist states when, after 1917, the territory of the fledgling Soviet state was almost literally swallowed up by the invading German army and the punitive Treaty of Brest-Litovsk, than it was after 1945, when it had defeated its greatest military threat and made itself more viable through its presence in Eastern Europe. It is curious from an international perspective to argue that the USSR was more of an international threat to capitalism when it was dependent on developments in the internal politics and class conflict within other states. Materially, the USSR's support for international revolution was negligible to non-existent in the years of its supposedly greatest challenge to international capitalism. It was only after 1945 that the USSR could provide significant material support to revolutionary forces. Moreover, in terms of continuity between 1917 and 1945, the Red Army's incorporation of Mongolia, Georgia and elsewhere into the USSR in the early 1920s, and the attempt to spread revolution to Poland might be seen to reflect a continuity in Soviet international relations realized in the incorporation and 'revolutions from above' in Eastern Europe after 1945.

In many ways, Mary Kaldor adopts a similar position to that of Cox in her focus on the internal conflict within each bloc in the Cold War. *Imaginary War*, Kaldor's principal theoretical contribution to Cold War theory, reflects her concern with the social basis of state power in both East and West, and the impact of the militarization of state and society.[42] The Cold War, or 'the East–West conflict' as Kaldor more usually calls it, was an outcome of the Second World War in the sense that war, or its preparation and image production, was the central defining characteristic of the postwar political order until 1989. Kaldor describes this period or political order as 'imaginary war'.[43] She suggests, like Cox, that this atmosphere of tension and hostility was something exaggerated, and although she recognizes that there were tensions between the blocs: 'The elements of conflict, however, were outweighed by the complementarity of the two systems: both needed the other in order to regulate domestic and interstate relations within both systems.'[44]

The 'imaginary war', the formation of military alliances after the Second World War and the integration of states into political and economic formations, what she calls 'Stalinism' and 'Atlanticism',[45] were attempts made by each ruling class to legitimize the particular form of social relations and reproduction of state power within each bloc.[46] This being the case, Kaldor focuses on the contradictions and conflicts within each social formation. Like Cox she disputes the real threat that each posed to the other. Indeed, if there was a threat to each social system it derived from internal tendencies and contradictions. In the case of Stalinism: 'The West represented an appealing alternative to Stalinism, though the main challenge to Stalinism came from revisionist communists.'[47]

Similarly, Stalinism never threatened to undermine capitalism and liberal democracy in the West. It was the critics of the postwar compromise between capitalism and social democracy based on a militarized alliance that were the greatest threat to the social system in the West, most exemplified by peace campaigners and the radical left. Implicit in this analysis is something of a mutuality of ideas and hopes for the replacement of the ideology of 'imaginary war'. Kaldor's analysis is imbued with a sense of idealism which is missing from Cox's analysis, an idealism that is placed upon the radical critics of each social system as manifested in the peace campaigners and the outgrowth of a semi-autonomous 'civil society' from the 1970s, exemplified by the dissident movements of Charter '77 and Solidarnosč in the Soviet bloc.

What linked the social developments and contradictions within each bloc to produce the emergence of social forces that had a common thread, which was anti-militarist and pluralist–democratic with a faith in a radical civil society, were the contradictions in the production of state power within each bloc. The production of state power was determined, according to Kaldor, not from the autonomous realm of politics à la Realism, but from the organization of the economy. What characterized the postwar organization of society was an industrial base of mass production and organizational uniformity. 'Statism' is how Kaldor describes the postwar world, and to greater or lesser degrees the separate blocs that emerged after the war were examples of this phenomenon. Under Stalinism the society and state form came closest to a militarized formation and this ultimately served to undermine the legitimacy of the social system in the East. The Cold War, then, was a period of the struggle to reform an unreformable system, each bout of reform leading to economic and then political liberalization (the German Democratic Republic in 1953, Hungary and Poland in 1956, Czechoslovakia in 1968, and Poland throughout the 1970 and 1980s) which threatened the social basis of state power.[48]

Atlanticism was another manifestation of 'statism', but instead of a contradiction based on economic reform and political repression, the conflict was much more limited to the economic sphere, between private property and the market and the role of the state in the management of the capitalist economy. Until the early 1970s the compromise between social democracy and capitalism lasted, but by the early 1970s there was a crisis of the state in the West. The consensus that the postwar capitalist order had been constructed under American hegemony came apart. Inter-capitalist conflict ensued as the United States began to lose its political and economic dominance, a process marked by the debacle in Vietnam and the end of the convertibility of the US dollar.

Kaldor's assessment of the Cold War in many areas brings to the fore concepts and concerns that dominate Cox's work. However, we can discern something quite particular in the explanation of a theory of the Cold War from *The Imaginary War*. Cox's class analysis focuses on the political agency of the state as an articulation of class power; whereas Kaldor focuses on social movements within civil society, East and West, as having a significant determining effect on the conduct of the Cold War and on its end.[49] This location of political agency in the peace movement in the West and the dissident movements in the East, however, was a little naive. Although one should not doubt the role of social movements in the ending of the Cold War, the focus on the metamorphosis of an autonomous sphere is exaggerated. First of all it was state action, principally the actions of the USSR, that removed the external veto on internal change. It was only within this political framework that an opening appeared that allowed the possibility that social movements might have an impact. Although social movements may have accelerated change in the East they did not cause it, and, even in this regard, by the late 1980s the peace movements in the West had well passed their point of being able to mobilize mass public–political support. It was states who were the main actors, indeed, as carriers of particular social relations and class interests. This was most clearly highlighted by the absorption of the German Democratic Republic (GDR) into the Federal Republic of Germany in 1990, once popular protest was quickly dissipated following the removal of the obvious and visible vestiges of communist–authoritarian rule.[50] But there was only change in the East. There was no corresponding change in the West.

Because Kaldor's argument relies on an implied symmetry in the Cold War between the contradictions within each system, she overlooks the gross asymmetry that was manifest in the events after 1989. The Soviet bloc quickly disappeared as a distinct and different set of social relations and was replaced by a set of social relations *imported* from the West: American popular culture with western European or Christian Democratic capitalism. This leads on to another problem with her analysis of the Cold War conflict. As with Cox, it underplays the real social and political conflict between two different social systems. Rather than, as she suggests, the existence of a different social system providing the legitimacy for the imposition of another social system (capitalism), there was real social conflict between the two. We can identify another asymmetry here as Kaldor does,[51] but the asymmetry was not only political, it existed in the social-economic sphere too. By overemphasizing the Cold War in Europe, as does Cox, Kaldor fails to give due weight to other parts of the world where the social conflict was much more evenly based and where, throughout the postwar period, there were victories and defeats for both sides in their attempts to internationalize their social forms.

Whereas Realism can be accused of ceding too much explanatory power to the autonomy of the international system, the Marxist approaches of Cox and Kaldor could also be accused of 'reductionism' by confining the Cold War to a kind of 'strategic functionalism'. Thus both, particularly Kaldor, have to downplay the differences between East and West; this is notably so in the conceptualization of military power as a largely domestic issue rather than an international one as well. This leads them to neglect the geopolitical interstices of the Cold War by 'absorbing' the external antagonism into questions of domestic politics. By failing to take seriously the international strategic–military conflict between the USSR and the United States these analyses cannot offer logically consistent explanations for some of the most significant and dangerous crises of the Cold War, as in Vietnam and Cuba, where their argument emphasizing the domestic dynamic of the Cold War is stretched to breaking point.

Fred Halliday departs from the work of Cox and Kaldor by locating the source of the Cold War in the international rather than the domestic realm, through focusing on what he regards as the international social conflict mediated by the states of each bloc and social system. Halliday offers a theory of the Cold War that is founded on the interrelationship between what he considers to be the two most important constituent features of the postwar international order. The first concerns the transformation in the nature of military power that the emergence of nuclear weapons heralded. This transformation was politically significant in that it came to be concentrated in the war-making capacities of two states after 1945, the United States and the USSR. The structural consequences for international order of this military–technological transformation were paralleled, indeed, augmented by the second constitutive feature, the different and opposing social systems by which each superpower was internally constituted.[52] The Cold War, then, was constituted by two different and antagonistic social systems, regulated by the transformed nature of strategic–military power.

Halliday argues that the domestic social interests of each superpower were present in each one's international relations, in the sense of when and where they intervened in world politics and the type of political forces they supported. Indeed, because of the 'universalizing' and expansive nature of each system [53]

> the very social interests embodied in the leading capitalist and communist states are present, in a fluid and conflicting manner, in the Third World; the result is that the clash of the two blocs is constantly reanimated and sustained by developments in these other states. [54]

Here we have one of a number of differences from the other Marxist-engaged theories discussed. Halliday places much more emphasis on the involvement of the superpowers in the Third World, which, for him, provides the principal reason for the intensity of the Cold War and the collapse of détente in the late 1970s. [55] Whereas on the social, military and ideological fronts in the crucible of the Cold War – Europe – things remained relatively stable until the upheavals after 1989, it was in the peripheral areas of the old imperial hinterlands that became the Third World where the Cold War conflict was far from imagined, and was at times particularly ferocious.

However, Halliday qualifies this insistence on the impact of American capitalism and Soviet socialism on world politics by stressing the regulating logic of the arms race and strategic conflict. Thus Halliday suggests that the international, at least in the forms of the arms race and strategic conflict, was *autonomous* of the internal constitutive features of each social system. [56] Although there was continuous antagonism from 1917 in socioeconomic terms, this only became internationally significant and defining of world politics after 1945, when the USSR had augmented its strategic–military power by means of its victory over Nazi Germany and expansion into Eastern Europe. This, for Halliday, is ultimately defining of the Cold War as he distinguishes the periods of intense geopolitical conflict as the real Cold War from less concentrated conflict that characterized other periods. For example he distinguishes the first Cold War of 1946–53 from the period of 'oscillatory antagonism 1953–69', the phase of détente between 1969 and 1979, and the second Cold War of 1979–85. [57]

There is much of substance and explanatory power in Halliday's analysis of the Cold War. In taking seriously the social constituencies of each bloc and the interaction between state and society, Halliday accepts many of the ideological claims of each superpower. His analysis is informed by a broader appreciation of what constitutes international relations than that of most other theorists of the Cold War. The strength of Halliday's approach to the Cold War is that he attempts to link the domestic nature of the superpowers to their international relations. He also seeks to link not only military power but also the convulsions of social revolution as the dynamic of the Cold War, making a truly international conflict. However, Halliday's understanding of the Cold War rests, as with Cox and Kaldor, on the identification of the postwar conjuncture as the start of the Cold War, thus severing political continuity in the USSR's international relations from the 1917 Bolshevik Revolution. This temporal decoupling is equally problematic with respect to an understanding of social revolution, with the successful revolutions in China, Vietnam and Cuba all having roots that pre-dated the Second World War.

However, it is particularly with regard to Halliday's notion of 'cold wars' that his theory of the Cold War is most questionable, in that by distinguishing between different periods of postwar history, Halliday appears to distinguish between a logic of military conflict and ongoing social conflict. The focus on 1945 and the periods of Cold War rather than détente, suggests that what really was defining of the Cold War was military conflict. In this sense, then, the conflict was contingent on military power, particularly that of the USSR after 1945. Not only does this concede too much to Realism, but it also detaches social conflict and social relations from the constitution of military power. However, political and international political conflict should not be reduced to military conflict; rather, military conflict should be seen as a manifestation of political conflict at its most acute and intense, and not as something separable or unique from that conflict. By ceding an autonomy to military power Halliday ends up having to disconnect the politics of 'inter-systemic' conflict from inter-state conflict. Thus, his version of the Cold War comes to mean strategic conflict between the superpowers, but something which is distinct; indeed it tends to operate autonomously in terms of the socio-ideological conflict of the Cold War.

A second concern is that he assumes a symmetry in the content and universalizing dynamic of the superpowers which tends to overlook the quality and nature of the international relations in which each superpower was engaged. That is, because each was constituted differently domestically, each dynamic of expansion was bound to be different and the consequences of expansion were to have different effects. This was most clearly evident in that after 1945 both superpowers expanded their respective spheres of influence into different parts of Europe, and that the nature of each side's expansion with respect to local state autonomy, the role of military power in domestic political relations, and the organization of economies in western Europe and the Soviet bloc were fundamentally different. The core difference was that whereas the USSR needed direct coercive–military power to expand, determined by the direct political–military authorities of the Soviet state, the United States *could* expand its influence *without* direct military power, and involving a political agency not directly identified or controlled by the US state.

This survey of the literature of the theorization of the Cold War has discussed a number of sources, and different intellectual and political traditions. In doing so it has highlighted the principal conceptual tools each uses to understand the Cold War. From this survey we can see that the Cold War provides a major conceptual *problématique* for IR scholarship. This is particularly the case with respect to how internal constitutive values and organizational forms conditioned the international relations of each superpower, and how far we can distinguish the internal from the external as providing the source of explanation in the Cold War. However, with the literature survey in mind, we can say a number of things that relate to a definition or understanding about what the Cold War was. First, the crux of the Cold War was a conflict located in the interaction between state and society at the international level. That is, the social forces contained within states were the principal agents of the Cold War. It was in these conflictual relationships located within different forms of political and economic organization that an understanding of the Cold War is to be found. Secondly, the most important source of conflict within state–society relations manifested itself in social revolution. It was here that the most dangerous ruptures of this period in world history were to be found. The contest, involving the superpowers, but also forces within the Third World, saw the challenge of revolution against a particular internal *and* international social order, and attempts to maintain that order. Finally, the Cold War was characterized by the dominance of specific currencies of international relations between 'states' in the form of military power and military conflict. The role of nuclear weapons and the strategic arms race were of central importance in both international and internal relations, and this needs to be understood if we are to conceptualize the Cold War.

With the above in mind, we have a general conceptual understanding of the Cold War. This being the case the following three chapters will be based on theoretical discussions of the state as a form of political rule and what we mean by 'politics' in the Cold War; the role of military power and conflict as the principal currency of the international relations of the superpowers during the Cold War; and the role of social revolution as a central dynamic in the Cold War that engaged the superpowers. The theoretical analysis will be followed in the final two chapters where a more historically informed approach will attempt to substantiate some of the theoretical positions put forward.

NOTES

1 What could arguably be seen as the three most important postwar IR texts (particularly from a teaching point of view) – H. Morgenthau, *Politics Among Nations: The Struggle for Power and Peace* (New York: Alfred A. Knopf, 1948); H. Bull, *The Anarchical Society: A Study of Order in World Politics* (London: Macmillan, 1977); and K. Waltz, *Theory of International Politics* (Reading, MA: Addison-Wesley, 1979) – do not in fact analyse the Cold War in any great depth,

and manifestly do not problematize the Soviet Union and its form of international relations. See F. Halliday, *Rethinking International Relations* (Basingstoke: Macmillan, 1994), p. 172.

2 'X Article: The Sources of Soviet Conduct', *Foreign Affairs*, 25, 4 (July 1947), pp. 566–82; *Realities of American Foreign Policy* (London: Oxford University Press, 1954); *Russia and the West Under Lenin and Stalin* (Boston: Little, Brown, 1960); *Memoirs, 1950–63* (London: Hutchinson, 1972); *Soviet Foreign Policy, 1917–1941* (Westport, CT: Greenwood Press, 1978); *The Nuclear Delusion: Soviet–American Relations in the Atomic Age* (New York: Pantheon Books, 1982); *American Diplomacy* (Chicago: University of Chicago Press, 1984).

3 *Diplomacy* (New York: Simon & Schuster, 1994).

4 *Strategies of Containment: A Critical Appraisal of Postwar American National Security Policy* (New York: Oxford University Press, 1982); 'The Emerging Post-Revisionist Synthesis on the Origins of the Cold War', *Diplomatic History*, 7, 3 (summer 1983), pp. 171–90; *The Long Peace: Inquiries into the History of the Cold War* (New York: Oxford University Press, 1987); 'International Relations Theory and the End of the Cold War', *International Security*, 17, 3 (winter 1992), pp. 5–58; The *United States and the End of the Cold War: Implications, Reconsiderations, Provocations* (New York: Oxford University Press, 1992); 'The Cold War, the Long Peace, and the Future', in M. Hogan (ed.), *The End of the Cold War: Its Meaning and Implications* (Cambridge: Cambridge University Press, 1992), pp. 21–38; *We Now Know: Rethinking Cold War History* (Oxford: Clarendon Press, 1997).

5 See Kissinger, *Diplomacy*, pp. 774–801; Gaddis, *United States*, pp. 160–8.

6 This focus led Gaddis to describe the postwar era as the 'long peace' because of the absence of war between the superpowers, largely due to the influence of nuclear weapons. However, such an understanding tends to overlook the connection between nuclear weapons and bloody conflicts in the Third World as suggested by the impact of the Vietnam War and the Cuban missile crisis.

7 See Kissinger, *Diplomacy*, p. 424; Gaddis, 'Cold War', p. 27.

8 However, it is important to note that Gaddis's most recent work, *We Now Know*, based on access to recently released Soviet archives, agues that Soviet foreign policy, particularly under Stalin, was based on ideological conviction more than state interest.

9 For an historical survey of Soviet foreign policy that is imbued with Realist assumptions see Adam Ulam, *Expansion and Coexistence: Soviet Foreign Policy 1917–1973*, 2nd edn (New York: Holt, Rhinehart & Winston, 1974).

10 Kissinger, for example, suggests that the peculiarity of American history, in that the United States was born of an idealistic revolution against colonial tyranny, imbues or tarnishes the pursuit of a genuine national interest in US foreign policy and the conduct of the Cold War with an excessive idealism. Indeed, he argues that it was this idealism and desire to cast the rest of the world in its own image that led to the calamities of US foreign policy during the Cold War, as in Vietnam. Gaddis invokes this argument too, tying it to a notion of overstretch which Paul Kennedy, in his *The Rise and Fall of Great Powers: Economic Change and Military Conflict from 1500 to 2000* (London: Fontana, 1989), has discussed. Similarly, Realist theorists, most notably George Kennan, have stressed the dictatorial and repressive nature of the Soviet state as being reflected in its foreign policy, in its cautiousness and its need to have an external threat to justify its own internal legitimacy. See Kissinger, *Diplomacy*, pp. 17–18; Kennan, *American Diplomacy*, pp. 110–13; *Memoirs*, pp. 322, 340–1.

11 See J. Mearsheimer, 'Back to the Future: Instability in Europe after the Cold War', *International Security*, 15, 1 (summer 1990), pp. 5–56, for a Realist analysis of the consequences of the end of the Cold War.

12 Halliday, *Rethinking International Relations*, p. 177.
13 Indeed, ignoring the rhetoric, the USSR was a traditional great power. See Kennan, *American Diplomacy*, pp. 107–23; *Nuclear Delusion*, pp. 141–53.
14 *American Diplomacy*, pp. 119–28.
15 W. Wohlforth, 'Realism and the End of the Cold War', *International Security*, 19, 3 (winter 1994–95), pp. 91–129, has tried to offer a Realist explanation of the end of the Cold War by focusing on the impact of Gorbachev's domestic perceptions of power and external threat as the reason for the USSR's 'withdrawal' from the Cold War. However, such an approach, particularly with respect to the subjective nature of perception, surely serves more to question the basis of Realist arguments in the external conditioning of great power behaviour than to defend it.
16 Both Kissinger, *Diplomacy*, pp. 774–801, and Gaddis, 'Cold War', p. 30, and *United States*, pp. 160–80, suggest this.
17 Gaddis, *We Now Know*.
18 See R. Garthoff, *The Great Transition: American–Soviet Relations and the End of the Cold War* (Washington, DC: Brookings Institution, 1994); idem, 'Why Did the Cold War Arise, and Why Did it End?' in M. Hogan (ed.), *The End of the Cold War: Its Meaning and Implications* (Cambridge: Cambridge University Press, 1992), pp. 127–36; T. Risse-Kappen, 'Did "Peace Through Strength" End the Cold War?', *International Security*, 16, 1 (1991–92), pp. 162–89; R. Ned Lebow and T. Risse-Kappen (eds), *International Relations Theory and the End of the Cold War* (New York: Columbia University Press, 1995).
19 See the work of Allen Lynch, *The Cold War is Over – Again* (Boulder, CO: Westview Press, 1992); R. Jervis, *Perception and Misperception in International Politics* (Princeton, NJ: Princeton University Press, 1976).
20 See R. Crockatt, *The Fifty Years War: The United States and the Soviet Union in World Politics, 1941–91* (London: Routledge, 1995), pp. 112–13, 209–12, 278–301.
21 Ibid., pp. 260, 301–4.
22 Ibid., p. 370.
23 See F. Kratochwil, 'The Embarrassment of Changes: Neo-Realism as the Science of Realpolitik', *Review of International Studies*, 19, 1 (January 1993), pp. 63–4; R. Ned Lebow, 'The Long Peace, the End of the Cold War, and the Failure of Realism', *International Organization*, 48, 2 (spring 1994), p. 250.
24 See J. Checkel, *Ideas and Political Change: Soviet/Russian Behaviour and the End of the Cold War* (New Haven: Yale University Press, 1997).
25 Lebow, 'Long Peace', p. 266.
26 Ibid., p. 276. See T. Risse-Kappen, 'Ideas Do Not Float Freely: Transnational Coalitions, Domestic Structures, and the End of the Cold War', *International Organization*, 48, 2 (spring 1994), pp. 184–214, where Risse-Kappen views the impact of alternative security paradigms representative of a global liberal international community, and how these had an impact on the different domestic structures of the USSR, the United States and the Federal Republic of Germany.
27 R. Koslowski and F. Kratochwil, 'Understanding Change in International Politics: The Soviet Empire's Demise and the International System', *International Organization*, 48, 2 (spring 1994), pp. 217–20; Kratochwil, 'Embarrassment of Changes', pp. 70–2.
28 Koslowski and Kratochwil, 'Understanding Change', p. 228:

> Just as the Cold War began in East-Central Europe with Stalin, so it ended there with Gorbachev revoking the 'Brezhnev Doctrine' ... Gorbachev's decision reconstituted the international system by changing the constitutive norms of bloc politics and thereby the rules governing superpower relations.

29 Ibid., pp. 234–42.

30 See D. Deudney and G. John Ikenberry, 'The International Sources of Soviet Change', *International Security*, 16, 3 (winter 1991–92), pp. 74–118; idem, 'Soviet Reform and the End of the Cold War: Explaining Large-Scale Historical Change', *Review of International Studies*, 17, 3 (1991), pp. 225–50.

31 M. Kaldor, *The Disintegrating West* (Harmondsworth: Penguin, 1978); 'Warfare and Capitalism', in *New Left Review* (ed.), *Exterminism and Cold War* (London: New Left Books, 1982), pp. 261–87; *The Baroque Arsenal* (London: André Deutsch, 1983); *The Imaginary War: Understanding the East–West Conflict* (Oxford: Basil Blackwell, 1990); M. Kaldor *et al.* (eds), *The New Détente: Rethinking East–West Relations* (London: Verso, 1989); M. Cox, 'Western Capitalism and the Cold War System', in M. Shaw (ed.), *War, State and Society* (London: Macmillan, 1984), pp. 136–94; idem, 'From Détente to the "New Cold War": The Crisis of the Cold War System', *Millennium: Journal of International Studies*, 15, 3 (winter 1984), pp. 265–91; idem, 'The Cold War in the Age of Capitalist Decline', *Critique*, 17 (1986), pp. 17–82; idem, 'The Soviet–American Conflict in the Third World', in P. Shearman and P. Williams (eds), *The Superpowers, Central America and the Middle East* (London: Brassey's, 1988), pp. 171–85; idem, 'Whatever Happened to the "Second" Cold War? 'Soviet–American Relations, 1980–88', *Review of International Studies*, 16, 2 (April 1990), pp. 155–72; idem, 'From Truman Doctrine to the Second Superpower Détente: The Rise and Fall of the Cold War', *The Journal of Peace Research*, 27, 1 (February 1990), pp. 25–41; idem, 'The Revolutionary Betrayed: *The New Left Review* and Leon Trotsky', in M. Cox and H. Ticktin (eds), *The Ideas of Leon Trotsky* (London: Porcupine Press, 1995), pp. 289–304.

32 F. Halliday, *The Making of the Second Cold War*, 2nd edn (London: Verso, 1986); *From Kabul to Managua: Soviet–American Relations in the 1980s* (New York: Pantheon Books, 1989); *Rethinking International Relations*; *Revolution and World Politics*.

33 See Cox, 'Western Capitalism', p. 142; Kaldor, *Imaginary War*, pp. 5, 112.

34 Halliday, *Rethinking International Relations*, p. 181.

35 For a comprehensive overview see M. Light, *The Soviet Theory of International Relations* (Brighton: Wheatsheaf, 1988).

36 Which was drawn directly from early Bolshevik debates, particularly as outlined in Lenin's *Imperialism, the Highest Stage of Capitalism* (Moscow: Progress Publishers, 1934).

37 Cox, 'Western Capitalism', p. 146: 'The struggle against the worldwide communist threat provided America with the necessary ideological *raison d'être* to mobilize its people behind the great tasks which lay ahead, whilst legitimising its imperialism abroad.' And in 'Cold War', p. 36: 'Without the Soviet Union, the rehabilitation of bourgeois rule on a world scale would have been impossible in the postwar period.'

38 See Cox, 'Whatever Happened to the "Second" Cold War?', p. 170; 'From Truman Doctrine to Superpower Détente', p. 35.

39 See Perry Anderson, 'Trotsky's Interpretation of Stalinism', *New Left Review*, 139 (1983), pp. 49–58.

40 See T. Cliff, *State Capitalism in Russia* (London: Bookmarks, 1988).

41 Cox, 'Revolutionary Betrayed', pp. 289–304.

42 See Kaldor, *Baroque Arsenal*; 'Warfare and Capitalism', pp. 261–87.

43 *Imaginary War*, p. 3.

44 Ibid., p. 112.

45 Ibid., p. 5.

46 Underpinning this understanding was the theory of a 'permanent arms economy' associated with, among others, M. Kidron, *Western Capitalism since the War* (Harmondsworth: Penguin, 1970).
47 Kaldor, *The Imaginary War*, p. 112.
48 Ibid., pp. 55–69.
49 Ibid., p. 236.
50 See F. Halliday, 'Interpreting the Cold War: Neither Geostrategy nor Internalism', *Contention*, 14, 1 (fall 1994), pp. 49–66.
51 Kaldor, *Imaginary War*, p. 108: 'there was an asymmetry between East and West, for Western democracy undoubtedly exercized a greater pull for people in East-Central Europe, than Soviet Socialism did for people in the West.'
52 Halliday, *Making of the Second Cold War*, pp. 24–45.
53 Halliday, *Rethinking International Relations*, pp. 170–80.
54 Halliday, *Making of the Second Cold War*, p. 33.
55 See Halliday, *Rethinking International Relations*, pp. 133–4.
56 Halliday, *Making of the Second Cold War*, pp. 30–6.
57 Ibid., p. 3.

PART I:
THEORY

3

The Politics of the State in the Cold War

The state and inter-state conflict have been at the heart of an understanding of the Cold War. As mentioned in Chapter 2 this has been mainly associated, particularly in stressing inter-state conflict between the superpowers, with Realist theory. However, it is my contention that the discussion of the nature of the state in most Cold War literature has not been sufficiently grounded in either history or sociology. Specifically, the focus of this chapter is the need to analyse the historical nature of the modern state, and the domestic social relationship between the state, as a set of political–legal institutions and society, particularly the social relations of socioeconomic production. Through such an investigation not only do we qualify and 'concretize' what we mean by the state, or more accurately, *a* state, but we can also identify the unique features of states that pertain to not only their domestic nature, but also, more importantly for the Cold War, their international relations.

The Cold War was both part of and an influence on the transformation of the international system, particularly in the period after 1945 that witnessed the spread of the sovereign state form as a universalized institutionalization of politics. However, this transformation was only really universal in a legal–diplomatic and territorial sense. Although the state became 'globalized', what this actually saw was the emergence of distinct types of political community that had representation as states in international relations, but whose social, economic, cultural and political content varied greatly. What this means is that in intellectual and political terms the notion of the state must be contested. This contestation relates to the process of the emergence of new states in the international system and their effect on that system, and how they have related to the pre-existing forms of state. However, it does not relate only to the proliferation of states, but also to the changing nature, both domestic and international, of the dominant states in the international system.

Although we can identify attributes of a state or more historically accurately, political–legal rule in the abstract, we need to investigate the peculiarities of states or political forms if we are to provide any historical explanation of them. What this means for the Cold War is that although we can all recognize that the state obviously played a significant role in the international relations of the Cold War, we also need to examine the exact nature of the states involved and, in particular, how the nature of each state conditioned its international relations, which in turn, helped determine the structural properties of that system.[1] Such an approach suggests not only that the state is a product of historical processes, but also that the state both is an agent of historical change and is in turn partly shaped by wider historical changes that it has not necessarily authored. International politics, then, in general and in the Cold War more precisely, should be seen in 'processional terms', in the sense of the way in which developments at what Waltz calls the 'unit level' condition the properties of the system, and where the evolution of the system can in turn condition/transform the behaviour of the agents – states – that make it up. This is what the Cold War was about, particularly in the sense of the relationship between two states, the United States and the USSR, that were domestically constituted in fundamentally different ways, and it is this that this chapter seeks to investigate.

This chapter will provide a critical overview of the main assumptions behind the Realist understanding of the state, and how this dictates a specific and very limited appreciation of the Cold War. The second half of the chapter will offer an alternative conceptualization of the state in the Cold War. This will be based on an historical inquiry into the origins of the modern state through an analysis of the relationship between the institutionalization of political rule and the organization of the economy, and how this relationship is mediated by the conflicts within the social relations of socioeconomic production. This will show the modern state as a distinct type of politics, and that the currency of politics associated with the state is directly associated with the organization of the relations of socioeconomic production. Moreover, with such an approach the meaning of 'politics' is opened up and contested through the challenges to the state form. This will be highlighted with the contrasting of the politics and international relations of the USSR and the United States respectively. What this will reveal is that politics is not necessarily limited to the state, and that what determines the nature of international politics is not the state itself, but how the state relates to the sphere of socioeconomic production, and the nature of this relationship.

Realism, the State and the Cold War in International Relations Theory

Realism as a theory of International Relations (IR) is mainly concerned with a focus on the state and the political relations between states. Both the units of international relations and the currency of those relations are identified with politics, and more specifically the politics of power.[2] What makes Realists distinct is their conception of power, and its relation to their understanding of the state. It is this that is *the* distinguishing feature of Realist approaches. This is important because Realism 'collapses' the notion of power with the state. Thus, when Realists talk about the balance of power they are not talking about power in general, but rather power as it is institutionally expressed within the organizational form of the state. Power, as the state, is what characterizes Realism. Realism does not separate power and thus politics from the state, and because of this it ends up reifying the state as the sole agent and focus of power. With such a limited conception of power, Realism fails to investigate the different forms of power, and how the state and state power can be characterized by more than just the bald assertions of Hobbes and Weber of absolute coercive power and the monopolization of the instruments of legitimate violence. This is particularly so with respect to the Cold War. Although Realists did not always ignore the domestic, the social or the ideological content of internal politics, in terms of international relations this tended to be more of a 'surface froth' rather than the 'matter' of international relations.[3]

Because of their notion of what power is, whether Realists seek an understanding from the structural properties of the international system or the bases of policy-making decisions within the state, they end up with an ontology that is quite ahistorical.[4] This being the case, Realists have an understanding of international politics as operating according to a logic of power politics[5] and the systemic limits to political action.[6] Following this logic of equating (coercive–military) power with the state, international politics becomes reduced to the working out of the balance of power. Other currencies of power,[7] particularly at the domestic level, are either detached from or ignored by international politics. It is not only the dubious separation of the domestic sources of power from international politics but also the tautology of the balance of power as international politics that leads Rosenberg to suggest:

> if power in a states system is ultimately military power, and the statesman is 'doing politics' only when attending to security-related issues, then the hypothesis that the statesman thinks and acts in terms of interest defined as power becomes unfalsifiable.[8]

Politics as the balance of power and the state are synonymous. The 'events' or issues that relate to international relations are to be found in the decisions and consequences of the decisions of state policy. The ontological fault line here most obviously lies in the reification of the status of the state which serves to 'screen out' the state–society (economy) relationship. It is, to quote Rosenberg again:

> The general weakness of the Realist descriptive method, which *can* perceive that the modern state seeks to mobilize the economy, but not

that the economy is also part of a transnational whole which produces important *political* effects independently of the agency of the
state.[9]

This understanding of politics is a little limited. It screens out other actors,
it bypasses other obvious definitions or logics of politics, and it treats the
political actors (states) as absolute and autonomous entities. Another
problem is that it reduces all change or actions to the political. This is not
a problem with the identification of the 'political', but becomes one with
the rather narrow understanding of the political in Realism.[10] In seeking
to explain everything through the interests of power, we end up obscuring
or tarnishing everything with the brush of power politics, which is only
recognized in its appearance of military and strategic competition. Politics
is taken as a recognized and uncontested categorization,[11] a concern that
is separate from economics and 'normative' content. However, the 'politics'
of Realism is extremely problematical because it fails adequately to discuss
what we may take to mean by politics and thus international politics.

For Realists the state, or the nature of the state, is something that is fixed
in the realm of international relations. Quintessentially the state is the state,
as it has always been. A state in international relations is a means of organizing a people in a limited territorial entity based upon the supreme
political authority of sovereignty, and the physical ability to preserve that
internal authority from external challengers. For all intents and purposes
the state in international relations is an agent of political violence, a shell
for controlling and directing political violence against other states.[12] In this
respect the 'state' or political community of classical Greek civilization is
no different from the state of nineteenth- and twentieth-century Europe.
In essence they are the same.[13] They have the same functions; they confront
the same internal and external limitations. The only things that have changed,
historically, are the means, and how the means to achieve the goals end up
inflecting or determining the system/structure in which these states exist.

Such an approach serves to obscure the real social and empirical content
of the state. This is also a consideration that affects how we regard the
primary currency of Realist international politics, political–military power
in the sense of the exact nature and form of these relations. For example,
how are these relations constituted? How do they relate to the wider social
and material production within that social order?

The application or threat of political violence in international relations
is something that is taken to mean the same universally. All forms of war
or applications of force operate according to the same logic regardless of
the state actor involved. However, the role of coercive or military power in
the international system is not a constant in international relations, as the
arguments of the 'democratic peace' literature have made clear,[14] and
the practical experiences of European integration highlight and the

institution(s) of multilateralism suggest.[15] Moreover, the actual application of military power in international relations is also related to the nature of domestic politics. This will become apparent in this and following chapters through a discussion of the impact of social revolution and its relationship with war on international relations. Thus, what Realists tend to suggest are uniform (state) policy outcomes and reflections of a common form of power[16] due to the structural discipline of anarchy are in fact more contingent and different. Not all states act in the same way, because they are not all the same, and because of their internally derived distinctions they are likely to react differently to international developments.

This can be seen in the role and nature of power in the international relations of the superpowers in Europe after 1945. In a basic sense both came to the 'European table' from a similar position: Europe was weak and devastated, and the United States and the USSR were each militarily preponderant in Western and Eastern Europe, respectively. However, as developments after 1945 soon highlighted, the way in which each side related to its European sphere of influence was very different. By focusing on power codified as coercive–military power and the political agency of the state, Realists end up overlooking the distinct quality of international political relations that came to characterize each side of the continental divide. This was most marked in the relationship between the United States and Western Europe, which reflected international political outcomes derived from the nature of the social relations of these types of capitalist state, which saw the development of international relations not reducible to the coercive relations of the (US) state. American influence in Western Europe was obviously much more pronounced after 1945, but this influence rested on a *foundational* political distinction between political authority and private property/market exchange. Although this was encouraged by the US state's support for European cooperation through the Marshall Plan, it also rested on the existence and possibility of increasing structural links between the private-property-based economies of Western Europe and the development of international trade and exchange relationships. The vehicle for this was the embryonic European Economic Community within the broader international economic structure of international trade managed through the Bretton Woods system of fixed exchange rates. US policy, then, was focused on *promoting* the distinction between the political and economic spheres, state and market.[17] Power, in this case, was diffused through different forms of agency located in the relationship between the political/public and economic/private spheres. This was markedly different from the institutionalization of power in that part of Europe which was Soviet-controlled.

The nature of political power and the degree to which power is defined in explicit and directly coercive–military terms in international relations by Realists, and the problems associated with this understanding are also to be found in the way in which Realists have tended to conceptualize the structural configuration of power in the postwar era, otherwise known as bipolarity. In the Realist understanding, the 'bipolar' distribution of power was derived from two poles of power in world politics that became manifest during the Second World War, identified with the United States and the Soviet Union. Thus, in this dimension of Realism the Cold War was the term used to describe the particular organized form of power relations in the postwar period, an international system dominated by the hierarchy organized around the United States and the Soviet Union.

The Cold War began with the expansion of political influence into the centre of world politics (Europe) after the Second World War, into the political vacuum left by the defeat of the Axis powers and the weakness of the other traditional European great powers.[18] Thus, the end of war saw a power vacuum in world politics which was filled by the Soviet Union and the United States, the two dominant states in the international system. But why did this 'condominium' of power lead to a political conflict? On one level Realism explains international conflict as inevitable and enduring because of the absence of an overarching authority in international relations. According to this perspective, all states are in some form of conflict with each other. However, in more explicit terms, conflict and competition for power relates to the operation of the mechanism of the balance of power where states act or react according to the imperative of attempting either to balance or to gain political/strategic advantage over others. Thus, the balance of power operates according to 'zero-sum' assumptions in that the expansion or increase in (military) power by one state is seen as a loss of power for another state, thus triggering a (hostile) response. This, simply put, provides the basis for the dynamic of the Cold War. The pursuit of political opportunity *qua* expansion of political power and influence is the enduring logic of the states-system, and the Cold War is but one episode in this, a distinct episode because it was framed within the structural context of two dominant states.

The problem with this way of understanding the postwar international order and how far that order was synonymous with or determined by a bipolar understanding of power, is that it not only rests on a symmetry with respect to the relative power capabilities of each superpower, but it also reduces the Cold War to the relations between these two states. Whereas in the differing forms of power that characterized US and Soviet relations with either side of Europe after 1945 the issue is the nature of power and its identification with the state, here, the issue again relates to the empirical comparison of US and Soviet power after 1945. Furthermore, it downplays the importance of not only other Western states, particularly Britain and France, in the early period of the Cold War, but also those states such as China, Korea, Vietnam and others that were the agents of revolutionary change that dramatically influenced the superpower relationship.

With respect to the empirical comparisons of each superpower's power in the immediate period after 1945, it would be difficult to identify a symmetry that the notion of bipolarity seems to suggest. In terms of nuclear weapons, the United States had a monopoly in 1945–49, and even after the ending of that monopoly by the USSR, it was not until the mid to late 1960s that one could argue that the USSR had reached a level of approximate parity with the United States. Thus, if bipolarity refers to strategic nuclear weapons, and the superpowers were certainly set apart from other states in this respect, then there is a clear empirical problem of identifying it. This also relates to a wider comparison of each superpower's involvement in the shaping of world politics after 1945 and the projection of military power within it. Whereas the foreign relations of the United States after 1945 were characterized, particularly with the announcement of the Truman Doctrine in 1947 and the writing of NSC-68 in 1950, by an aggressive involvement in the shaping of postwar world politics through the use of diplomatic, economic and military instruments, the USSR, particularly with Zdhanov's 'Two Camps' doctrine, was preoccupied with issues and developments largely within the Soviet bloc. Indeed, it was not until some time into Khrushchev's leadership that the USSR began to take bolder initiatives in the Third World, and even then Soviet influence continued to lag behind Western strength in the Third World. Moreover, it was not until the 1970s 'arc of crisis' that the USSR really challenged American international power through its involvement in and support of revolution in the Third World.

Finally, bipolarity, by reducing the Cold War and international politics to the superpower strategic relationship, has to marginalize the role of other states. This is particularly important with respect to some of the major crises of the Cold War, in Indo-China and the Middle East, in the 1950s. Although American power was to prove decisive in dealing with these crises, up until this period, some way into the Cold War if Realists are to be believed, colonial powers, notably Britain and France, had been at the forefront of containing communism and radical nationalism and thus actual and potential Soviet allies and communist influence. The involvement of other states also relates to those revolutionary states, notably China, Korea, Vietnam and Cuba, that acted outside the 'bipolar relationship', but fundamentally helped to shape the US–Soviet relationship, as superpower involvement in Korea in 1950–53, in Indo-China in 1954–75, and in Cuba after 1959 highlighted.

Even on its own terms as an explanation of the political relations between states, Realism reduces the Cold War to the logic of anarchy/self-help. Yet it cannot explain why some states were hostile to others whilst other states were in alliance with others according to shared internal characteristics.[19] This is probably the gravest of ontological oversights, the lack of analysis of how the domestic and international relate to each other, which serves to inflect when it does not determine the politics of the state in international relations. This is most clearly shown by the presence of particular states that have overthrown or fundamentally restructured both their internal and external relations in the same process through revolution, and in so doing created a new form of politics. This to some extent has been addressed by the 'English School' of Realism, to which I turn next.

The Realism associated with the theorists of 'International Society' or the 'English School', principally related to the work of Hedley Bull, attempts to offer an alternative to the positions of Morgenthau and Waltz. Bull in particular offers an alternative understanding of what constitutes the international.[20] What constitutes the international are the specific political relations between distinct political entities according to a logic derived from a particular normative idea based on the independence of sovereign states. Thus, although Bull is conscious of the structural limits of international society, these are not *constitutive* of that society, rather international society is based on a set of shared basic values and norms that are found, ultimately, in the members of the society, sovereign states, and how they interact with each other. Thus, the 'self-help' system of Waltz is overcome by a mutual understanding of 'society' and the political order that follows from this.[21] Although clearly stating that power and its applications are the ultimate basis of order in international society,[22] Bull attempts to historicize the notion of power and how power is mediated. He suggests that power is manifested through particular political and economic values that are constitutive of the states that make up international society, and thus inflect the system as a whole with a particular political persuasion. These commonalities are in essence the rules and institutions of international relations that 'order the anarchy' that prevails in a political system with no supreme authority.[23] Whereas for the other variant of Realism, politics is determined by the system-wide features of 'anarchy', according to the 'English School' politics is determined by the political values and organizational forms that go with particular attributes of power. Power thus becomes inflected with values beyond 'power' itself.

Although the 'English School' has an understanding of international relations whose ontology is state-centric, it seeks to infuse the notion of the state with a particular kind of normative or political–cultural–legal content.[24] Although the state is the dominant actor in international relations, it is a historical subject, endowed with a peculiar 'modern' content,[25] which makes it so important and distinct. The state is sovereign, and in being sovereign is imbued with an empirical content that leads it to act in particular ways in international relations. This content derives from its membership of an international society. Such a society is inclusive of only certain political forms. This type of political form, the modern sovereign state, is the product of a particular historical–social process (modernity). What is important, and what makes the 'English

School' different from other forms of Realism is not the concept of an 'international society' rather than a system of states, but the fact that the political relations between the members of this society are not only regulated by themselves but by particular modern institutions that grew out of and emerged from the international expansion of this political form which originated in sixteenth-century Europe. Thus, the history of international relations is that of the successful proliferation of a particular kind of political form, the sovereign state.

Power politics and war, although recognized as being within the 'anarchy *problématique*', are not the only manifestations of power, and in some respects may not even be the basis of international order. The political/normative objective of the international society and its members (states) is the preservation of order, a political order based on sovereign states.[26] The instruments of war, international law, diplomacy, the balance of power and the role of the great powers all fit into the logic of the maintenance of a particular kind of political order. Thus, power is 'moderated' by the need to preserve order among states. What this means is that international relations is based on a specific understanding of the international and the political. Power has a normative element in terms of the preserving of international society, which is a unit of collective good. The 'self-help' of Waltz and the 'power-maximization' of Morgenthau are tempered by Bull's concern to stress the need for orderly relations between states, based on a common and collective notion of society which is both inclusive and exclusive.

The 'English School' attempts to historicize the concept of the modern state through a discussion of its proliferation. However, this historicization is still problematic. The problem lies mainly with the limits of the discussion, in that the 'English Realists' tend only to explain the proliferation of the state as a political–legal–territorial construct. International society theorists fail adequately to theorize the penetration of these ideas and institutions within a wider social context which is paralleled by the expansion of capitalist social relations. They can explain the proliferation of the legal–territorial forms of state as they appear on the map and achieve membership of the United Nations. However, they do not fully explain the permeation of this type of politics and its institutionalization as it actually happened. The political forms in question, the notion of a sovereign state with a rule of law based on certain conceptions of right, freedom and citizenship, cannot be separate or abstracted from the wider social processes within which they were embedded. Just as these political forms and concepts of rights, relating to a specific concept of the individual, developed out of specific historical social conflicts in Europe, so the spread of these forms to other parts of the world saw conflicts and attempts to resist their adoption, and attempts to offer alternatives to them.

The form of the modern state emerged alongside capitalist social relations. The modern state is, then, a capitalist state in the sense that, as a political form it has a specific social and political relationship with individuals and society[27] distinct both from pre-capitalist political forms derived from feudalism and also from non-capitalist political forms that emerged out of the Cold War. The modern state is a product of a social conflict where economic relations of production and exchange were separated from direct forms of political authority[28] that were present under feudalism in Europe. Whereas pre-capitalist and pre-modern forms of political authority were directly involved in, indeed, responsible for, the social relations of economic production (i.e. economic production was a directly political question based on direct relations of coercive power between lords and peasants), under capitalism and under the politics of the modern sovereign state capitalist economic relations have been effectively removed from directly political relations, because the economic relationship between workers and capitalists is different and legally separate from the relationship between workers or citizens and the state.

However, although this was a social transformation that had profound consequences for the organization and meaning of politics, this does not mean that the political and economic spheres are separate. Because the social relationship between workers and capitalists is based on exploitation and on the recurring problems of crises within the capitalist economy, the social relations of material production are not fully autonomous in terms of the state. This relationship between the state and the economy does not only refer to coercive state intervention when the social order is threatened by class conflict, but in the wider social relations of capitalist production and exchange, notably through the rule of law, the protection of private property and the maintenance of an infrastructure. The point, then, that an 'English School' understanding of the state tends to ignore is the need to analyze and understand the political relationship between the spheres of rule and socioeconomic production that conditions the nature of the state and the politics of the state.

The state appears separate, and the 'English School', like Realism in general, takes this as in fact to be the case. However, the process of the development of capitalism involved using the political power of the state as a means to quash attempts at preventing the separation of the direct producers (peasants) from their means of production. The state acted to assist 'primitive accumulation' through enclosures and other political acts whose social and economic consequences included the laying of foundations for capitalist social relations.[29] The state is the political appearance of capitalism. Although it appears separate, it is heavily tainted by the unfolding logic of the emergence and penetration of capitalist social relations. The modern state, in terms of the sovereign state as described by international society scholars, is then, in essence, a capitalist state.

This relationship and the type of politics that emerges from within it are also important for the international proliferation of the sovereign state, which has been a major preoccupation of the 'English School'.[30] This is important because although by the late1960s most of the map of the world was made up of the patchwork of sovereign states, many of these political forms were not states that resembled advanced capitalist states. The unfolding of modernity that had been achieved some time before by the latter has still not been fully realized by many other states. Thus, a focus on a legal–territorial concept of the state can lead to an overlooking of the very different and uneven nature of the political entities called 'states', and thus of politics in the Third World. This is not to suggest that the end of the colonial era was not an important political transformation in international relations, but rather to suggest that the picture is more complex and contradictory than focusing on the legal–territorial understanding of the term 'state' may suggest.

It is not enough, then, to say that we have an international society of sovereign states just because colonies became independent and secured representation at the UN. This is even more problematic if we consider the fact that a number of 'states' actually transformed their internal/external constitutive forms through social revolution. These entities had diplomatic representation, but were they states in the sense that I have just described, or were they some other political entity, even though defined by the territorial shell of the sovereign state?

David Armstrong[31] is a notable exception in this regard. A Realist in the mould of the 'English School', Armstrong has developed an understanding of revolution that seeks to overcome many of the problems with Realism. Like Bull, Armstrong is concerned to focus on the maintenance of *order* in the international system, arguing that it is the existence of an international society that best facilitates orderly conduct between sovereign states.[32] It is the dominance of order in international relations that curtails the ability of states and social forces to change the constitutive values, rules and conduct of international relations through social revolution. What is refreshing about Armstrong's analysis is that it actually begins with the assumption that revolutions do have an impact on international society by challenging the existing concept or norm of order; this recognition is almost unique among Realists.

However, Armstrong's understanding of revolution and his specific reference to the Soviet Union and its conduct in world politics are qualified, and this qualification weakens the boldness of his original exploration of revolution. For example, Armstrong emphasizes the importance of (mis)perception and communication as being imperative to maintaining order, and the language of revolutionary states only serves to problematize this.[33] Yet, to give Armstrong credit, he does suggest that in some respects revolutions *do* pose a unique threat to international order. He recognizes, albeit with qualifications, that the Bolsheviks were not distinct as international actors only in their political rhetoric. He accepts that in the 'dualism' of the Soviet involvement in world politics, in the form of the 'peaceful coexistence' between states and the 'proletarian internationalism' that sought to transcend the politics of states through class, the Soviet Union and Comintern did pose a serious threat to the order of international society.[34] However, his acceptance is contingent upon and limited to the events during and immediately after the Revolution, and for the most part Armstrong suggests that the Soviet revolution in the form of a state as an international actor was 'socialized' by the constraints of the international system and the need for cooperation through acceptance of the norms of international society.[35] In these arguments, Armstrong tends to endorse the general Realist understanding of revolution and thus of the Cold War.

In suggesting that revolutions can and do have an impact on the internal constitutive forms within a society, Armstrong seems to be undermining one of the defining features of Realism, the separation of the domestic political sphere from the international. However, Armstrong fails to explore fully the character of domestic politics that includes social relations and sociopolitical structures, and not just internal values. Moreover, he does not recognize, ultimately, anything beyond the evolving *formal* political relations between states as the mechanism for the evolution of international society. Because of this, Armstrong fails to address why it is that the United States has become the dominant state and principal enforcer of the external and internal values of international society, in terms not only of political order, but of the wider institutions, norms and values that define human relationships.

Armstrong confines his notion of norms to formal political relations between states, and does not address the other norms of private property and capitalist social relations as internal *and* international norms. Thus, he overlooks the nature of the social transformation of Russia that 1917 ushered in, and how this created a distinct type of state with a particular form of politics, which rested on a transformed social space. This situation remained throughout the Cold War, and it did not change until after 1989. Because Armstrong tends to concentrate on the external political relations, particularly the 'export of revolution', he ends up missing some of the complexities of the Soviet Union. Just because the USSR may have ceased to pursue a foreign policy that rested on the aggressive direct export of revolution did not mean that it had become 'socialized' like any other state. Of course the shift in Soviet policy reflected a recognition of the problems and risks associated with this policy, but one cannot, as Armstrong does, jump to the conclusion that the Soviet Union was, ultimately, no different because of the political and legal constraints of international society. The appearance of normality, the participation in diplomatic forums and the acceptance of certain legal norms obscured the fact that the Soviet Union was characterized by a different form of international relations, based on a different internal politics.

What Armstrong recognizes is that there is a domestic–international political linkage, a dynamic that helps to explain the evolution of the institutions and practices of international society. However, this does not mean that international society theorists accept that revolutions in one degree or another subvert the norms and institutions of that international order. They do not. Indeed, for all of them, *all* revolutions are 'socialized'.[36] That is, they are forced to conform to the organizing principles of the international order that all Realists are agreed on, the sovereign state, and also that that revolutionary state will always conform to the rules and practices that membership of the international society/order requires.

For example, in Bull's most cited text, *The Anarchical Society*, he fails to recognize the importance of domestic constitutive values as having an impact on the Cold War. He makes it clear that the Soviet Union participated as a sovereign state in the five 'institutions' of international society.[37] The USSR was reflective of the broader 'revolt against the West'. Yet, for Bull this was *within* the confines of the institutions of international society; indeed, much of this revolt adopted and applied the language and norms associated with international society to justify revolt. Thus, because of the use of pre-existing norms (i.e. the demand for what already existed, at least in theory, from national self-determination to legal protection), Bull and others suggested that the Soviet Union was like any other state in its *international* relations.[38] In this respect, then, Bull, like Waltz and Morgenthau, appears to reduce power and politics to the organs and logic of the state.

The politics of the state in this tradition of Realism is given a political/normative content that derives from the historical development of the political relations between the members of international society. Because of its historical development, in particular the postwar developments that saw a near tripling in the number of sovereign states (with a wide and conflicting variety of internal constitutive political norms), international society's concept of order has evolved and taken on a number of normative dimensions that reflect the changing nature of international relations.[39] The Soviet Union and the Cold War are but one episode in this history. However, although this makes for a much more open and illuminating potential research programme for Realism, it still suffers from some of Realism's major problems. International society continues to have a limited ontology of politics that stems from the separation of the political from the economic and thus ends up ignoring one of the major aspects of domestic politics. In particular this aspect relates to capitalism, which is an internal aspect of a society's constitutive definition, but which is also part of an international system that does not stop at the territorial limits of a state. These issues will be discussed more substantively in the conclusion to the chapter. The following section will develop some of the issues discussed above with a more explicit reference to the Cold War.

Reconstructing a Politics of the State in the Cold War

This section of the chapter will go beyond the Realist notion of the state in the Cold War by building on the foundations provided by the critique of Realism. It will seek to provide an Historical Materialist conceptualization of the state in the Cold War by renegotiating the boundaries and terrain of politics. In a precursor to what follows, politics *qua* the state will be reconstituted in terms of social relations. What this means is that the separation of politics (the state) and economics (production, distribution and exchange) will be replaced by the conceptualization of politics as 'the unity in the separation' of the political/public sphere of the state and the private/economic sphere of production.

Such a conceptualization of politics is drawn from the work of Marx and Engels,[40] a conceptualization that begins with the politics of 'humanity's interaction with nature', that is, the material and social relations of production which lie at the heart of any understanding of human/social relations. However, more precisely, the underpinning of what one means by the state and thus what constitutes politics in the Cold War is located in the relationship between the formal institutions of political power and the 'informal' politics located within the sphere of socioeconomic production and the relationship between this sphere of social life and the state. What follows will argue that it is the case that not only should politics not be confined to the agency and relations of the state but that it should also include the non-state sphere. However, it will also be argued that the politics of the state is itself qualified and conditioned by its relationship with the domestic sphere of socioeconomic production. Moreover, the nature of the politics that characterizes states, particularly if they are dominant states, can and will condition the social and political complexion of the wider international order. What *constitutes* international relations, then, is in large part derived from the nature of social relations and the institutionalization of politics within great powers.

The analysis of the Cold War becomes an examination of the international political and economic relations of capitalism and the interaction between these two 'aspects of politics'. What determines the character of this is not only war, as Realists tend to argue, but also the outcome of the social conflict centred on, but not confined to, that between capital and labour and, in particular, the degree to which that conflict can be maintained within existing social and political structures. Revolutions are the most obvious example of a possible historical outcome of this conflict. Related to this, and the second factor that conditions the relationship between the state and socioeconomic production, is the recurrence of capitalist economic crisis, as in a 'slump' or recession, and how this affects the state's supervision of the capitalist economy. What is significant about this relationship and how it conditions the nature of politics is that the character of the state is not determined solely by the agencies of the state or the policies of government, but rather, in a wider social and international context, by the economic operations of the capitalist economy founded on the logic of accumulation through 'horizontal competition' between firms.

These factors reveal themselves within domestic politics, although they also tend to have profound international consequences, as the 1929 crash and the post-Bretton Woods recession of the 1970s highlight. Moreover, what these internal developments also signify is not only the degree to which domestic social relations and politics are characterized by the agency and currency of politics derived from the state, but also how far the international relations of and between capitalist states are defined by the more direct politics of state agency, or a more *indirect* politics not confined to the state, but including other political agents and currencies of relations derived from capitalist social relations.

As mentioned, one historical product of the tensions and conflicts within capitalist social relations, particularly as they reveal themselves in international relations, social revolution, not only exposes how social conflict can be transformed into explicitly political conflict and the overthrow and construction of a new state, but also introduces a new and different type of politics. Therefore, an analysis of the Cold War and the nature of the state or states in the Cold War will need to analyze those (revolutionary) states not constituted by the political–economic relationship of capitalism, which would suggest a different type of international relations. Thus, the determining factors of the history of international relations, typified by the history of the Cold War, are reflected in the changing, evolving and conflicting development of the state.

The 'hard', 'outer' shell of the Realist state obviously plays a part in this history, but not in the way set out by Realists. The currencies of nuclear weapons, conventional forces and other forms of the state are present, but in a social context.[41] The prosecution of organized political violence by the state is not separable from the strategies of the social reproduction of that state. Thus the state in these terms, and its military or political expansion in Realist terms, is transformed to reflect the actual social characteristics of states. The state is not seen as reacting according to the laws of anarchy that appear to ensure a uniformity of political outcomes *à la* Waltz, but rather the state reflects domestic and international relations based on the contradictions and conflicts within the expansion and consolidation of capitalist social relations and the peculiar types of political–state forms that such a process and conflict throws up.

Capitalism, International Politics and the State

In the Realist account of politics the state tends to be 'cut adrift' from the broader social structures and relations between people. Once this occurs, politics and history become enshrined in the separate public authority of the state, which relegates the actual history of people to the private sphere. The history of social struggles involving classes is airbrushed from the historical record. The state does not embody human content or agency, but rather, it is understood as a purely organizational form of power. What is obviously missing in this account of the state and its emergence is the fact that the actual historical presence of the state within a society is a product of a particular social–historical process, which is associated with the unfolding of the logic of a capitalist modernity.

For Realism, the state is a category or an ideal-type in the sense of the state being a general political form endowed with general organizational attributes that make it act in a general way. While we must obviously have abstract categories and criteria for talking about something, concepts that furnish meaning to a theory, we must also apply these concepts and, ultimately, realize them through an historical and specific under-standing of types of state or forms of political rule. This is an historical investigation and it implies change and agency. Therefore the notion of the state in IR needs to be seen in 'processional' terms, as something that has emerged because of the presence and operation of particular kinds of agency, and something that has been subject to change as well as initiating change.[42]

The history of the state is thus contingent and alive, and from this perspective is not reducible to 'politics' as conventionally understood; neither is it reducible to an idealized form separate from society or the social relations between people. Rather, the state should be seen as a 'processional form', an institutional mechanism associated with the emergence of capitalist social relations based on the separation of the direct and immediate public power/authority from socioeconomic production.[43]

The capitalist state as the formal institutionalization of politics rests, then, on the historical separation of political authority from socio-economic production. What this means is that although politics tends to be designated as a concern with state policy, this rests on a foundational distinction between public and private authority and power. Moreover, although the capitalist state does not tend to participate, *directly*, in the relations between capitalist production and exchange, it can and does act as a 'social relation of capitalist production'. Indeed, without the rule of law, the defence of private property and the regulating functions of the state, capitalism as an economic system could not function.[44] Thus, there is a relationship between the state and the operations of the economy which serves to promote the reproduction of the social relations of capitalism, relations *defined* by the separation of direct political power from socio-economic production, and the social relations of power and conflict within this sphere.[45] As I have already mentioned, the reproduction of capitalism rests on this separation, but a separation that, particularly in moments of structural economic crisis and intense sociopolitical conflict, *depends* on the interventions of the state. Because of this relationship with the ongoing developments and occasional convulsions within the capitalist economy, what we mean by politics and political agents needs to include the politics of socioeconomic production, which, most importantly, is not confined to the spatial limits of the state.

Thus, whereas the formal and direct politics of the state are anchored and limited to the territory of the state, the informal and indirect operations of capitalist economic activity, codified into horizontal competitive relations between firms and hierarchical vertical relations between capital and labour, are transnational and go beyond the spatial and political limits of the state. Not only is the nature of politics under capitalism unique in the sense that it rests on a distinction between politics and economics, public and private, but it is also distinct in that state sovereignty is *not* absolute, but rather rests on a facilitation of international exchange based on social relations that do not necessarily require the direct sanction or authority of the state. The exchange of commodities through international trade reflects not only social relations between people, but also a much wider social structure that rests, at the international level, on the foundational distinction between political rule and capitalist production and exchange. Although states provide a legal framework in establishing and regulating these relations, they are not the primary agents. The agents in this international social relationship are owners and producers, buyers and sellers. These are not formal 'political' agents, but individuals and firms, whose locus of activity is not the realm of the public sphere, but the private sphere of economic gain and self-interest.

What this means is that the social character of states is conditioned not only by domestic developments but also by international developments. This situation relates to those states that were subject to and products of imperialist domination and also to the advanced capitalist states engaged and entangled within major economic relationships. The inter-war period, particularly after the 1929 Wall Street crash, highlights this, with the shift away from more open international trade and the introduction of political measures to protect domestic industries, and much greater state intervention in the management of the domestic economy, thus transforming the relationship between state and economy, and the state and the international system. It was also evident in postwar developments within Western Europe, particularly in the Marshall Plan, and American pressure and encouragement for European states to not only work together in pursuing economic reconstruction, but also in a manner which corresponded to wider American political and economic interests.[46]

In the context of the postwar era of American 'hegemony', the transformation of the international order had a distinctly American capitalist quality about it. These qualities reflected the domestic nature of American politics and American capitalism, features highlighted not only in the

American framing of the new social order in the western half of Germany, but also in their attempts to press Britain to end its discriminatory (imperial) economic practices that frustrated American attempts to construct a more liberal and open international economic order. However, what distinguished this American form of hegemony was not necessarily the relative power of the United States over its rivals, though this was obviously significant, but the fact that it did not rest on, and was not fully characterized by the direct and coercive sanction of the state, but rather, the deployment of American economic largesse via existing or newly established states and capitalist economic structures in Europe.

Although the organs of the US state were the primary agents of the postwar transformation of Western Europe and US–European relations, US foreign policy rested on the support of American capital, particularly the incentives to American banks to invest overseas. It was not only this domestic support, but also the fact that once established the new international economic order would be guided by the dynamic of capitalist competition between firms for markets and resources, based on the pervasive capitalist 'rationality' of profitability and accumulation. It was this economic strength that provided an economic form of political leverage that was largely absent from the international relations of the USSR, particularly in American concerns to prise open the formerly closed markets of European colonies.

Despite the fact that postwar international economic order was politicized through forms of protectionism and a managed international trade regime (Bretton Woods), these controls did not amount to a complete transformation of the public–private, state–economy relationship. The United States had compromised over the need for degrees of state intervention in the management of world trade and within the European economies, yet its long-term goals remain wedded to a more liberal international economic order.[47] Moreover, by deliberately limiting the explicitly political nature of its economic policy, the United States sought to avoid political tensions emerging with European states in the application of the European Recovery Programme (ERP). Thus, the United States emphasized basic economic goals that focused on production increases rather than the more political concerns of redistribution.[48] By encouraging European economic integration, the United States sought in the longer term to reduce the political autonomy of European capitalist states, which would lay the foundations not only for reduced political tensions between them, but also, ultimately, for the removal of barriers to trade between Europe and the United States.[49]

The private political dimension to the restructuring of Western capitalism after 1945 was not confined to the material, but also other non-state sources. These included the establishment of American-style trade unions and labour–management relations, along with the encouragement given to the initiatives of influential private citizens such as Jean Monnet's 'Committee for the United States of Europe'.[50]

This episode in the international political relations between capitalist states highlights the fact that they are based on the interaction of the spheres of (private) economic activity and public political rule. What determines this relationship and its political outcomes largely depends on the domestic political and economic pressures placed upon it, and whether or not the conflicts that emerge within it can be confined to the existing public–private, state–economy relationship. The maintenance of the capitalist social order rests, then, on the preservation of the sphere of private socioeconomic relations.

Capitalist development from the eighteenth century onwards has witnessed major changes within the relationship between state and economy, for the most part involving the state acting to limit or regulate capitalist economic activity because of intensifying class conflict or responding to economic crises as in the depression of the 1930s and the recession in the 1970s. What these issues highlight is the evolving nature of capitalist development and the possibilities for its reform, especially within the context of a democratic political system. However, whereas capitalism has been subject to varying degrees of democratic supervision mainly because of working-class and democratic pressures on the state, it has also been confronted with crises that have incited revolutionary challenges not only to capitalist economic activity but to the authority and power of the capitalist state that have resulted in the reconstitution of the state–economy relationship through the overthrow of capitalist social relations.

What the history of capitalist modernity, and thus of the modern sovereign state suggests, then, is that the state is a contested political form subject to social redefinition. What this in turn suggests is that the state is a historically recent form of political rule in global terms, and an institution subject to change (and not necessarily revolutionary change 'from below', but also structural change orchestrated by the state itself, as recent and ongoing developments in the European Union tend to highlight). This is something that is reflective of the history of capitalist modernity, witnessed in the internal social and political transformations within developing capitalist states led by Britain from the eighteenth century onwards and within the international expansion of capitalism from the postwar transformations of colonialism and imperialism to an international order of sovereign states.

The challenges to power relations within capitalist states obviously relates to the nature of the dispensation of power, and how far such threats can transform that configuration of power, and the degree to which changes can be confined within the capitalist structures of political and economic, public and private power/authority. The pressures on the state, however, are not only consequential in terms of the political outcomes, for example the state's role in managing the economy and/or the state's ability to represent the interests of particular social groups or classes, but also (and this can also relate to the consequences of the political contestation of the state, especially if the outcome is a military-backed coup d'état) in the transformation of the nature of the state, in the sense of the deployment of coercive and military power to suppress dissent/revolt. Thus, when social/class antagonisms cannot be confined to an economic question resolvable at the source of that conflict, the workplace, and if that conflict becomes 'politicized' in the sense that it not only directly involves the state, but becomes a *question of the state*, then the foundational distinction of capitalist politics between politics and economics is dissolved. The outcomes of such episodes of sociopolitical conflict have either been fascism and military dictatorship or communist revolution.

However, such outcomes are not an inevitable product of the contradictions and conflicts within capitalist states. Indeed, what has characterized the politics of the advanced capitalist states, particularly after 1945, has been relative political stability and the absence of not only a direct political contestation of the state and social order, but also, largely because of this, the absence of a directly coercive politics within these states. Thus, the United States and the other advanced capitalist states, particularly (West) Germany and Japan, have been ordered by a domestic politics that is liberal democratic where public authority does not rest on directly coercive power, and where social conflict tends to be either confined to, or managed within the existing social structures of capitalism based on the division between political–economic, public–private. What this means is that the nature of the capitalist state is *not* geopolitically determined by the structural imperatives of the system and the need to defend its territorial integrity, but rather that the nature of the state, which co-defines the structure of the international system, is also determined by configuration of politics within it, and, particularly, the extent to which social life and politics are determined by the agency of the state and if they are, to what degree state politics is a directly coercive politics. The presence and reproduction of a non-state sphere of social relations, that is not necessarily limited to economic production, encourages not only non-state forms of power and order, but also politics, and, moreover, a politics that is, in essence, transnational.

By contesting the state as a political form, from both an intellectual and a political perspective, it is evident that the politics and international relations of capitalist states are qualitatively different from those between non-capitalist 'states', and those between capitalist and non-capitalist 'states'. This is quite clear, even with more orthodox interpretations of international relations. In terms of the international society approach the relations between Christendom and the Islamic world were different from intra-Christian relations.[51] However, in terms of an international society (i.e. a global system represented by sovereign nation-states as the form of political rule), we can go beyond the distinctions recognized by orthodox approaches to IR, and conceive of the relations between political forms as being derived from their social relations. What this means is that politics, in terms of the nature of the state (political rule within a given society/territorial entity), is only explicable in terms of how it reflects and is part of the social relations of socioeconomic production. Thus, during the Cold War international relations were not about the political relations between states, but about the forms of political relations between different types of political authority, which reflected differing ways of organizing social life, based on socioeconomic production. Although we need to discern the relative absence of directly coercive power in and between the politics of the advanced capitalist states, we also need to recognize how this was *contingent* on the successful management of class conflict within existing social structures. If and when such conflict cannot be managed within existing social structures then the state and politics are reconstituted.

One of the most important ways in which societies were reconstituted and ways of organizing social life altered was, as I have already suggested, through social revolution. It was these developments in the Cold War that provided the dynamic of the political relations of the Cold War that the United States and the Soviet Union were part of. It is in the politics of the social revolutionary state as a form of political rule, and the conflict with capitalist forms of political rule which stemmed from this, that the explanation of the Cold War is to be found.

The Revolutionary 'State' as an Alternative Form of International Politics

Revolutions have provided the discipline of IR with its most visible examples of both the contestation of the state as a form of political rule, and the transformation of the state through a reconstitution of social relations between state and society/economy. Although on one level these types of political rule have assumed the territorial 'shell' of the state they have been qualitatively different, and have realized an alternative form of politics derived from a different set of social relations.

The USSR and other revolutionary states were ordered by a very different form of political authority than was the case in capitalist states. The most important and defining distinction was that the basis of capitalist production and social relations in the private ownership of the means of production and the 'free' market in labour were abolished. The socio-political transformation inaugurated by the 1917 Bolshevik Revolution produced an economy structured by centralized state planning and state-collective ownership of the means of production. Autonomous social institutions were eliminated as society was *ordered* in all spheres of social life by the pervasive and uncompromising presence of the coercive–bureaucratic apparatus of the Party-state. Revolutionary transformation saw not only the destruction of the autonomous spheres of social life, be they capitalist or traditional–feudal, that ended up transforming the structural relationship between state and society; it also amounted to what Theda Skocpol has identified as the construction of a new type of 'mass mobilizing' state.[52] The political authority of the state that had just been smashed by revolution was reconstituted in a much stronger fashion and extended into all areas of life. The state was now absolute in its legal and political reach.[53] There was no longer any conceptual or political distinction between public and private, political and economic.

The politics of those states that emerged out of communist social revolution was structured in such a way that centralized political power was determining in the same way that the 'fragmented sovereignty' of capitalism was determining of capitalist states. Thus the presence of the state, and particularly its coercive organs, was not confined to the formal institutions of rule and political order, but was also found in those areas of social life that were the preserve of the private or 'non-political' sphere in liberal-democratic capitalist states. Culture, and more significantly, the social relations of production and exchange, were directly determined by the sanction of the Party-state. Production, distribution, exchange and consumption were not determined by the 'anarchy' of the 'economic' decisions of individual buyers and sellers, producers and consumers, but rather by the five-year plans of the state. What people ate, where they worked, what they produced, how they produced, and what they were paid and so forth were determined by the decisions of directly political authorities.[54]

The problem within this structural relationship, that compounded the fact that political dissent was brutally suppressed, was that socioeconomic questions that in capitalist states did not manage directly to involve the politics of the state were explicitly political. Because of the lack of any private 'political' sphere, all questions were reducible to the state and this being so whether the state could contain the ethnic, cultural, social, economic and political tensions and contradictions within existing social structures became much more problematic. With these tensions, the state alone was directly responsible (and blamed) for problems that were not usually/always public or political in capitalist states. Whereas economic, ethnic, social and cultural issues were largely determined by the 'politics' of the private sphere, these issues were expressly public and political in the USSR. Because of this, not only did social tensions and conflicts appear more acute in the USSR, but also the ability to deal with them was limited to the coercive structures of the state,[55] a situation that only served to weaken further the state's political legitimacy.

However, the contradictions that came to dominate the politics of the Soviet Union were derived not only from its sociopolitical constitution, but also from its material backwardness and ideological project. These contradictions that 'governed' the history of the USSR were present at its creation, most evidently in the objective of the construction of socialism from a socioeconomic base of relative backwardness, and international goals of the security of the Revolution and its expansion. These two sources of pressure, one internal, the other international in origin, were evident in Stalinism.

The 'project' of Stalin related not only to the internal goal of rapid economic development to ensure 'socialist construction' under Party-state leadership, but also to the need to ensure the external defence of the USSR. Internally, the Soviet Union faced food shortages and the conflict in the countryside over the role of private property and the distribution of peasant surplus produce to urban areas.[56] This was problematic for the Bolsheviks in terms of their project of socializing the means of production and abolishing private property, but became increasingly acute with the concern over their core political–economic objective, the need for the rapid development of the USSR's productive forces. Although the Bolsheviks had relaxed state control of the economy through the introduction of the 'New Economic Policy' (NEP) in 1921, and despite the fact that this served to boost short-term economic growth after the ravages of war, revolution and civil war, the problem was that, in the longer term, the NEP threatened to bolster not only capitalist social relations in the countryside, but also class forces that might challenge Bolshevik political supremacy.[57]

Stalin was aware of the imperative of rapid material development and also the potential social and political threat to the Bolsheviks by the continuation of NEP and its 'encouragement' of capitalism. This concern also related to the international threats to the Soviet Union, which derived historically from Russia being a victim of its own social and industrial backwardness. As Stalin made clear:

> To slacken the pace would be to lag behind; and those who lag behind are beaten ... The history of old ... Russia ... she was ceaselessly beaten for her backwardness. She was beaten by the Mongol Khans, she was beaten by the Turkish Beys ... she was beaten by the Anglo-French capitalists ... she was beaten by all – for her backwardness. We are fifty or a hundred years behind the advanced countries. We must make good this lag in ten years. Either we do it or they crush us.[58]

These threats had been manifest in the early years of the Revolution through Western hostility and support for the 'Whites' in the civil war. They continued after the civil war with the relative isolation of the USSR in international relations. This isolation/hostility was to take a new and more threatening form in the 1930s, not only because of the anti-Bolshevism of the Nazis but also because of the Japanese invasion of Manchuria in 1931.[59]

It was the combination, then, of domestic and international politics that was to force the Soviet Union to pursue a strategy of rapid and intense (and costly, in human and social terms) industrialization and modernization. For the Bolsheviks this required the development of the Soviet Union's productive forces *above all else*. As they stood after 1917, and with a backward agricultural sector and a distorted, fractured industrial base, the productive forces could not, according to the Bolsheviks, sustain or support socialism. The productive base of the social formation required development in order to allow the realization of the *material* construction of socialism defined as a social formation founded on a productive base superior to that of capitalism.[60] On this reading the project of the Soviet Union was identified with the surpassing of the existing capitalist social formations[61] in terms of production. This socioeconomic imperative meant that such a project inevitably led to forms of political coercion to develop the productive forces.[62] This coercive imperative turned into a military operation, a civil war between the state and the peasantry, that was played out with the deaths of millions through famine and the slaughter of many more by the Red Army and the secret police (the NKVD).

The Soviet social formation was, then, baptized not only by the violence of the 1917 Revolution, but also by the Revolution's outcome in a state dominated by the role of politically sanctioned force or coercion as a means of social transformation. Social and political transformation, that for Marxists had always been something that emanated from social struggle and socioeconomic structures, was now replaced by the direct, political sanction of the state and its coercive apparatus. For Stalin, then, force was no longer the midwife, but the mother of the new society.[63]

Although property was socialized, and the rule of capital had been abolished, the social relations that came to the fore under the Bolsheviks reflected the contradictory nature of being socialist in terms of the replacement of the market by centralized planning, the abolition of private property, and the elimination of wage labour, but also reflecting a project that required the state to enforce particular coercive, quasi-capitalist techniques to ensure a rapid development of the Soviet Union's productive base.[64] This explains the analysis of the Soviet Union and Stalinism in particular as a 'revolution from above'. The Party-state, through its control of the coercive apparatus and its domination of society, ensured the top-down implementation of revolutionary modernization while preserving some of the socialist gains of the revolution. The nature of this socio-economic transformation and the fact that it was led by the coercive agency of the state exposed an acute contradiction in the Soviet social formation, consequent on the nature of Soviet politics, its relative material backwardness and its international vulnerability.

In the first instance, because of the state-economy relationship production could not be regulated in a non-coercive or 'non-political' way through the combination of the social 'disciplining' of a flexible labour market and unemployment, and production carried out by competing (private and international) units of production. Moreover, if the political authorities were to avoid using direct coercion to secure economic objectives,[65] then it was likely that they would have needed to plan to ensure that the material life of working people, Party members as well as non-Party members, was improved, or at least maintained at existing levels. Without this, labour indiscipline, and other forms of producer alienation were likely to undermine economic performance and material growth. In its most extreme form the alienation of workers manifested itself in acts of overtly political militancy through strike action or physical attacks on the property and persons of the apparat.[66]

Although the USSR claimed to be a Workers' state, in practice the Soviet working class did not democratically control the state. The Soviet Union, as a social formation, saw a relationship between the bureaucratic institutions of the Party-state and socioeconomic production where the former was seen as an instrument of revolutionary praxis.[67] Because the state was led and dominated by the Party, so that it claimed to be a state of the working class, it sought to determine the production strategy on behalf of working people. In effect, however, the relationship between the Party-state and the social relations of production (i.e. the relations of the working people) was characterized by tensions and alienation, which derived from the fact that the direct producers did not politically control their own social relations, and thus their own collective (and individual) social realization. The politics that stemmed from such arrangements was premised on this political divorce between the direct producers and the alienated political power of the Party-state. It was because of this relationship between the working class and the ruling authorities that the Soviet Revolution was never able *fully* to reconstitute social relations.

Thus, although the role of violence and the 'terror' in Soviet industrialization was quickly removed in the post-Stalin era, the social damage had largely been done, and the intellectual and political paradigm that guided Soviet economic policy was entrenched. The objective remained rapid material accumulation, and despite no longer requiring systematic and orchestrated Party-state violence, it did continue to rest on the coercion of working people who were effectively *ordered* by the ruling authorities and their local Party functionaries as to what and how to produce. The coercive nature of Soviet social relations were mitigated, however, by continued economic growth until the 1970s particularly with significant increases in per capita food consumption, and the range and availability of consumer goods.[68]

Khrushchev and Brezhnev implemented reforms to build on these improvements (and they were, indeed, in relative terms, huge accomplishments), by focusing on attempts to increase efficiency and productivity, through the decentralization of decision-making and the promotion of local 'enterprise' autonomy. However, these reforms never managed fundamentally to improve Soviet economic performance. Although they did not require the level of coercion that characterized Stalinism, they continued to fail to address the lack of effective popular supervision and control over the means of production. Thus economic growth continued to be stifled by social relations that rested on producer alienation and the ever present prospect of managerial-state force to intensify modernization, triggering popular anger and the necessity of coercive intervention by the ruling authorities.

The Soviet Union, like most of the other revolutionary states, which in many respects adopted aspects of the 'Soviet model', was characterized throughout its existence with this tension located in its contradictory and tension-induced form of social relations. Because of the Bolshevik determination to modernize and 'out-produce' capitalism, the Soviet Union located itself in a frame of reference that identified with capitalism, as the *material* object of its project. The history of the Soviet Union, which culminated in the *perestroika* of Gorbachev, reflected this tension and the dominance of a theoretical and practical paradigm based on the belief that socialism would only be realized with the fullest development of its productive forces. The Soviet Union, then, was trapped in the shadow of capital. Its productive strategy, in effect, attempted to emulate or use techniques, forms of technology and foreign expertise with which to 'perfect' socialism. Social relations (i.e. the political and social relations of the direct producers at the source of production) were not recognized as being in themselves a productive force. Instead, in practice, labour was treated as just another instrument of production,[69] rather than as the basis with which to revolutionize the social relations of society.

The problem of maintaining social and political order was not limited to the USSR's domestic politics, but also manifested itself in the wider Soviet bloc and the international communist movement. Whereas the CPSU could derive a major degree of political legitimacy from being the creation of 1917 and having secured victory in the 'Great Patriotic War', such legitimacy was largely absent, and was manifestly so in 1954, 1956, 1968 and 1980–81, when Soviet military power, or the threat of it, was used to crush dissent in Eastern Europe. These crises were a product of the tensions and conflicts within local political rule in the region. However, the nature of politics in Eastern Europe, in its clear difference from politics in Western Europe, rested on the nature of Soviet expansion into the region after 1945, and the fact that, as in the Soviet Union after the 1917 Bolshevik Revolution and Stalinism, politics in Eastern Europe rested on the elimination of non-state sources of politics and the organization of socio-economic production, to varying degrees, according to the Soviet model.

Unlike the social relations within and between the advanced capitalist states, which were not confined to the agency or political relations of the state, the social relations within and between Soviet-type states were restricted to a politics of the state. This meant that not only was the 'space' for difference severely limited, on account of all things 'being political' due to the all-encompassing nature of intra- and inter-Party-state relations, but also that if either local Party-state leaderships or indigenous social forces, as in Eastern Europe in 1954, 1956, 1968 and 1980–81, attempted to redefine internally social relations through the establishment of institutions not directly controlled by the Party-state, they were likely to be seen by the Soviet leadership as a way of undermining the Soviet political order. Because of the nature of the Soviet form of politics, in both the relationship between state and society and between the state and the outside world, such autonomous institutions were likely to redefine not only domestic politics, by establishing a realm not subject to direct Party-state control, but also international relations with other states and other agents not controlled by the Party-state.

The nature of the USSR and similarly constituted states was such that not only were they organized in a different way from capitalist states, but that the institutionalization of politics, indeed, what was considered to be politics, was very different. The problems associated with a direct and overt politicization of all aspects of social life, by definition not only turned all opposition and dissent into political challenges to the state, but also exposed these types of state to more acute contradictions. These internal tensions were magnified by the ideological project of rapid material development, which forced the state to act in an even more coercive manner to achieve growth targets, which in many instances further distanced working people from it, and also by the fact that it was confronted by a general level of external hostility.

Just as the politics of capitalist states emerged out of the relationship between political rule and socioeconomic production and the international system, so the politics of the revolutionary Soviet state was defined by its internal social constitution and how this related to the world. However, because of the 'separation' of the society/economy from direct political control, social and economic contradictions within capitalist states were not always political in the sense that they directly challenged or threatened the existing sociopolitical order. This was not the case with the Revolutionary Soviet form of politics. The direct and all-encompassing nature of Party-state power over and within society reduced the space of 'non-politics'. Non-state activity, be it cultural, economic, or social, challenged the social and political supremacy of the Communist state from within because it was not subservient to or controlled by the state's organs.

However, the consequences of this type of activity did not relate solely to the internal relationship with the Soviet state, but had profound international ramifications, because such activities and groups involved in them could develop links with other non-state international organizations located outside the USSR within the civil society of capitalist states. The conditioning nature of the domestic politics of capitalist and Soviet-type states profoundly affected their respective international relations and the development of the relationship between these two forms of state into the Cold War.

Conclusion: The Real Politics of the Cold War

The real politics of the Cold War consisted of more than just the formal political–military conflict between the superpowers. The external projection of military power was important, as the many international crises of the postwar period – Iran (1946), Berlin (1948), Korea (1950–53), Vietnam (1960–75) and Cuba (1962) – obviously highlight. However, by restricting the Cold War to this form of international political conflict, we not only reify the agency of the state, we also reduce politics to the state. Moreover, we end up, as Realists tend to, conceiving the Cold War as a form of symmetry, when, in reality, not only was the projection of international power by the superpowers uneven, but what that power actually consisted of was markedly different.

Seeing the politics of the Cold War as being embedded in the social constitution of power within the United States and the USSR and how this conditioned each side's international relations also pertains to the need to see ideology, or the directing agency of the currency of ideas, as more than just an autonomous factor in shaping policy and action. Ideology was significant in the international relations of the Cold War, not only because politicians and leaderships were motivated to act through the power of ideas, but also because ideology was realized within a set of institutions and social structures that conditioned the autonomy of individual actors and was also defining of ideology. As I will attempt to show in the following chapter on military power, Soviet revolutionary ideology was conditioned by the fact that the expansion of that ideology was via a set of socio-political structures and institutions which ended up *limiting* the practical autonomous power of the ideology of revolutionary internationalism.

Ideology only matters in politics when it actually motivates political behaviour, the consequences of which are the construction of social structures and political institutions. To talk about communist ideology and its impact or lack of it on foreign policy necessarily implies the existence or creation of the social and political structures of communism. If ideas are detached from a sociological and political context they become an agency without a 'subject'. What I mean by this is that we can only talk of the explanatory power of ideology in political actions by recognizing that ideology is the practical institutionalization of ideas.

The international politics of the Cold War was, then, dominated by the social and political nature of the superpowers and how they related to each other and other international developments. Both were products of capitalist modernity. The United States was a highly developed capitalist state, conditioned by the combination of the economic logic and impulse of capitalist accumulation and the formal politics of liberal democracy. The USSR was a product of international capitalist crisis, specifically war between developing capitalist states, and the combination of internal and external pressures of the imperative of capitalist modernization. However, it was also conditioned by the objective of materially superseding capitalism, and until this was achieved the direction of Soviet policy would be guided by the nature and level of capitalist development in the advanced capitalist states.

Because these states were differently constituted they also differed in their respective international relations. This, I have already suggested, is how each superpower came to condition political developments in Europe after 1945. Whereas the Soviet Union was effectively limited to a politics of the state, based on a directly coercive form of power, the United States was characterized by an international 'politics' and 'economics' not reducible to the state. The international politics of the Cold War, then, was not confined to the agency and relations of the state. Rather, it reflected the interaction, antagonism and conflict between two different and mutually hostile forms of political rule. Again, the example of postwar Europe is salient. The United States could and wanted to facilitate international relations and establish an international relationship with (Western) Europe through state and non-state 'political' activity that defended and promoted a distinction between state and society, public and private; indeed, US security was seen to rest on this.[70] This contrasted with the Soviet objective of security and expansion that could not permit any social or political autonomy within the states of Eastern Europe that would have served not only to weaken internal Soviet control, but also to allow these states to construct autonomous international relations outside Soviet control.

The outcome was political conflict and military competition, because these two states not only were differently constituted and had developed very different forms of international relations, but were also driven by different ideological agendas. In this sense conflict was inevitable, but not because of the balance of power or bipolarity. Rather, conflict emerged out of the antagonistic international political objectives of each state and *how* they came to realize them. Whereas American influence or 'hegemony' was constructed without the necessity of a direct political, physical and coercive presence in Western Europe, Soviet interests necessitated a direct, physical and coercive political presence. This direct political *and* military presence in Eastern Europe was about not only external physical defence, but also social and political control within the Soviet bloc, as the incidents that punctuated Soviet hegemony in 1954, 1956, 1968, and 1980–81 clearly highlighted.

Soviet power and its expansion necessitated the deployment of a direct and coercive apparatus of power. In contrast, the politics and political power of the United States could expand *without* the need for a directly coercive physical presence. Thus, the *expansion of capitalist social relations* after 1945 was *an international politics of expansion*. Whereas Realists talk of the expansion of power and securing advantage, what was really happening, ultimately, with *and* without military power was a politics of expansion based on capitalist social relations that did not always require a direct coercive American political presence. The international conflict centred on the issue that whereas Soviet power and international expansion required the destruction of all forms of non-state 'political' activity and relations, American capitalist political expansion demanded quite the opposite, the expansion of the non-state 'political' sphere.

Soviet international relations, then, were identified, correctly, with the elimination of any form of autonomous private sphere that offered the possibility of an alternative currency of politics. This association of a form of society, socialism, with a particular state, the USSR, meant that socialism was not identified as an alternative model to capitalism, but as a type of society inextricably linked to the USSR. Without a complete 'Sovietization' of social life, the social order was likely to be undermined by the presence of alternative currencies of politics. Whereas under capitalist social structures there is a degree of social autonomy, although the degree to which this extends to politics as such has always varied, the expansion of the Soviet social system did not and could not allow this.

This derived from the dynamic of Soviet political expansion, which was distinguished by its own and distinct *internal* logic. What this meant was that, because socioeconomic production was centrally organized and co-ordinated by the bureaucratic apparatus of the Party-state both within and between communist revolutionary states, the dynamic of material accumulation and thus socioeconomic expansion was always confined to the institutions of the state and determined by it. Expansion, then, took on a qualitatively distinct character because it was always determined by the political authorities for explicitly *political* ends. Expansion was not economic, but expressly political. In this sense the USSR was a self-limiting economic machine. Its economy could not expand on its own, and thus because it was limited to political expansion, it was never able to foster a global set of social relations. Because Soviet economic expansion necessitated a direct political expansion of the Party-state bureaucracy as well, it also demanded either a local-indigenous revolutionary overthrow of the state (as in China, Vietnam and elsewhere) and then the establishing of subordinate/dependent relations with the USSR,[71] or a direct Soviet political occupation, as in Mongolia and Eastern Europe. In other words, military violence and war were virtually the only means of international political expansion, based as it was on the destruction of an existing state and then its reconstitution.

Just as Soviet Bolshevism had managed to silence (and liquidate) any opposition, both capitalist and socialist, within the Soviet Union, it also could not tolerate international opposition. International socialist opposition or rivalry, be it Chinese or Dubček's 'socialism with a human face', threatened to undermine the contradictory relationship between the Party-state, as the agent of socialist transformation and international revolution, and the masses in the Soviet Union. This became increasingly problematic for the relations between the Soviet Union and other revolutionary states, because each could not tolerate an alternative or different path within the international communist movement. Such a situation would have obviously undermined the form of political rule within each socialist state, because all of the social formations concerned had not resolved the contradictions of the relationship between the political institutions and the development of productive forces.

In many respects, then, the international relations between revolutionary states reflected the situation of the possibility of international disputes carrying the same weight as an internal dispute with an internal political opposition. Because relations were confined to inter-Party-state relations, the impact of disagreement was much more pronounced. This was compounded by the contending 'factions' within each revolutionary leadership that were usually associated with support for a specific international line. Doctrinal disputes amounted to attacks on a leadership and as a consequence the domestic position of that leadership. Just as much as Soviet disfavour (particularly under Stalin) led to purges and changes of leadership, so the Sino-Soviet dispute reflected the possibility of externally assisted internal change, which all revolutionary leadership attempted to guard against.[72]

Because of the particular relationship between politics and economics in these types of state, international relations reflected the internal tensions between 'socialist' (i.e. material construction) and class relations rooted in an antagonism based on the alienation of the Party-state form of political rule as a relation of production. The Sino-Soviet split, then, and the way in which this was mediated in international relations to the point of military conflict in border clashes, and support for rival factions in national liberation struggles, formed part of the conflict over rival forms of socialist construction that the Soviet Union and China pursued. The conflict concerned the role of the institutions of political rule, with the Party-state rather than the working class as the agency of class mobilization and 'socialist construction'. This was as much an international problem as it was a domestic one. In the Soviet Union and China the respective communist parties were the forces of class struggle, but in international terms the Soviet Union regarded itself as the sole representative of the international communist movement. Just as within the Soviet Union the institutions of the Party-state directed and determined the social relations of the working class (what it considered as class praxis through improved worker productivity) and the nature of socialist construction, in the same way the USSR attempted to do so in the wider relations of the international communist movement. The USSR took it upon itself to determine the conduct of the international revolution, which continued to be bound up with the material and political strength of the Soviet bloc.[73]

The contrary was the case in the international relations of the United States. The United States and capitalist states in general operated according to a very different logic and form of political expansion that were not limited to a direct physical presence within a particular area. Because of the separation of the spheres of social life, capitalism as a social relation and the politics that derive from this can expand relatively autonomously without the need for a direct physical–political form of agency. The crucial economic distinction, then, between the United States and the USSR was the fact that the American economy, like capitalist economies in general, expanded according to the accumulating drives of capitalist competition. Although the state is not completely divorced from these developments, the relative privatization of capitalist production allows production, accumulation and thus expansion to be largely determined by the horizontal competition between capitalist firms. Thus, what marks out capitalist production is its own internal logic of expansion that is not explicitly politically driven. Expansion is driven by the economic imperative of competition, which allows an expansion that is not limited to areas of direct (national) political control. Capitalist expansion is inherent to capitalism as a social system. It does not rest on political decisions, but on the competitive workings of a market characterized by 'anarchy'. The most important point in contrast to the USSR is that the anarchy of capital is not limited to the state, but is extra-territorial, and thus in one sense supersedes the political power and politics of the state.

The rule of capital and capitalist social relations expand through commodities and the exchange of commodities and the relations and politics that follow from the 'mutual dependence mediated by things'. The form of political rule of capitalism is reflected in separate states, but is not recognized by capital and capital is not limited by it. The separation of the spheres of social life under capitalism allows forms of expansion to take on an apparently non-political character when the consequences and actual process of that expansion *are* political. American capitalism expanded prodigiously without appearing to do so as such, because it expanded into forms of political rule that did not regard such social relations as directly political, though in practice they certainly were. Capitalist social relations only become politicized when they are directly contested, and the (American) capitalist state, internal and external, only showed itself to be the agent of capital when the social antagonism within capitalism between workers and owners spilled over from its economic origins to the social order itself. It was only through such self-conscious political agency (which I will discuss in Chapter 5) that economic crises became political crises within and between states.

NOTES

1 In this respect this chapter is broadly located within the same 'critical theory' project of the so-called 'constructivist' approach to International Relations exemplified by Alexander Wendt, *Social Theory of International Politics* (Cambridge: Cambridge University Press, 1999). However, whereas constructivists tend to focus on the role of ideas in shaping structures, as opposed to Realists who, it is argued, emphasize material interests, the approach offered here emphasizes the social relationship between political rule and socioeconomic production.

2 Morgenthau, *Politics Among Nations*, pp. 5–12, 22–35. Although Waltz does not use Morgenthau's understanding of power, at least explicitly, his concern with security, its military definition and projection in a 'self help' system obviously relates to power or more explicitly for Waltz, the balance of power. See Waltz's discussion of the balance of power in *Theory of International Politics*, pp. 102–28, and the military definition of power, pp. 161–93.

3 Kissinger criticized US foreign policy for its inconsistent and flawed attempts to project American domestic ideals on to international relations – what he labels as 'Wilsonianism'. However, he suggests that not only was this morally problematic but also unscientific: see *Diplomacy*, passim. Gaddis in his later work intimates the importance of domestic ideals as a guide for foreign policy, but continues to stress the 'essential relevance of nuclear weapons' as a structural device that insured the long-term 'working out' of domestic change in the USSR. See *United States*, pp. 105–18. Kennan always stressed the need for US foreign policy to be true to the domestic ideals of the United States, but this was always framed in reference to the state, *American Diplomacy*, pp. 126–8.

4 What this means is that the Cold War is treated as an episode within a broader story of political power, to which states of all social and political persuasions are forced to conform, because of the organizing principles of the international system. See Gaddis, *United States*, p. 45; *Long Peace*, p. 217; Kissinger, *Diplomacy*, p. 426.

5 See Morgenthau, *Politics Among Nations*, pp. 25–9.

6 See Kenneth Waltz, *Man, the State, and War: A Theoretical Analysis* (New York: Columbia University Press, 1979), pp. 160, 238; idem, 'Realist Thought and Neorealist Theory', in C. Kegley Jr (ed.), *Controversies in International Relations Theory. Realism and the Neoliberal Challenge* (New York: St Martin's Press, 1995), pp. 75–80; *Theory of International Politics*, pp. 39, 58–66 and *passim*.

7 Most importantly power derived from economic ownership that is not reducible to the state.

8 Rosenberg, *Empire of Civil Society*, p. 19.

9 Ibid., p. 13.

10 Ibid., pp. 11–19.

11 Ibid., pp. 4–6.
12 For an historical sociology of the modern state that dwells on this historical development, the state as an institution for war, see M. Mann, *States, War and Capitalism: Studies in Political Sociology* (Oxford: Basil Blackwell, 1988); C. Tilly, *Coercion, Capital and European States, AD 990–1990* (Oxford: Basil Blackwell, 1990).
13 See Morgenthau, *Politics Among Nations*, pp. 5–8; Waltz, *Theory of International Politics*, p. 66; *Man, the State, and War*, pp. 80–123.
14 See M. Doyle, 'Liberalism and World Politics', *American Political Science Review*, 80, 4 (1986), pp. 1151–70; Wendt, *Social Theory*.
15 J. Ruggie, 'Multilateralism: The Anatomy of an Institution', in J. Ruggie (ed.), *Multilateralism Matters. The Theory and Praxis of an Institutional Form* (New York: Columbia University Press, 1993), pp. 24–36.
16 Waltz, *Theory of International Politics*.
17 For discussions of these developments, see G. Lundestad *'Empire' by Invitation: The United States and European Integration, 1945–1997* (Oxford: Oxford University Press, 1998); M. Hogan, *The Marshall Plan: America, Britain and the Reconstruction of Western Europe, 1947–1952* (Cambridge: Cambridge University Press, 1987); C. Maier, 'Alliance and Autonomy: European Identity and US Foreign Policy Objectives in the Truman Years', in M. Lacey (ed.), *The Truman Presidency* (Cambridge: Cambridge University Press, 1989), pp. 273–98.
18 See Kissinger, *Diplomacy*, pp. 424–6; Gaddis, *Strategies of Containment*, p. 4; idem, *Long Peace*, p. 49; Lynch, *Cold War is Over*, pp. 15–16.
19 See Halliday, *Making of the Second Cold War*, p. 41.
20 *Anarchical Society*, p. 51.
21 Ibid., pp. 24–51.
22 Ibid., pp. 101–26.
23 The Cold War therefore was not treated as a broadly distinct period, but rather in terms of the peculiar nature of the postwar international order. The Soviet Union had certain tensions with international society, but it was essentially a member of that society. Bull, *Anarchical Society*, pp. 204–5.
24 Ibid., pp. 40–51.
25 Thus the state is based on a particular model of domestic and international legitimacy. In terms of the former this reflected the just expression of a political community usually understood as a nation, and in terms of the latter, recognition of sovereign independence by other states.
26 See Bull, *Anarchical Society*, pp. 8–20.
27 See Rosenberg, *Empire of Civil Society*, pp. 123–58 for an extended discussion of the nature of the capitalist state.
28 As Marx makes clear: 'the *establishment of the political state* and the dissolution of civil society into independent *individuals* – whose relations with one another depend on *law*, just as relations of men in the system of guilds and estates depended on *privilege* – is accompanied by *one and the same act.*' K. Marx and F. Engels, *Collected Works*, Vol. 3 (London: Lawrence & Wishart, 1975), p. 167.
29 See K. Marx, *Capital*, Vol. 1 (Harmondsworth: Penguin Books, 1990), pp. 873–940.
30 H. Bull and A. Watson (eds), *The Expansion of International Society* (Oxford: Clarendon Press, 1985).
31 D. Armstrong, *Revolution and World Order: The Revolutionary State in International Society* (Oxford: Clarendon Press, 1993).
32 Ibid., pp. 5–6.
33 Ibid., p. 6. Armstrong does not pursue this point, but by raising it seems to suggest, as many liberals have done, how to respond to revolution by ignoring the rhetoric of revolutionaries, which is regarded as something only for domestic consumption.

Such an understanding belittles the impact of revolution on international relations and fails to understand the principal concerns of revolutions to exactly reshape the international order; this has always been a constitutive feature of social revolutions. See Halliday, *Revolution and World Politics*, pp. 1–23.

34 Armstrong, *Revolution and World Order*, p. 134.

35 Ibid., pp. 120–7, 135–47.

36 Armstrong, *Revolution and World Order*, pp. 302–3; Bull, *Anarchical Society*, pp. 311–15; idem, 'The Revolt Against the West', in Bull and Watson, *Expansion of International Society*, pp. 217–28.

37 Bull, *Anarchical Society*, pp. 204–5.

38 Ibid., pp. 208–27.

39 See Armstrong, *Revolution and World Order*, p. 7; R. J. Vincent, 'Order in International Politics', in J. Miller and R. J. Vincent (eds), *Order and Violence: Hedley Bull and International Relations* (Oxford: Clarendon Press, 1990), pp. 38–64; P. Lyons 'New States and International Order', in A. James (ed.), *The Bases of International Order* (Oxford: Oxford University Press, 1973), pp. 24–59.

40 See E. Wood, *Democracy Against Capitalism: Renewing Historical Materialism* (Cambridge: Cambridge University Press, 1995), pp. 19–48.

41 To treat these forms of political power on their own terms, detached from anything apart from the 'logic of anarchy', exposes the limitations of traditional 'International Theory'. The case should be instead to treat these forms of politics within the wider world within which they exist and by which they are shaped. For example, nuclear weapons are constantly discussed purely in terms of the operation of deterrence. A much richer understanding of the historical notions of these forms of weapons could be derived from specifying the historical uses of such weapons. See, for example, on this point D. Ellsberg, 'Introduction: Call to Mutiny', in E. P. Thompson and D. Smith (eds), *Protest and Survive* (New York: Monthly Review Press, 1981), pp. i–vi.

42 Thus we can identify not only different types of political form, from royal dynasty to empire and federation, but also distinctions within the organizing parameters of the modern sovereign state between liberal and fascist, and capitalist and communist. However, for Marxists, what directs our attention is the organization of socioeconomic production and how this conditions the nature and institutionalization of politics. See P. Corrigan *et al.*, *Socialist Construction and Marxist Theory: Bolshevism and Its Critique* (London: Macmillan, 1978), p. 9.

43 See Wood, *Democracy Against Capitalism*, pp. 36–44.

44 This is not a controversial point. Classical, Neo-classical, Keynesian and Marxist political economy all agree on this point. What distinguishes them is how they understand the nature and dynamic of this relationship.

45 See J. Holloway and S. Picciotto (eds), *State and Capital: A Marxist Debate* (London: Edward Arnold, 1978), pp. 2–16; Wood, *Democracy Against Capitalism*, pp. 59–97.

46 See Ruggie, 'Multilateralism', pp. 24–35; R. Pollard, *Economic Security and the Origins of the Cold War: The Strategic Ends of US Foreign Policy, 1945–1950* (New York: Columbia University Press, 1985); R. Latham, *The Liberal Moment. Modernity, Security, and the Making of the Postwar International Order* (New York: Columbia University Press, 1997). Hogan, *The Marshall Plan*.

47 Thus by 1958 not only had the major western European governments made their currencies freely convertible, but six were to form the EEC and seven EFTA.

48 Latham, *Liberal Moment*, pp. 145–6; C. Maier, 'The Politics of Productivity: Foundations of American International Economic Policy After World War Two', *International Organization*, 31, 4 (1977), pp. 607–33.

49 US economic policy towards Europe after the war also needs to be seen from the

wider perspective of US anti-colonialism, and the generally successful realization of its objective of overseeing the dismantling of European empires with their respective discriminatory trade regimes. Moreover, as R. Cox, *Production, Power, and World Order: Social Forces in the Making of History* (New York: Columbia University Press, 1987), pp. 214–19, argues, the proposed international financial architecture that rested on economic power provided major international leverage over the expansionary economic policies of national governments.

50 Cox, *Production, Power, and World Order*, p. 215. Such methods were also employed within the USA, particularly to isolate radical and communist elements within the labour movement and tie US labour relations into a broader US anti-communist ideology. See M. Rupert, *Producing Hegemony: The Politics of Mass Production and American Global Power* (Cambridge: Cambridge University Press, 1995).

51 See Bull and Watson, *Expansion of International Society*, pp. 1–9.

52 Theda Skocpol, *States and Social Revolutions: A Comparative Analysis of France, Russia and China* (Cambridge: Cambridge University Press, 1979).

53 See C. Lefort, *The Political Forms of Modern Society: Bureaucracy, Democracy, Totalitarianism*, ed. and intro. J. Thompson (Cambridge: Polity Press, 1986).

54 For discussions of the political economy of the USSR and Soviet bloc see the following: B. Fowkes, *The Rise and Fall of Communism in Eastern Europe* (New York: St Martin's Press, 1993); C. Harman, *Class Struggles in Eastern Europe, 1945–83* (London: Bookmarks, 1988); J. Kopstein, *The Politics of Economic Decline in East Germany, 1945–1989* (Chapel Hill: University of North Carolina Press, 1997); A. Nove, *An Economic History of the USSR, 1917–1991* (Harmondsworth: Penguin, 1992).

55 Not in all cases, as the Soviet system did manage to ensure a range of social and economic benefits to the population. However, attempts to question Party-state orthodoxy in relation to cultural activities, economic measures and so forth were not tolerated.

56 I. Deutscher, *Stalin: A Political Biography* (London: Penguin, 1988), pp. 302–15, states that in the mid-1920s farmers sold to towns only a third of the produce that they had sold prior to the war. By the late 1920s this situation had reached the point where famine threatened the population of the USSR's major cities.

57 See C. Bettelheim, *Class Struggles in the USSR*, I: *First Period, 1917–1923*, II: *Second Period, 1923–1930* (Hassocks: Harvester Press, 1977–78); Deutscher, *Stalin*, pp. 297–342.

58 See Stalin's speech 'The Year of the Great Breakthrough', November 1929, in E. H. Carr, *The Russian Revolution from Lenin to Stalin (1917–1929)* (London: Macmillan, 1979), pp. 170–1.

59 Without the drive for rapid industrial development, the USSR would not have been able to sustain the onslaught of German military power after June 1941. As it was, even with forced industrialization, Stalin's targets for pig-iron production by the early 1930s were only finally met in 1941. See Deutscher, *Stalin*, p. 322.

60 See Corrigan, *Socialist Construction*, pp. 24–50 for an excellent survey of how modernization or 'capitalist tendencies', based on a development project defined in terms of materially outproducing capitalism by 'catching-up and overtaking', dominated Bolshevism and the Soviet model.

61 Khrushchev's often misquoted speech at the UN in 1960, specifically the 'we will bury you' remarks, referred to his belief that the Soviet Union would out-produce the United States and thus 'bury capitalism to history'. See the work of Isaac Deutscher for an illuminating discussion of these themes of modernization and development in Bolshevism, in particular, *Ironies of History: Essays on Contemporary Communism* (London: Oxford University Press, 1966).

62 In a number of respects, the Soviet model incorporated a number of inegalitarian, quasi-capitalist traits. For example, labour power, most obviously under Stalin, was commandeered as an instrument of the plan by the Party-state, with little or no input from the workers. This tendency developed into a fetish of productivity, notably the Stakhanovite system that attempted to foster labour productivity through a hierarchy of wage differentials. See Lefort, *Political Forms of Modern Society*, pp. 70–8; I. Deutscher, *The Unfinished Revolution, Russia 1917–1967* (London: Oxford University Press, 1967), pp. 41–60.

63 Deutscher, *Stalin*, p. 342.

64 See Corrigan, *Socialist Construction*, p. xvi.

65 See Corrigan, *Socialist Construction*; Deutscher, *Stalin*, pp. 334–8, for Stalin's labour code and the role of direct coercion in labour productivity.

66 For an extended commentary see H. Ticktin, *The Origins of the Crisis in the USSR: Essays on the Political Economy of a Disintegrating System* (Armonk, NY: M. E. Shape, 1992); T. Cliff, *State Capitalism in Russia Today* (London: Bookmarks, 1988). Instances of the economic origins of political threats to the Soviet socio-political order were even more prevalent in Eastern Europe, where the politics of material contradiction were imbued with anti-Russian/Soviet nationalism, particularly in Poland.

67 Thus, for the Bolsheviks, Lenin as much as Stalin, the state was conceived as the major agency of socialist construction 'in both its production and political facets. It was both the motor of construction and the instrument of class struggle developing the forces and revolutionising the relations of production through its fiscal and planning machinery, whilst securing the political conditions for this stratagem through its repressive and ideological apparatuses.'
Corrigan, *Socialist Construction*, p. 44.

68 Halliday, *Making of the Second Cold War*, pp. 138–9.

69 See P. Corrigan *et al.*, 'The State as a Relation of Production', in P. Corrigan (ed.), *Capitalism, State Formation and Marxist Theory* (London: Quartet, 1980), p. 2.

70 Ruggie, 'Multilateralism', pp. 24–36; Pollard, *Economic Origins*, pp. 133–66; Latham, *Liberal Moment*, pp. 142–92.

71 As P. Dibb, *The Soviet Union: Incomplete Superpower* (Basingstoke: Macmillan, 1986), p. 33, suggests, the coercive and hierarchical nature of Soviet relations with 'allied' states not only caused problems in inter-communist relations but also raised fears of Soviet imperialism among many other states.

72 Thus, in China, Cuba and other revolutionary states, internal political leadership was directly related to the external orientation/international line towards the USSR. International disputes between leaderships or sections of them usually affected internal political order, with purges and the removal of those identified with the 'dissident' international line. This was what happened in the 1960s in China, particularly after the public acknowledgement of the Sino-Soviet split, and also in Cuba in the 1960s.

73 Stalin made this quite clear in a speech in August 1927, when he talked of 'Revolutionary Internationalism': 'An internationalist is one who, unreservedly, without wavering, without conditions, is ready to defend the USSR, because the USSR is the base of the world revolutionary movement, and to defend, to move forward, this revolutionary movement is impossible without defending the USSR' (quoted in Nation, *Black Earth, Red Star*, p. 36).

4

Military Power and Strategic Conflict in the Cold War

The previous chapter sought to reconstitute the politics of the state in the Cold War by conceptualizing the state as a political form derived from the parcelization of power that characterizes capitalist social relations. The conceptualization of the modern state, then, needs to go beyond an understanding of it as a legal–territorial entity, but also as an historical and social subject that emerged from, and was conditioned by, social processes and social conflict. One of the principal features of the state is the centralization and monopoly of organized violence, most manifest in the structures and organization of military power. Much of the previous chapter's analysis was suggestive of this issue: the role and determining force of coercive military power in the politics of the state. This chapter continues the preceding chapter's analysis by explicitly focusing on military power and how far the international relations of the Cold War were defined by the currency of military power and strategic conflict. This is important because much of the analysis of the Cold War which takes as its starting point the military personality of all states, particularly the superpowers, has understood it as an episode of strategic conflict dominated by nuclear weapons.

Despite a general agreement on the importance of military power as the defining feature of the Cold War, however, the exact nature and explanatory relevance of it has been disputed. Whereas Realists have focused on the role of military power in international conflict, Marxists have tended to stress its domestic role both in stabilizing and encouraging economic growth in capitalist economies through arms production (otherwise known as 'military Keynesianism') and in the management of domestic social and political conflict.[1] The strength of the Realist approach lies in its recognition that the Cold War was a genuine international conflict involving the superpowers, and that a significant, if not at times determining, role in this relationship was the international relations of military power. The strength of Marxist approaches is that they highlight the fact that military power cannot be detached from its 'anchorage' in domestic politics, nor can it be analyzed in isolation from other sources of social and political power. The problem with both of these perspectives, however, is that in one way or another each has a tendency to be 'reductionist' – in the sense that whereas one reduces the Cold War to largely strategic concerns, the other reduces it to domestic issues. Realists are inclined to ignore or to marginalize the impact of domestic politics, in particular the structural domestic socioeconomic presence of military power and how this conditions not only the meaning of domestic politics but also international politics. Thus, the external–geopolitical 'policy outcomes' of states are contingent upon, if not at times determined by, the nature of domestic politics and whether or not domestic politics is dominated by military power. Marxists, on the other hand, are prone to be reductionist in collapsing manifestations of external conflict into the domestic political priorities of each ruling class. Thus, for most Marxists, the international crises of the Cold War were not, ultimately, about inter-state military competition, but about the machinations of the dominant ruling classes and their efforts to preserve their power in the domestic sphere and bloc.

This chapter will try to overcome these problems by engaging with both sets of literature, and suggesting an alternative way of understanding the role and nature of military power in the Cold War. The Cold War was defined by military power not because of the ongoing (transhistorical) strategic conflict derived from the anarchical structure of the international system, as Realists tend to suggest, nor from the domestic need to use military power to maintain internal political power, as many Marxist have asserted, but rather because of the international consequences of the domestic natures of certain types of states. What was defining for the role of military power in the Cold War was the presence of the USSR, and the emergence of other similarly constituted states through social revolution that effectively abolished any non-state 'private' sources of politics. From the perspective of capitalist states like the United States, the reconstitution of domestic politics based on a transformed social relationship between political authority and socioeconomic production meant that they could not influence the politics of these states through non-state and non-military sources of political power. The only way in which the United States could achieve its objectives in its relations with the USSR and revolutionary states was through coercion based on military power. From the perspective of the USSR, because it had abolished the sphere of politics not reducible to the state, the only way in which it could realize its international objectives was through the external projection of coercive political power based on superior military power. Thus, *the Cold War was militarized because of the nature of social and political transformation within states*. It was for this reason that the absence of social revolution was the prerequisite for the possibility of an international relations system not based on military power and strategic conflict, and why eruptions of social revolution provided the main dynamic for the role of military power and strategic conflict in the Cold War.

The next two sections of this chapter will give an overview of and criticize Realist and Marxist analyses of the role of military power in the

Cold War; this will be followed by an analysis of how military power is socially constituted and how it came to have a different impact on the international relations of the USSR and the United States.

Military Power in the Cold War

The determining influence of military power in the Cold War reflected a number of technological, social and political issues that crystallized at the end of the Second World War. The most important military development was the successful use of nuclear weapons by the United States in August 1945. Alongside this military–technological advance were other developments that would lead to a restructuring of international military power in the postwar era. These developments consisted of the following: the military pre-eminence of the superpowers over other states, and the development of strategic conflict between them; the restructuring of international capitalist military relations under US leadership, formalized in the 1949 founding of the North Atlantic Treaty Organization (NATO) that contributed to the emergence of pacific relations between the advanced capitalist states; the proliferation of military conflict in the form of national liberation – revolutionary struggle concerned with state formation and social transformation in the colonial world.

The postwar era, then, saw a transformation in both the form and substance of military power and war, which were to play a critical role in the Cold War. However, what needs emphasizing is that all of these military developments were couched within wider historical and social developments. That is, although the world objectively became a more dangerous place after 1945, that danger was not reducible to the presence of certain military technologies, but rather was due to the nature of the international social and political turmoil and struggles that this period witnessed, which were not outside the shadow of the bomb.

Because of the changes enumerated above, military power was removed from the political conflicts between the advanced capitalist states to a degree that a forceful thesis emerged, entitled 'democratic peace', that argued that 'liberal democracies' did not fight wars with each other.[2] This was an unprecedented historical development and an outcome of the Second World War that reflected the transformation of international capitalism, and the inseparable developments of nuclear weapons and the increased Soviet threat. However, although military conflict was removed from relations between advanced capitalist states, military power was to play a critical and sometimes defining role in the international relations of the Third World. The *systemic* subjugation of peoples in Asia and Africa, which was strongly conditioned by coercive power, came to an end after 1945. Yet, during the process of decolonization international military power became an important issue in determining the ultimate outcome of national liberation struggles.

National liberation and revolutionary struggles in the Third World, then, became the principal arena for the application of military power in the Cold War. The transformation in the form of international capitalist social relations that decolonization reflected also reconstituted capitalist military power, since no longer was international capitalist expansion *conditional* on formal and direct political dominance. It was this transformation and the role of the superpowers in it that provides the main, though not complete, spotlight for the role of military power in the Cold War. Moreover, these developments were imbricated with the strategic nuclear relationship between the superpowers.

This being the case, one of the most important questions relating to the developments in the Third World and the Cold War is how far nuclear weapons determined the course of the Cold War. The point that needs to be made in addressing this issue, identified by Fred Halliday,[3] is that the transformation of military power heralded by nuclear weapons was couched within a more radicalized postwar social context,[4] based on the collapse of European colonial power and the rise of national liberation movements. Obviously, the potential destructive power of nuclear weapons makes them classifiable only on their own terms, and they obviously limited political and military conflict, but they did not, in themselves, define that conflict; they contributed to it.[5]

The presence, development and 'use' of nuclear weapons in the Cold War by the 'superpowers' obviously made the world a much more dangerous place to live in. Nuclear weapons, then, conditioned the international military conflict between the USSR and the United States. However, this conditioning and restraining of military power did not prevent their political use.[6] The use of nuclear weapons in the Cold War was not, in general, a product of the direct conflict between the superpowers, but rather reflected the conflicts within the international expansion of capitalist modernity and the conflicts this wrought in the Third World.[7] This was the terrain of conflict where military power was used and was sometimes determinate.

These issues are important because they contribute to the question posed above and at the beginning of this chapter about how the Cold War could be defined in terms of military power. Nuclear weapons did not emerge in a vacuum, but rather within the exigencies of war, and for the Soviet Union in a world where they were encircled and threatened by nuclear bases. In this sense military power in the form of nuclear weapons could be seen to have an international derivation. However, this recognition does not mean that nuclear weapons, as a form of military power, were autonomous and located solely within the realm of the international. Although they emerged within an international conjuncture their function and determining effect on the Cold War was not defining internationally, but was part of a wider set of relations that were not reducible to military power *alone*. Thus, nuclear weapons and superpower military power more broadly defined could, arguably, be seen to have helped determine the emergence and outcome of a number of crises and conflicts during the Cold War.[8] However, the determining of events like the Vietnam War and the Cuban missile crisis cannot be detached from wider issues that conditioned the *use* of military power. As will be argued in the subsequent discussions of US and Soviet military power, military power had a different formative impact on each one's internal and international relations in the Cold War. The role of nuclear weapons and military power were important in this regard, but were determinant in *different* ways for each superpower. This being the case, derived from the political substance of each as a distinct form of political rule, nuclear weapons featured differently in each one's international relations. Thus if military power was defining of the Cold War, it was only so in terms of the realization of each superpower's overall political objectives.

Geopolitical Determinants of Military Power in the Cold War

The central assumption of Realist analysis of the Cold War is that it reflected a historical continuity, not a rupture, in the competitive relations among states, based on the barometers of military power and strategic conflict. This argument focuses on the military dominance of the United States and the Soviet Union after the Second World War. Bipolarity dominated the interpretation of the Cold War as military competition through the arms race and technological advances in military capabilities, and how this was refracted and realized in distinct, but transhistorical forms of inter-state conflict. The Cold War, then, saw the application of different and changing military capabilities. This included the armed encircling of the Soviet bloc after 1947 by US-led military alliances and strategic nuclear bases, the encampment of the Red Army in the military 'buffer zone' of Eastern Europe, and the search for global military base facilities. This was part of the wider search for military allies, the preserving of, and expansion into, spheres of interest in the emerging world of decolonized states, and the direct military interventions and deployment of military force in the Third World. All of these account for the dynamic of the Cold War and the enduring forms of military power that pervaded it. What was distinct in terms of the participants in the Cold War, principally the United States and the USSR, were the competing national– strategic interests and how these related to domestic politics.[9]

Seen in the above light, the superpower projection of military power was comparable. They reflected the structural dominance of each in its respective sphere of political influence and in world politics generally. Following this, the projection of military power was primarily about the securing of certain strategic and political objectives for a particular state. These objectives reflected comparable political interests, which amounted to: military base rights/alliances, access to the local economy in terms of a market for goods and access to raw materials, and strategic loyalty (i.e. providing a bulwark against any rival superpower influence in the area and/or local forces sympathetic to one or other superpower).[10]

For Realists, the strategic arms race was not only the principal relationship of the Cold War, but was largely determined by it.[11] Nuclear weapons and military power regulated the conflict between the United States and the USSR because strategic leverage accrued through an advantage in their production and deployment. This transformed the possibility of great powers imposing their political will through the direct application of force, as in the past, but it did not transform the essence of inter-state conflict. The competing for allies, raw materials and strategic access continued, but it was conditioned by the need to ensure a level of strategic-nuclear advantage over foes.

The problem with Realist arguments over the role and impact of military power in the Cold War is that, (i) they tend to assume that the nature of each side's international relations were essentially the same; and (ii) even if we accept the former premise, it rests on a dubious assertion that the actual material content of those relations was comparable. On both counts Realist assumptions are questionable. I have already discussed the former in some depth in the preceding chapter, so shall now concentrate on the latter.

The second point above relates to how far the actual military 'content' of the international relations of the superpowers in the Cold War was comparable. If the Cold War was largely about superpower strategic conflict then this would need to be justified by some kind of international military-strategic relationship of competition and conflict between the United States and the USSR. Yet if Realists are to be believed, up until the 1960s at least, well into the Cold War, the USSR was not competing on the same strategic-military terms as the United States. Although both sides pursued similar policies in the research and development of strategic weapons (the arms race), the actual international significance of these developments was rather one-sided, in the sense that the USSR did not have an effective strategic military capacity until sometime in the late 1960s. Hence, until the USSR reached a recognized level of 'parity' in the late 1960s in the strategic arms race, there was no 'level playing field' in the Cold War and the content of strategic competition between the two superpowers was characterized by asymmetry. The USSR had a territorial strength in that it maintained a large military presence in Eastern Europe, but one cannot look at this presence purely from a strategic perspective.

The Red Army was more active *within* the Soviet bloc than outside it for the whole of the Cold War.

This argument may be countered by the fact that the USSR was active in the Third World from the late 1950s–early 1960s onwards, and in the early 1970s during the 'arc of crises' manifestly so. However, the projection of Soviet military power was in *response* to revolutionary seizures of power in a number of states in the Third World. The international context is important in that not only was the international role of Soviet military power contingent on international developments that it could not always direct or control, but furthermore in that it was dependent on the expectation of the likely nature of the US response. The US strategic-military posture had been undermined by the defeat in Indo-China, which provided, for the first time in the Cold War, an international conjuncture where the United States was concerned to limit the deployment of military force. If and when the United States returned to a more aggressive posture, as it did in the early 1980s, the international context changed and in doing so altered the possibility for the prescriptive use of Soviet military power.

More important, though, is the fact that the 'strategic' strength of the USSR was augmented by not only its own military power, but also the level and success of the contestation of the international capitalist order through social revolution. Realists tend to blur the distinctions between the Soviet challenge to the United States and that offered by the dynamic of social revolution, which was largely autonomous of the USSR. Although the USSR's strategic position did benefit from revolution, the content of its international relations did not include revolution. In this sense then, not only do Realists underplay the asymmetry in the content of each superpower's international relations, but they also fail properly to conceptualize the contributing impact of social revolution, which was not reducible to either superpower, yet was a major factor in the Cold War.

Domestic Determinants of Military Power in the Cold War

Marxist writing on the Cold War has also emphasized the defining influence of military power and strategic conflict. Much of this analysis is founded on the assumptions of classical Marxism, and in particular the debates over the 'warlike tendencies' of (capitalist) imperialism.[12] What distinguishes this approach to the Cold War, however, is the identification of the constitutive social elements of military power. Military power and strategic conflict are not, in themselves, defining of the Cold War, only insofar as they reflect, in a military form, the wider constellation and contradictions of a given sociopolitical order.[13]

The principal focus of these arguments is an analysis of the role of coercive–military power in the constitution of each superpower's domestic/ bloc politics, and how the threat of the 'other' was used to help preserve internal political order and contain radical–revolutionary impulses within each bloc.[14] The Cold War, then, was not seen as a social or strategic conflict between the USSR and the West, but rather as a system that allowed for the dominance of each ruling class, domestically and over their respective allies, assisted by the manipulation and exaggeration of an external political–military threat. The inherent contradictions and war-like proclivities of capitalism were contained through US military and economic hegemony, which would not have been possible without the appearance of a Soviet military threat. Likewise, the stability and *domestic* strength of the USSR rested on continuing to project external hostility towards the West, without which the tight internal discipline of the USSR and the Soviet bloc would have collapsed under the system's inherent contradictions.

Although these analyses highlight an area and set of sociopolitical issues largely ignored by Realist analysis, they do so at the cost of reducing the Cold War to either a 'strategic functionalism' or, *in extremis*, con-spiracy theory. The fixation on internal sociopolitical conflict within the two constituent blocs of the 'Cold War system' reflects a tendency to overlook two major issues that relate to the impact of military power on the international relations of the Cold War. First is the tendency of implying symmetry in the internal social relations of each superpower. Thus there is a tendency to downplay the differences between the capitalist form of state and the Soviet or 'socialist' form of state. Instead, each ruling class needs to use the state, particularly its coercive institutions, to help maintain political leadership both within each superpower and also within the wider bloc. Military power, then, is not primarily a currency of inter-national relations, but rather the basis of a domestic sociopolitical order.

The problem with this is that although they suggest that the USSR was more defined by a coercive politics to maintain political order within itself and the Soviet bloc than was the case in the United States and the West, one would have assumed that developments within the external realm would have been *engineered* to justify the continued levels of political surveillance, control and military occupation. However, although the Soviet Union always sought to justify its military presence and political control in the language of security and threat, it is difficult to identify a consistent pattern, or any pattern for that matter, where, after Stalin's death, the USSR deliberately provoked international crises so as to help justify internal repression. Although the Soviet leadership was well versed in the propaganda of threat and encirclement, some of which they did exaggerate, they did not pursue *policies* that deliberately tried to maintain or increase the level of tension. If anything, Soviet policy was concerned to limit the potential for any direct military conflagration with the West.

Yet, when the USSR did use military power, it was precisely to support other revolutionary states, as in its support for the Cuban and Vietnamese revolutions, and its intervention in Afghanistan, which was at the risk of seriously upsetting the 'strategic arrangement' it supposedly had with the West.

This highlights the second problem with the tendency to downplay the external and military sources of the Cold War. Here Soviet support for the Cuban revolution was not only about consolidating the bloc by incorporating Cuba into it but about using Cuba as a means to challenge US strategic power by directly threatening the United States with a 'first-strike' capability. The outcome of this, and the US response to it, are well documented; what this example highlights is that military power was not just a purely domestic issue. Rather, for the USSR it was the principal means with which to cultivate international relations, and because of this it contributed to an international dynamic of competition and conflict that went much further than servicing domestic politics.

Another line of Marxist argument has focused more explicitly on the militaristic tendencies within capitalism, particularly those associated with the thesis of the 'permanent arms economy'.[15] This argument, which influences those of Kaldor and Cox, states that the material production of military power in the advanced capitalist economies had more to do with the domestic health of these economies than with dealing with international military preoccupations or threats. The claim is that because of the inherent problems within capitalist economies associated with managing demand and maintaining economic growth and employment, the state spends money on armaments to help ensure economic growth and employment to the overall benefit of the economy. Militarism, then, is an innate feature of capitalism, and this argument tends to follow on from Lenin's theory of imperialism and the origins of war in 1914 and 1939. The manipulation of an external military threat provided the justification for this military expenditure, but the reality was that this was an internal economic need, not an external political one.

The problem with this argument is that it tends to assume that the American economy was dominated by the military sector to such a degree that increased production and consumption in this sector would have had general effects on the wider economy. This tends to assume what needs to be explained. The evidence is far from clear-cut as to the necessity of militarized production to maintain the economic health of capitalist states. As Smith has argued, there is evidence to suggest that the growth and employment rates of the major capitalist economies after 1945 were evenly balanced between those states that had high levels of military expenditure and those with low levels.[16] Moreover, as Halliday has argued, it is difficult to distinguish the different areas of military expenditure and their impact on the wider economy, where nuclear weapons accounted for a smaller

amount of expenditure than conventional weapons, yet the wider economic consequences of expenditure on the latter were more pronounced.[17]
Finally, there is also the problem of the period of time in question and the
'time lag' from expenditure to its subsequent impact, thus leading to the
question as to how far military expenditure was the reason for increased
economic activity.

The American economy was obviously affected by military production
with respect to the massive amount of public money channelled to
production and research, and the overall expenditure on armaments.[18]
Resources that went to the military sector obviously did not benefit the
civilian sector. However, not only did this not structurally undermine the
American economy, but some aspects of military production did have
wider spin-offs, with technological benefits for the rest of the economy.[19]
The American civilian economy, however, continued to lead the West in
terms of most economic–consumption indicators. Although, by the late
1960s, it was being caught up by its main capitalist competitors, these
developments never managed to bring into serious question the economic
health and political stability of the United States. Moreover, even when
American domestic economic health was problematic, the economy continued to be attractive to international investors. External investment was
such that both the state and private bodies could borrow money from the
external sources of the world market, as the Reagan administration did
in the early 1980s to fund much of its massive arms expenditure. The
structural social relations of capital were such, then, that the American
economic or material capacity to produce armaments was not confined to
the domestic limits of its economy as was that of the USSR. American
capital and the state could seek out alternative sources of credit and
material support to balance, if necessary, domestic civilian concerns.
Moreover, the structural relationship of state and economy/production in
the United States also meant that the political questions that continued to
weigh upon the CPSU leadership relating to levels of domestic economic
consumption were largely resolved by the relative separation from politics
of production, distribution and consumption.

Military production in the United States did not, then, mean that it was
a militarized–industrial society. The vastness of the American economy
and the fact that it was part of a larger international whole meant that,
structurally and socially, its configuration and dynamic were very different
from that of the centrally planned 'socialist' economies of the Soviet bloc.
Moreover, military power was less of an internal political factor in the
domestic generation of the American liberal–capitalist sociopolitical order.
So, in both political and economic terms, military power constituted the
politics and economics of the United States to a much smaller extent than
in the USSR.

The United States and the USSR were similar in terms of each depicting the other as an external military threat and of the ideological and military responses to that threat, but the wider social and thus political consequences to this material preoccupation were not shared equally. The production of Soviet military capacity and the development of its technological–material base were determined by the Party-state's control of the economy through socialized property relations and production based on central planning. Military power was produced within the domestic constraints of the Soviet economy and its material capacity. The USSR's material backwardness was fundamental in this respect in contributing to the nature of the production of military goods in the economy. This material backwardness was what Stalin was most concerned about, as, in an article published in 1929, Stalin made clear:

> Do you want our Socialist fatherland to be beaten and to lose its independence? If you do not want this you must put an end to its backwardness in the shortest possible time and develop genuine Bolshevik tempo in building up its Socialist system of economy. There is no other way. That is why Lenin said during The October Revolution, 'Either perish, or overtake and outstrip the advanced capitalist countries.'[20]

The relationship between the production of military power and material backwardness was not, however, guided only by the external need for the rapid creation of a modern technologically sophisticated military machine to defend against and defeat capitalist foes. It was also the need of a coercive-military apparatus to cope with the internal sociopolitical conflict resulting from forced collectivization and rapid industrialization. In this sense, then, the material constitution of the USSR was predicated on the twin concerns of the coercive basis of the internal sociopolitical order and the necessity of the Soviet social formation being organized socially and materially for external military defence.

Soviet economic development, *ab initio*, was distorted by the necessity of a type of material development that prioritized the production of military goods. Not only was the Soviet economy characterized by relative backwardness vis-à-vis the economies of the advanced capitalist states, but because it was removed from the operations of the world market it did not have the same access to external sources of credit or types of technology and products as did Western states. What this meant was that military production was not only founded on a weaker material base, but also that military production would be a relatively much greater burden for the Soviet economy to bear than it was for the advanced capitalist states.[21]

However, it was not only this problem of material backwardness, but also the *form* of the social relationship between the Party-state and the economy that conditioned the production of military goods. Military production ate into the material resources that otherwise could have gone to other areas of investment and consumption. Because the political authorities were directly responsible for the production of military goods in particular and economic production in general, economic questions, notably the level of and improvements in economic provision, were directly political questions. This being the case the concern to ensure that the political tensions derived from economic questions would not manifest themselves in direct and open conflict between the Soviet people and the Party-state meant that planning and the material possibilities of military production had to be sensitive to these issues. Indeed, the constitution of Soviet military power was, in many respects, conditional on Soviet domestic politics. Khrushchev's decision to reduce conventional military forces and focus on the development of nuclear forces was related to channelling more resources into accelerating economic development, thus realizing economic objectives that he had set in the late 1950s. Moreover, the organization of Soviet military power, particularly the presence of Soviet conventional forces in Eastern Europe, reflected the necessity of military power to maintain communist power there.[22]

The problems within the USSR and the Soviet bloc over the burden that military expenditure placed on the performance of the economy as a whole, and thus on material provision for the Soviet people, should not be exaggerated, however. Despite the relative economic hardships and the wider problems of the planned economy, Soviet military power from the late 1960s continued to consolidate and grow.[23] Thus, although the wider economy did suffer because of the provisions made for military production this did not prevent the USSR from maintaining high levels of defence spending and resource allocation. However, what it did highlight was the continued structural weakness of the civilian economy. Although the USSR could generally match the United States in military terms, in general economic terms it still lagged behind on most economic indicators.[24] This reflected one of the central political contradictions of the USSR. Although the USSR could continue to extract resources to produce the means of military power, by continuing to do this at such high levels it further undermined the general political goal of the development of the USSR's productive forces. Because military power was unlikely ever to be determining, in the sense that if either side in the Cold War had used it directly against the other it would have triggered a massive retaliatory response and 'mutual state suicide', wider economic issues, particularly the strength of the economy, what Isaac Deutscher called the 'Great Contest', were more likely to be.[25]

The USSR was caught in a political paradox of its own making based on the external compulsion to produce more military power, but in doing so threatening to undermine the material basis of the domestic socio-political order. Because the ruling political authorities were directly responsible for all aspects of social life, the inability to separate military provision from social provision and political rule meant that the state was directly pressured externally and internally. In the case of the former, the USSR was forced (within its existing social formation and form of political rule) to increase its military capacity to secure any autonomy at the geopolitical level. Yet this served to undermine the ability of the state, internally, to maintain social and political stability by meeting and improving on existing levels of social and material provision. The fact that there was no private sphere to meet any of these economic and political pressures meant that the production of Soviet military power and its strategic use was always contingent on the level of domestic stability.

To summarize this section, then, the United States and the USSR were differently constituted by military power in the explicitly political sense of the nature of domestic political order and in the more socioeconomic sense of the nature of military production. In the case of the United States, because of the liberal-democratic capitalist nature of the sociopolitical order, political power was fragmented and social conflict was largely confined to the private, non-political sphere, which meant that direct political and military power was not necessary to deal systematically with social conflict. This was not the case in the USSR, where, because of the 'collapsing' of social, economic, ethnic and cultural issues with the political, based on the absence of any autonomous private–economic sphere, social conflict was always political conflict, which necessitated the direct involvement of state power and systematic public coercion.

The differentiation in social and political power in capitalist states also qualified the economic impact of the production of armaments, which not only related to the limitation of the politicization of military production, but also in the sense that such production could be economically assisted by transnational capital beyond the domestic capacity of the United States. This was not the case with the USSR. The problems of maintaining domestic political order were exacerbated by the burden of military production, and the fact that military production was effectively confined to the material capacity of the Soviet Union. As the next section will show, the political and economic contradictions that stemmed from this were augmented by the fact that Soviet international relations necessitated the production of a strong and technologically sophisticated military power to have any effective international relations.

However, the bigger problem of many Marxist-based analyses that have addressed the domestic quality of military power is that they have tended to neglect the geopolitical interstices of the Cold War by 'absorbing' the external antagonism into questions of domestic political conflict. By failing to take seriously the international strategic-military conflict between the USSR and the United States these analyses cannot offer logically consistent explanations for some of the most significant and dangerous crises of the Cold War, where the argument that the Cold War was some kind of mutual accommodation is stretched to breaking point.

Social Relations of Military Power in the Cold War

Military power is constituted both domestically and externally. Externally, it is established in the necessity of states to defend, or at least make preparations to do so against possible military threats from other states. However, the nature of this international dimension of military power is conditioned by how it is internally constituted, in terms of how the matériel of military power is produced, and the effect this has on wider socio-economic questions, and also in the more openly political sense of its role in the maintenance of the existing sociopolitical order. The domestic significance of military power not only conditions its significance as a *currency* of international relations, however, but also 'colours' the nature of the international system. Thus, states largely defined by a politics based on military coercion are likely to be confronted by other states similarly constituted, and the structure of the system and the relations that sustain it will be largely confined to the currency of military power.

It should be clear then that military power should not be detached from its domestic social context; moreover, the degree to which a state's domestic politics are configured by coercive military power will to a great extent determine not only the nature of its international relations, but also the way in which other states can or cannot relate to it. This is what characterized the Cold War, and made military power a defining feature of it. Military conflict was, then, a defining feature of the Cold War, because one state, the USSR, was effectively constituted by coercive-military power. This being the case, not only did this mean that Soviet expansion was effectively confined to the external projection of military power, but also that it could only be contained by military power. It was not only the fact of US military preponderance over the other major capitalist states after 1945 that helped guarantee pacific inter-capitalist international relations, but also the fact that these states were so constituted that American interests could be realized without the need for direct coercion or conflict. This was not the case with the USSR or other revolutionary states. Non-state relations were blocked by the different, 'absolutist', form of sovereignty in the USSR. The militarization of American attempts to construct a postwar liberal international order, then, was largely due to the fact that the USSR could not be incorporated into the new American (multilateral) liberal international order, whereas West European states could. As Robert Latham has argued:

> whereas Britain and France had the capacity to shape negotiations and affect the course of liberal relations, only the Soviet Union had the capacity to disrupt the process itself without being subject to effective discipline.[26]

Without the ability to condition Soviet politics other than through military intimidation, the United States was, in effect, forced to confront the USSR in a hostile manner. For the USSR, to have conducted international relations as the United States desired would not only have meant a Western socio-economic presence in Eastern Europe, but ultimately would have fundamentally undermined the Soviet form of politics and the centralized–absolute power of the Party-state.

The internal constitution of politics within the United States and the USSR had two significant consequences for the Cold War. The first was that whereas the United States was not limited to an international politics based on military power, the USSR was. Secondly, each superpower was driven by a different logic or dynamic of expansion and its consequences. Whereas the USSR could only expand politically in an explicit and direct manner (i.e. as a political–territorial form), the United States could expand its political influence and power without necessarily expanding as a state-territorial presence, but through an alternative form of politics based on capitalist social relations.

The Social Constitution of the American Form of Military Power in the Cold War

The role of coercive-military power in the international relations of the United States during the Cold War was largely *contingent* on the domestic sociopolitical constitution of other states. Military power was the dominant form of American international relations *only* with respect to those political entities that had closed off the possibility of cultivating relations through non-state sources of politics. The Soviet form of state-society relationship reflected this par excellence, and after 1945 this also came to include a number of other states, from China to Cuba. Military power and strategic conflict, then, were directly imbricated with the consequences of internal social and political conflict. It was the outcomes of these conflicts at the domestic level that had an international impact that provided most of the conjunctures when the United States used military power in the Cold War.[27]

Revolutionary change, as in the examples of China, Cuba, Vietnam and elsewhere in the Third World, rested on the direct politicization of those spheres of social life not previously dominated by the state. This expansion of the coercive power of the state not only abolished the internal sources, but also the external sources of non-state power, derived from ownership of private property, political and cultural associations, and religion. The only way of relating to these types of state was directly through state-to-state relations.

These political relations became explicitly coercive and antagonistic, not only because of the domestic nature of the revolutionary state based on its expropriation of foreign and local private property and the breaking-off of established political links, but also because of its international nature, especially its goal of internationalizing the revolution.[28] The greatest instance of this was the Bolshevik-founded Comintern and the establishment of an international organization and cadre network of activists committed to socialist revolution. Even when the Comintern was being directed more by Soviet security concerns than revolutionary expansion in the 1930s (though such a distinction may not *always* have been a contradiction), the organizational existence of communist revolutionary agency, outside the borders of the USSR, as in China and Indo-China, meant that local communists could and did act with degrees of autonomy based on local social and political circumstances that facilitated revolutionary struggle. In all cases of communist, or what became communist, revolution, as in Cuba, revolutionary states established channels and promoted the 'export' of revolution: the Chinese in their crucial support of the Viet Minh after 1949 that was to prove a turning point in the war with the French; the Vietnamese in their programme and support for an Indo-Chinese Revolution which included not only South Vietnam, but also Laos and Cambodia; finally, Cuba in its support of revolutionary struggle in Latin America, and in its direct military interventions in southern Africa and the 'Horn' of Africa in the 1970s.

Revolutionary states largely conformed to the political paradigm of Bolshevism, which rested on the elimination of any non-state political sphere. Thus, how these states attempted to 'export' revolution was imbricated with the coercive-military form of their domestic politics, thus making a military response likely. Because revolutionary states had insulated themselves from alternative political currents within, and politics was limited to the coercive form of the state and a 'maximalist' ideology that was hostile to existing international norms, the United States was effectively 'forced' to use military power either to contain or to overthrow it, thus not only preventing its international expansion but also offering the possibility for domestic counter-revolution. Coercion and force were more apposite than dialogue and compromise because, by their nature, revolutionary states were not interested in a modus vivendi or compromise. Just as much as revolutionary crises within states exposed the coercive basis of the state and politics, so in their international relations they provoked a coercive response by challenging the existing international system.

Thus, the augmentation of state power combined with a 'universalist' and belligerent ideology alongside the removal of the structural ability either to manage or to prevent domestic change, challenged the basis of American power and provoked a hostile political response founded on the same form of politics that tended to characterize the politics of the revolutionary state. International law, diplomacy, and economic incentives or sanctions alongside the language of compromise were ineffectual because, at least in the short term, these were not political currencies that the revolutionary state was likely to be influenced by. Just as much as social revolution exposed the acute nature of political conflict and the inability to resolve political problems through existing institutions and mechanisms within states, so they also exposed the deep fractures in international relations that equally could not be resolved through existing channels or forms of relations. Thus, in this respect political conflict and military power were the outcome. Just as much as the USSR was 'disciplined' by military power, so were other revolutionary states.

What motivated an American *strategic* response to social revolution, however, was not due to internal consequences of revolutionary change alone. It was the importance of Soviet involvement that contributed to making a local or regional crisis into one of strategic significance. Although we do not have to accept the historical arguments of American Cold War ideologues who blamed and found a 'Red under every bed', neither should we accept the position of many liberals who argued that the USSR was not really interested in supporting international revolution. As Soviet attempts to 'sneak' nuclear missiles into Cuba and the consequences of Soviet support for North Vietnam showed, revolutions provided an important way of challenging the United States. Indeed, as Soviet thought on international relations highlighted in the notion of the 'correlation of forces' as the barometer of international power in the Cold War, the expansion of Soviet international power was closely associated with the local challenges to the international capitalist order and not only the possibilities of weakening Western power, but also the prospect of securing political relationships with these states.[29] In this sense regional change became part of a shifting global front that provided the USSR with avenues of international political influence.

Prior to 1945, American hostility to radical–revolutionary change had been largely confined to the Western hemisphere,[30] where the United States had used military force to intervene in the internal politics of a number of states undergoing major structural change. The United States had intervened systematically, using military force, throughout Latin America in the early part of the twentieth century, most notably in Mexico, Cuba and Nicaragua.[31] This behaviour can be seen to reflect a consistency in American international relations pre- and post-1945, particularly in US attitudes towards certain radical and revolutionary forms of domestic political change. The use of coercive-military power either to prevent or to contain and overthrow radical and revolutionary domestic socio-political transformation was evident prior to the promulgation of the Truman Doctrine. In effect the Monroe Doctrine had by the early 1900s been turned into an explicitly counter-revolutionary doctrine after the removal of European colonial power from the Western hemisphere that was to precede the global focus of the 1947 Truman Doctrine.

What facilitated the extension of American international power was the combination of a weakening of the other major capitalist powers that meant that the United States would be able to challenge their political and economic dominance in many parts of the world, with the weakened ability of these powers to combat radical and revolutionary movements, as with the British in the eastern Mediterranean and the French in Indo-China. Thus, because American interests were largely confined to the Western hemisphere up to their involvement in the Second World War, American hostility to revolution played itself out there. But with the change in the relationship of the United States to the colonial powers and the challenge to colonial power in the colonies, the realm of American counter-revolution was extended.

After 1945, the American commitment to a liberal-capitalist conception of state sovereignty became 'globalized' through the Truman Doctrine from what had previously been limited to the Western hemisphere. With decolonization the majority of emergent states conformed, to a greater or lesser degree, to an internal sociopolitical structure that permitted American international relations to be based both on the formal currency of state-to-state relations and on 'political' relations through the private capitalist sphere. In these cases, military power was *not* defining of American international relations. What this meant was that the United States, because of the way it was internally constituted, could relate to other states not only via the political structure of the states system, but also through the international structure of the capitalist private sphere. This it sought to do through establishing its international power not through direct bilateral or political relationships, based on an explicit hierarchy of power and American dominance, but rather through multi-lateralist institutions based on American political design.[32] Even what came to be the most important institution for the projection of American international military power, NATO, was formalized as a multilateral institution that managed to combine American strategic and political interests, yet restricted the nature of US dominance. US power was, then, institutionalized in a unique way such that American hegemony was 'softened' by its liberalism. This was not charity and it was not a case of self-sacrifice, rather it reflected not only the nature of American domestic politics and its form of power, but also the fact that the United States *could* achieve its international objectives, in most cases, through forms of leverage that did not necessitate direct coercion and an ideological vision that, although anti-communist, was not dismissive of a regulatory role for the state in limited areas.[33] Thus, American international power could *expand* its political influence not only through the politics of the state cemented by military power in formal alliances, but also through the political outcomes of capitalist exchange and competition. This currency of international relations was founded on the competitive and accumulative drives of capital consequent on the horizontal and 'anarchic' competition between firms for markets and resources. This dynamic was largely autonomous of the state; instead investment, production and consumption decisions taken by capitalist firms were largely based on the pervasive criteria of profitability and accumulation.[34]

In the immediate postwar period the autonomy of international market exchange between the major capitalist states was restricted, mainly because of the global imbalance between the American and the other Western economies. This imbalance was addressed by a combination of public and private initiatives that rested on American economic largesse through the Marshall Plan and the American economy's management of trade imbalances thus ensuring liquidity in the international trading system. The Marshall Plan was the 'benign' means to ensure open access for American capital, assisted by incentives for American banks to invest overseas. However, the fact that European economies were dependent on American dollars to purchase (American) goods provided great economic leverage with which to press for either the reduction or removal of *political* barriers to trade.[35]

American private economic power was, until the late 1960s, founded on the convertibility and dominance of the US dollar. Although this reduced the political autonomy of other national currencies, because the United States was willing to shoulder the burden of balance of payments deficits, it was accepted by European states and contributed to the 'long boom'.[36] The United States, then, conceded the need to ensure political stability based on economic growth, which was initially funded by the political decision to provide credit to other capitalist states. Thus, although the American economic vision of international free trade was compromised, economic recovery quickly 'set in' in Western Europe and Japan, promoting political stability which helped to marginalize the domestic communist threat, thus reducing the possibility of the need to use direct coercion in intra-Western relations but not in external relations with the Soviet bloc, which became increasingly hostile and militarized after 1945.

US military power, then, was primarily an international political concern and its economic production was not fundamentally about domestic socioeconomic issues, but about having the military potential to meet international military challenges. Not only was US military power primarily an international political issue, but it was also not determining of American international relations. International politics reflected the configuration of American domestic politics. However, the nature of domestic politics was not a result of a predisposition against military power, but the fact that the sociopolitical order did not need to rely on public coercion and military power for its continued existence. The absence of public coercion was a consequence of relative domestic political stability and the fact that social conflict was contained in such a way that it did not usually challenge the social order. When there was a possibility of genuine social crisis with the impact of the Great Depression in the 1930s, the state was able to intervene through the New Deal to stabilize the economy and preserve the social order without the need for systematic public coercion. Therefore, American international relations emanated directly from the structures and institutions of domestic politics. This relationship was evident not only in the structural sense of the political–economic relationship, but also in the social and political content of that relationship, as the New Deal social 'class consensus' provided the ideological content and vision for the construction of new international institutions and a liberal-capitalist international order.

Where military power was the determining factor, however, in American international relations was in US responses to revolution. This was the outcome of an international political *process* that began and was imbued with diplomatic, economic and legal intervention, and it was the nature of the developments within revolutionary states and their international consequences that was to lead to forms of military confrontation between the United States and social revolution. In this respect military power and strategic conflict were not separable from the domestic social and political developments in revolutionary states, indeed they were analogous. Just as much as social conflict which ended up challenging the state provoked a military response, so when international social conflict could not be contained by non-military instruments because such conflict directly challenged states and thus international political order, an international military response occurred. The nature of this form of political power was not separable from other currencies of political power, legal, diplomatic or economic. It was distinct only in the sense that the military manifestation of political power was reflective of the most acute and intense form of conflict, yet the sources of that conflict were socially determined.

The Social Constitution of the Soviet Form of Military Power in the Cold War

Coercive-military power played a much greater role in the domestic constitution of the USSR in both the maintenance of the sociopolitical order, and in the material contradictions that flowed from the production of military power. The coercive nature of Soviet politics not only derived from the 'negative' absence of an autonomous sphere of social life not reducible to the authority of the state, but also because of the contradictions of this type of social formation that necessitated a greater role for public violence. This being so, the Soviet form of international relations came to rest, and be identified much more so with military power.[37]

This, as I have discussed in Chapter 3, was a result of the combination of external military pressure and the necessity of the use of force in the USSR's rapid social transformation after 1917. In many respects the consequences of this were such that, arguably, one could label the USSR's as a 'war economy'.[38] Although the proportion of economic activity dedicated to military production was never to attain the levels reached during the Second World War, the logic of external military competition continued to dictate large areas of Soviet economic activity after 1945. Indeed, while for the whole period prior to 1945 the USSR was, in effect, 'catching up' with the military capacities of the major capitalist states, after 1945 it actually contributed to that competition, by deploying its military power overseas and competing for strategic advantage against the United States.[39]

Even in the USSR itself, where the Red Army was not used in the way that it was in Eastern Europe, and where it had a much greater degree of legitimacy (largely from the 'Great Patriotic War'),[40] the stability of the sociopolitical order rested on the continued delivery of the social and material gains derived from the Bolshevik Revolution. The maintenance and improvement in material living standards was obviously undermined not only by the maintenance of high levels of military spending, but also by the fact that the economic base from which it produced military power and the material living standards of the Soviet people was squeezed and limited to the productive power of the Soviet economy. As long as the USSR could maintain high levels of economic growth then it had the chance of meeting both political exigencies. However, the most signifi-cant contradiction derived from the domestic–international nexus, where increased international success, which rested on military power, only served to burden further the productive capacity of the domestic economy. Soviet economic and military support for its allies in Eastern Europe and elsewhere provided a further burden to the domestic economy.[41]

The social constitution of the domestic politics of the USSR ensured that the *form* of Soviet international relations was limited to a politics confined to the directly political sphere of the state. The problem, however, was that this form of international politics was identified with the elimination of any form of autonomous private sphere that offered the possibility of an alternative currency of politics.[42] Thus, for the USSR to expand as a political form, it had to ensure not only the control of the machinery of the state but also the social liquidation of the realm of socio-political activity not directly reducible to the state. Without a complete 'Sovietization' of social life, the social order was likely to be undermined by the presence of alternative political currencies. These offered not only the possibility of cultivating an alternative form of domestic politics, but also the opportunity for alternative currencies of international politics to condition domestic political developments. Inevitably, then, 'Sovietization' was a coercive process and, as in the case of Eastern Europe, necessitated the deployment of military power.[43]

Although Europe was divided into two military alliances, NATO and the Warsaw Pact, while the former was *in practice* largely geared towards the perceived external threat, the latter was an organ of internal bloc discipline and social control. The Warsaw Pact guaranteed (Soviet) 'socialist sovereignty', and particularly after the 1968 promulgation of the Brezhnev Doctrine was publicly acknowledged by Soviet officials to be an institution of intra-bloc policing as much as external defence.[44] Moreover, it was not only the guarantor of 'socialism', but also of Soviet power in Eastern Europe, as it was the USSR, and not the other member states, that determined when ideological–political deviation from Soviet conceptions of socialism warranted military intervention.[45] Coercive and military power was, then, constitutive not only of domestic politics but also of international politics, because to ensure the elimination of non-state sources of domestic politics occasioned the use of force to dismantle the private sphere and, because of this, the ability to deal effectively with all those sociopolitical conflicts that had previously been largely resolved by non-state sources of 'coercive' (private) authority.

The form of Soviet international relations was fundamentally limited because they were directly tied to the Soviet state. Although the USSR did use other forms of military power, such as arms shipments and economic instruments through trade concessions and material and financial aid to seek international influence, such means of political influence were, ultimately, unable to secure an effective expansion of the Soviet system.[46] The only way in which the USSR could expand its international influence was through cultivating political relations with states where military and economic aid was used to promote closer links with the USSR. However, these relations were not able to alter the sociopolitical structures within these states. Although the USSR provided significant economic and military aid to countries such as India, Syria, Egypt and Indonesia, it was not able to use this aid to alter the structure of domestic politics. In effect the domestic sociopolitical regime tended to stay largely unaltered, allowing capitalist states, including the United States, to continue to cultivate political relations through both the private and public spheres, using the currencies of military and 'commodity' power. This issue was important for Soviet international influence, what the Soviet leadership understood as the 'correlation of forces', because there was no way in which the USSR could guarantee long-term political influence or support in these types of state. Thus, despite substantial military and economic aid, without a complete (revolutionary) domestic transformation there still persisted the likely possibility that either the regime itself would reorientate itself away from the USSR, as Egypt, Indonesia, and Algeria did, or the presence of domestic sources of non-state politics, as in the bazaar, through Islam, or the continued presence of the social relations of capitalist exchange would offer the possibility of alternative international sources of domestic politics to emerge, thus undermining, if not eliminating, any Soviet presence.[47]

There was nothing to prevent the USSR cultivating political links, even alliances, with non-revolutionary states, such as India, but these links did not rest on a common ideological or political basis. Moreover, what came to determine the strength and substance of these relations was the degree to which such relations boosted economic development of the states concerned (i.e. how far Soviet aid and the example of the 'Soviet model' continued to offer a successful path to political and economic development). However, the fundamental problem that plagued the social relations of the Soviet system, which did not quite restrict capitalism in the same way, was not only that 'socialism' was identified as an alternative model to capitalism, but that it was inextricably linked with the USSR. Because of the unification of the spheres of the state and society/economy under Soviet socialism, there was the constant concern among many Third World states to maintain a degree of political autonomy from the USSR, either by maintaining forms of liberal-democratic political structures, as in India, or by eliminating any internal communist threat, as in Egypt and Iraq. The USSR's interventions in the Third World, and in particular in Afghanistan after 1979, exposed this problem of socialism equating to a form of Soviet empire.[48] The nature of these relations, then, contributed to Soviet influence but not to the expansion of the Soviet system. This could only come through the direct territorial expansion of the USSR or through social revolution.

The internal nature of the USSR, particularly the political unification of the spheres of public and private, political and economic, necessitated a much greater coercive presence that was to have major repercussions for the way in which the USSR was to relate to the wider international system. This was especially so in a world of nuclear weapons, and at a time when for the most part, until the late 1960s, the USSR was in a position of strategic disadvantage vis-à-vis the United States.[49] Thus, one could argue that because of the way in which the USSR was internally socially constituted not only was military power more defining of Soviet international relations, but also, because of this, the USSR was much more conditioned by geopolitical calculations than other states. It was only when the USSR had reached a level of strategic parity with the United States, paralleled by the coincidence of the consequences of the US defeat in Vietnam that, for the first time in its history, the USSR had the means to project its political power more aggressively, and the geopolitical context of American political weakness permitted it to do so.

The sensitivity of Soviet international relations to geopolitics and, specifically, external military threats because of the way in which the USSR was internally constituted meant that the USSR could only afford to pursue an aggressive or expansionist international relations not only when it had the military wherewithal to project itself, but also when it was unlikely to provoke a hostile military response from its capitalist foes, and if it did, it could deal with such a response. This was recognized by Lenin in his report on foreign policy to the Bolshevik party in May 1918:

> We possess great revolutionary experience, which has taught us that it is essential to employ the tactics of merciless attack when objective conditions permit ... But we have to resort to temporizing tactics, to a slow gathering of forces when objective circumstances do not favour a call for a general merciless repulse.[50]

The postwar conjuncture is significant in this respect because it provided a limited geopolitical space for Soviet international expansion based on the military occupation of Eastern Europe after the defeat of Nazi Germany. The expansion of Soviet international power was through the direct use of force after wartime victory. Whereas American political influence prevailed in Western Europe without a direct political occupation, the USSR had to rely on the use of military power, along with the coercive–administrative structures of communist bureaucracy, to ensure a Soviet-style political order. In effect, the USSR used its military power to ensure a bureaucratically orchestrated revolutionary sociopolitical transformation. The use of military power was effective and conducive in this conjuncture, but as a means to ensure wider Soviet international influence it was severely limited. The limitation derived not only from its 'imperialist' appearance,[51] but also, more significantly in the context of the postwar international order, from the fact that any external projection of military power was likely to provoke a hostile US military response. The geopolitical constraints on the Soviet use of military power largely derived from US strategic preponderance, particularly in the possession and use of nuclear weapons. This superiority was used to coerce the Communist powers in a number of crises in the postwar era – Iran in 1946, Berlin in 1948, Korea in 1953, Indo-China in 1954, Cuba in 1962, Vietnam in the late 1960s and the Persian Gulf in the early 1980s.[52]

However, although Soviet postwar expansion was significant it did *not* reflect a discontinuity in the nature of Soviet international relations. Rather it reflected, as did the periods after 1917 and in the 1970s, that when the USSR confronted an international political and military environment conducive to Soviet international expansion it seized such opportunities. The end of the Second World War provided a geopolitical conjuncture that allowed the USSR to expand. However, as much as it permitted expansion into Eastern Europe it did not, and could not, facilitate political expansion into western and southern Europe, or northern Persia. This was because Soviet political encroachments, be they based on the Red Army in the latter or the local communist parties in the former, would, in all likelihood, have aroused a hostile military response from the major capitalist states, and the United States in particular, as the USSR's behaviour in Eastern Europe and Soviet support for North Korean invasion of South Korea had done in 1950.

The apparent inconsistency in Soviet policy after 1945 was a product of the shifting geopolitical context and the likelihood of a US military response to Soviet aggression. This was what occurred in 1948–49 over Berlin, with the US mobilization of its strategic nuclear forces and its willingness to risk a direct military confrontation with the USSR over access to West Berlin. The expansion of Soviet power in Europe beyond the Iron Curtain would, then, have almost certainly triggered war with the United States. However, whereas the United States and West Europeans had shown themselves willing to use force in Europe (for example, in Greece, Turkey and elsewhere), with successful communist revolution in China the Asian geopolitical context appeared less hazardous for the projection of Soviet power. This was 'confirmed' with the interpretation of Acheson's speech on US foreign policy in January 1950. The apparent lack of American interest, confirmed by Acheson's speech and the 'acceptance' of the Chinese Revolution by Washington, provided the green light for the projection of Soviet power.[53]

Thus, it could be argued that Soviet foreign policy was consistent from 1917 until the end of the Cold War. It was so in the sense that the ability of the USSR to pursue its international objectives and support revolution was contingent on a geopolitical environment that allowed it to do so without the threat of major war, which for most of its existence, the USSR would probably have lost. Why and where the USSR supported revolutionary forces and directly challenged the international capitalist order was where it could do so without risking a hostile military response.[54]

The nature and continuity of Soviet international relations and its sensitivity to geopolitics was reflected in that in the immediate years after the Bolshevik Revolution the fledgling Soviet state did not remain dependent on the revolutionary potential of the European working class as a means to ensure international expansion. The direct power of the new state spread revolution through force of arms into Mongolia, Georgia and elsewhere, and attempted to do so in the brief war with Poland in 1920. Whereas Soviet 'adventurism' may then have been possible, it was not possible when the USSR confronted the military threat of Nazi Germany from the 1930s onwards, and when it subsequently encountered the US military–nuclear threat after 1945.

What these historical developments highlight is that the USSR was always likely to be confronted by a hostile international environment, which not only reduced the possibilities of the USSR influencing international developments, but also risked provoking a hostile US military response if and when it did. Because of this, the projection of Soviet international power, be it in support of international revolution or the direct expansion of Soviet power, as in Eastern Europe and Afghanistan, rested on the institutional fusing of ideology and military power. It was not the case of distinguishing when Soviet ideology rather than realpolitik was operative or not, but rather the fact that the expansion of 'ideology' rested, indeed depended, on military strength. The unification of ideology, economic production and exchange, political organization with military power meant that the USSR did not have international *economic* relations. Rather its economic relations were subordinate to and were centrally organized through the coercive bureaucratic apparatus of the Party-state. In this sense the penetration of Soviet (political) influence and expansion via economic relations was dependent on a corresponding directly political presence. This inability to construct a political order through economic relations was apparent in the postwar period, when the USSR in effect prevented the states of Eastern Europe from participating in the Marshall Plan. Not only would Marshall aid have undermined Soviet influence and drawn these countries into the newly emerging international capitalist order, but also it would have prevented the USSR from exploiting its political domination of Eastern Europe and the unequal trading arrangements, which saw major Soviet exploitation of these economies to boost its postwar reconstruction, that existed until Stalin's death.

Thus, both Halliday's distinction between state interests and ideological interests, and Deutscher's[55] focus on the economic competition between capitalism and communism, the 'Great Contest', do not identify adequately the nature and international limitations of the Soviet economic form. Because production and the social relations of production were directly tied to the political form (the Soviet state), the Soviet economy could only internationally expand through direct (i.e. territorial) expansion. Economic as political expansion was obviously achieved differently under capitalist social relations and forms of politics, but the Soviet Union could not compete internationally in the sphere of material production alone. This had to be accompanied by political expansion. However, this was highly problematic because of the political and military costs that such 'expansion' would incur.[56]

Because of the nature of Soviet international relations and particularly their sensitivity to the character of the geopolitical context, the only way in which the USSR could expand and could challenge American-capitalist power was through its support of social revolution. This provided a means for securing political links between similarly constituted states based not only on shared assumptions about capitalism and political-economic development, but also on their mutual confrontation with US military power.

Although the USSR was not consistent in its support for social revolution, this, in itself, is not a reason to dismiss Soviet policy as either conforming to *raison d'état*, or the servicing of domestic political concerns. The tendency to reduce Soviet foreign policy to either the structural imperatives

of the international system or the manipulative and opportunistic machinations of a ruling class preoccupied with its domestic position, overlooks
the mutually constitutive relationship between the nature of Soviet domestic
politics and the character of the international system. Because of the way
the USSR was constituted and the way it organized its international
relations, inevitably, the form of its support for revolutions was always
susceptible to geopolitical pressure. Thus, Soviet support for international
relations had to address the likely military consequences of such support.

As much as the expansion of Soviet power was conditional on a favourable geopolitical environment, because of the nature of Soviet international relations, so Soviet support had to be sensitive to the possibility
of provoking American counter-revolution. This sensitivity was particularly acute when the USSR did not want to be in a position of provoking
a direct military confrontation with the United States through its support
of a revolutionary state. The cautiousness that the USSR showed in its
initial response to the Cuban revolution concerned not only the social and
political character of the revolution, but also the concern not to provide a
pretext for the likely US strangling of the revolution that showed any
obvious symptoms of communism.[57] It was only when the revolution
began to take on a much more socialist orientation in 1960 that relations
developed.

The case of Cuba is also suggestive of how domestic revolutionary
sociopolitical change was an important means by which the USSR might
challenge American strategic power, thus providing a local spark to fuel
strategic conflict between the superpowers. It was not only the possibility
of constructing socialism within the Soviet bloc that made Cuba important
for the Cold War, but also the fact that it was seen by the USSR as a means
to challenge American strategic superiority and, in the same act, politically
incorporate Cuba directly into the 'discipline' of the Soviet system. The
positioning of nuclear missiles in the Caribbean was the means of ensuring
that. Through a Soviet military presence, the Cuban leadership would 'stay
loyal' to Moscow, and it would do this because of the military protection
provided by the missiles.[58] The stationing and targeting of the missiles
would also have challenged if not fundamentally eroded American strategic
nuclear advantage, thus providing the USSR with much more geopolitical
space with which to project itself internationally without the fear of the
use of or threat of using nuclear weapons by the United States that had
formerly limited if not prevented Soviet action. The importance of 'revolutionary bridgeheads' for the USSR was also highlighted in south-east
Asia, where the Soviet-backed Vietnamese defeat of the United States and
its South Vietnamese allies helped provide not only a spur to détente, but
through this process a geopolitical space in which the USSR could be more
assertive.

For the Soviet system to expand, it had to gain 'footholds' in other revolutionary states. Yet its reliance on the success of international revolution meant that because of the likely hostile response of the United States, revolutions in effect produced a contradictory outcome. Social revolutions overthrew capitalism but they also produced a transformation in the form of capitalist power from the currency of exchange relations to one dominated by military power. This was seen not only in the US presidential 'security doctrines' that responded to revolutionary upheavals and/or Soviet expansion, but also in the direction of postwar international politics in Europe. Although NATO was formalized in 1949, it was only after the outbreak of the Korean War and the perception of Soviet involvement that the United States finally began committing serious military resources to western Europe.[59]

This US military response was compounded by the inability of the USSR to realize fully its objectives in its relations with revolutionary states without the use of military power. However, the (military) form of Soviet expansion was the only way in which the USSR was able to challenge US power, because without it the USSR would have continued to be confined to a limited geopolitical autonomy through US military preponderance. Moreover, there was little possibility that the United States would limit or reduce its strategic arsenal *until* the USSR was recognized as a more or less equivalent strategic–military power. Thus, the USSR *had* to be seen to be a genuine military threat before the United States was likely to negotiate arms limitations with it. It was only when the USSR had reached parity, at the time of the US defeat in Indo-China, that the time seemed right for the United States to reconsider the use of military power to secure its international goals.

This is not to suggest that the USSR was an inherently passive or pacific political actor during the Cold War, but because of the form of its politics and the degree to which this was constituted by military power, it was caught in this paradox. To strengthen its international position it was restricted to the cultivation of directly political relations with other revolutionary states, most of which were involved in forms of conflict with the United States either direct (as in Vietnam) or indirect (as with Cuba in Latin America). However, by doing this it served to provoke increased US hostility that weakened the likelihood that the USSR would be able to engineer an international agreement which would reduce the possibility of direct military conflict with the United States. This had not only international consequences, but also domestic ones, which were important for a sociopolitical formation like that of the USSR. The only way in which the USSR could maintain its form of Party-state political authority was by ensuring the passive acceptance of the population. In the long term this was only possible through material growth, whereby the social needs and demands of the Soviet people were met by the system's social–material provision. This was increasingly undermined by the domestic social and material resources used to maintain not only military power, but also military and economic support for other revolutionary states.

The role of military power in Soviet international relations was derived from the absence of any alternative (autonomous) sources of politics which would help determine international developments.[60] Although military power was defining of domestic politics, this did not mean that international relations were subordinate to questions of domestic sociopolitical order. Instead, the limitations on the use of Soviet military power stemmed from the military disadvantages it faced, from 1917 until the early 1970s, because of the superior military strength of its international foes. Thus, what determined Soviet support for international revolution was not, primarily, the domestic preoccupations of the CPSU, but the international military consequences of such support. The geopolitical consequences of Soviet military power also had profound domestic consequences. Increased production of armaments served to undermine social and political stability because of the strains military production posed on meeting class-based socioeconomic objectives which were the fundamental basis of domestic political order. Although social revolution offered a means of international expansion and a challenge to American international power, because the ways in which the USSR sought to incorporate revolutionary states into the Soviet bloc were limited, they also ended up provoking US military hostility, which further fuelled the dynamic of the strategic conflict of the Cold War.

Conclusions

This chapter has sought to highlight the specific nature and role of military power in the Cold War. It has argued that military power, if it is not to be treated as a technological object, should be contextualized from the point of view of the specific social and historical moment within which it is found. From this it is possible to argue that geopolitical conflict was not derived from balance-of-power calculations or misperception, but rather because of the conflict that emerged between different forms of international politics, which were consequent on domestic revolutionary sociopolitical transformation. The strategic conflict of the Cold War was about the ways in which different types of state related to each other and how those international relations were conditioned by the social constitution of those states. Military power and strategic conflict were, then, imbued with distinct social characteristics derived from the domestic politics of states.

The most important domestic social relationship in this respect was that between the sphere of rule and formal political authority founded on the *ultima ratio* of coercive–military power and the sphere of socioeconomic production. The nature of this relationship not only defined the nature of politics, but also the degree to which coercive-military power was determining of that politics.

The Cold War took on an international militarized form because the USSR was effectively limited to an international politics of expansion based on military power, and because the United States and other capitalist states could not secure their international political objectives with respect to these types of state through other means. This was not just an issue of trying to condition political and economic developments within the USSR through non-military means, but was also due to the fact that during the Cold War, Western coercive–military power limited and prevented the expansion of Soviet international power. The Cold War continued to be dominated by military power and strategic conflict, although the USSR was effectively frustrated in its direct use of military power beyond the Soviet bloc, because the USSR was able to expand and challenge American and international capitalist power through the proliferation of social revolution. And as long as the USSR could sustain its international contestation of the US-led international capitalist order without the likelihood of direct military (nuclear) conflict, then the Cold War would continue.

What follows from such an understanding of the nature of the USSR is an alternative way of approaching the Cold War, which would see it as essentially reflective of a continuity in the nature of Soviet international relations. The significance of the postwar conjuncture was similar to the international significance of 1917 and the period of increased Soviet international (military) activity in the 1970s. What these historical conjunctures highlight is the major crises in the international capitalist order that initially produced the context within which the USSR emerged and which then permitted it to expand internationally after 1945 and in the 1970s. However, these episodes of expansion reflected the nature of Soviet international political strength *and* weakness, because Soviet international power was *contingent* on a geopolitical environment based on the nature and level of external military threat. Thus, the ability of the USSR to determine international developments not only rested on the military capacity to project itself, but also on a geopolitical context that permitted it to do so because of either the military weakness of its capitalist foes or their unwillingness to check Soviet expansion through military power.

The problem and defining contradiction of the nature of the USSR and its international relations, however, was that Soviet international successes only served to increase Western hostility and, in particular, a hostility manifested in military power which, in a world of nuclear weapons, imposed geopolitical limits to what the USSR could do. The problem was not confined to Soviet international relations but also extended to domestic politics, where the political and economic costs of international expansion weighed heavily on an economy and pattern of social relations where the domestic political legitimacy, and thus stability of the regime, rested on fulfilling domestic material goals that increased military spending only served to jeopardize. This internal problem concerning political legitimacy was such that on a number of occasions after 1945 the USSR had to use military force to ensure political order within the Soviet bloc.

Because of the geopolitical limits to what the USSR could itself do, the challenge to international capitalism rested on social revolution. This provided the 'processional dynamic' of the Cold War, where revolutionary sociopolitical transformation was the tinderbox of strategic conflict. The fact that international conflict was dominated by the challenges to, and transformations in, social and political order within states, and their international consequences in the involvement of the United States and the USSR, provided the defining uniqueness of the Cold War. Once this challenge had 'spent itself' or been exhausted through the burden of military hostility, the dynamic of the Cold War and its relationship with strategic conflict, as happened by the late 1980s, came to an end.

Thus, because of the domestic nature of the USSR and states like it, the Cold War was synonymous with military conflict. Yet, because of the inherent dangers in the international use of military power, as highlighted by the 1962 Cuban missile crisis, military power would not and could not be determining of the Cold War and its outcome. What was ultimately decisive in the Cold War, then, was the ability not only to reproduce a domestic sociopolitical order not based on the necessity of systematic centralized coercion, but also to construct and sustain an *international* order not based on the structural need to enforce order and expand through military power.

The Cold War was dominated by military power because of the inability of the United States and capitalist states either to incorporate or to discipline states based like the USSR on social revolution, into the social relations and structures of the international capitalist order. The only way in which they could discipline the USSR and revolutionary states was either through containment or through counter-revolution, both of which means were based on military power. However, capitalist states used international military power not only because of the nature of states like the USSR, but more importantly because of the *form* taken by the active attempts by the USSR to expand internationally either directly or through the support it gave to revolutionary movements and states. The USSR expanded when it could, when the geopolitical threats to its projection of military power either were absent or could be met. However, in the long term the burden of Soviet international success only served to undermine the domestic basis of that success, thus providing for the historical conclusion to the Cold War.

NOTES

1 See Cox, 'Western Capitalism', 'Cold War'; Kaldor, *Imaginary War*; D. Horowitz, *Imperialism and Revolution* (London: Allen Lane, 1969); M. Kidron, *Western Capitalism*; idem, *A Permanent Arms Economy* (London: Socialist Workers Party, 1989); T. Vance *et al.*, *The Permanent War Economy* (Berkeley: Independent Socialist Press, 1970); S. Melman, *The Permanent War Economy: American Capitalism in Decline* (New York: Simon & Schuster, 1974).
2 Primarily associated with the work of Michael Doyle, 'Liberalism and World Politics'.
3 Halliday, *Making of the Second Cold War*.
4 See G. Kolko, *Century of War: Politics, Conflicts and Society since 1914* (New York: The New Press, 1994), pp. xvi–ix, 374.
5 Although it is speculation, without nuclear weapons it seems quite incontestable that, in a different form, there would have been (continued) political–military conflict between the USSR and the United States after 1945. Nuclear weapons did not determine the US–Soviet conflict, as M. Davis has stated:

> That conflict [between the different social formations of East and West] would have existed and developed into a Cold War, even if nuclear weapons had never been invented. The Bomb has shaped and mis-shaped its evolution, and may yet put an end to it altogether. But it is not its spring. This lies in the dynamic of class struggle on a world scale.

('Nuclear Imperialism and Extended Deterrence', in New Left Review (ed.), *Exterminism and Cold War* (London: New Left Books, 1982), p. 42.)
6 See Halliday, *Making of the Second Cold War*; Davis, 'Nuclear Imperialism', pp. 35–64 for a more extended discussion of the political uses of nuclear weapons.
7 See Davis, 'Nuclear Imperialism', pp. 35–64.
8 Arguably, the existence of nuclear weapons could be seen to have reduced the potential for superpower military conflict. Thus, instead of international political issues being resolved militarily by the superpowers, issues were resolved through alternative currencies of politics and military power that involved different forms of political agency (i.e. other states or political movements).
9 For a discussion of this with respect to the United States see Gaddis, *Strategies of Containment*, and, for the Soviet Union, Kennan, 'X Article'.
10 Some scholars have conceived the political–military expansion of the superpowers as forms of 'imperialism'. Thus the Soviet responses to social and political upheaval within its sphere(s) of interest, mainly in Eastern Europe after 1945, were seen as being anti-revolutionary and imperialist, as were American attempts to quash revolution in Latin America and elsewhere. This Realist position shares, ironically, many similarities with the work of much analysis of the Soviet Union from a 'state capitalist' perspective. See Cliff, *State Capitalism*; P. Binns *et al.*, *Russia: From Workers' State to State Capitalism* (London: Bookmarks, 1987) for such an approach.
11 What Gaddis christened the 'long peace'. See Gaddis, *Long Peace*; C. Kegley Jr, *The Long Postwar Peace: Contending Explanations and Projections* (New York: HarperCollins, 1991).
12 For a summary of these debates see A. Brewer, *Marxist Theories of Imperialism* (London: Routledge, 1990).
13 Kaldor, *Imaginary War*, pp. 3–7; Cox, 'Western Capitalism'; Halliday, *Making of the Second Cold War*, pp. 24–45; Kidron, *Western Capitalism*.
14 Kaldor, *Imaginary War*, pp. 49–116; Cox, 'Western Capitalism', pp. 141–50, 'Cold War', pp. 25–40.

15 Melman, *Permanent War Economy*; Vance, *Permanent War Economy*; Kidron, *Western Capitalism, Permanent Arms Economy*; P. Baran and P. Sweezy, *Monopoly Capital: An Essay on the American Economic and Social Order* (Harmondsworth: Penguin, 1968).

16 R. Smith 'Military Expenditure and Capitalism', *Cambridge Journal of Economics*, 1, 1 (1977), pp. 61–77.

17 Halliday, *Making of the Second Cold War*, pp. 122–33.

18 A report in the *Guardian* newspaper (2 July 1998), based on figures released by the US Department of Defense, stated that since 1940 the US economy had spent over $19 trillion on military hardware.

19 The Internet is an obvious example of what began as a product of the military sector having a profound and stimulating impact on the wider capitalist economy. This was also found in the strategic defence initiative (SDI) project, where a number of European governments were concerned over the civilian benefits, and thus competitive advantage accrued, of this high-technology research.

20 Stalin, cited in D. Holloway, *The Soviet Union and the Arms Race*, 2nd edn, (New Haven, CT: Yale University Press, 1984), pp. 6–7.

21 Despite the problems of accuracy, there is general consensus that the USSR spent approximately double the amount (in all aspects of defence) spent by the United States on defence. This deprived the USSR civilian economy of large amounts of investment goods and qualified scientists. Moreover, significant areas of industrial production were devoted to military production, including machine tools, metallurgy and the chemical industry. See Dibb, *Soviet Union*, pp. 80–9.

22 See C. Jones, 'Soviet Allies in Europe: The Warsaw Pact', in R. Menon and D. Nelson (eds), *Limits to Soviet Power* (Lexington, MA: Lexington Books, 1989), pp. 131–55.

23 Dibb, *Soviet Union*, pp. 142–7; Holloway, *The Soviet Union and the Arms Race*, pp. 3–14, 109–30.

24 Not only was the Soviet economy less productive than Western economies, but the Soviet people had a lower standard of living. Moreover, by the late 1970s growth rates were declining on the back of falls in productivity. See Dibb, *Soviet Union*, pp. 2–3, 71–80; Halliday, *Making of the Second Cold War*, pp. 36–9, 137–45.

25 The Soviet leadership was explicit in this regard, from Khrushchev's 'we will bury you' promise in 1960 to Brezhnev's statement to the CPSU's 26th Congress in 1981: 'As we know, the decisive sector of the competition with capitalism is the economy and economic policy'. Quoted in Dibb, *Soviet Union*, p. 70.

26 Latham, *Liberal Moment*, pp. 133–7.

27 In the early postwar period the revolutionary seizures of power in China and Korea contributed not only to an American commitment of military power, but also to the complete restructuring of US strategic policy with NSC-68. These revolutionary crises were followed by others that were to trigger US strategic responses encapsulated in presidential national security doctrines, from Truman over the eastern Mediterranean to Reagan over Afghanistan and Central America.

28 See Armstrong, *Revolution and World Order*; Halliday, *Revolution and World Politics*, pp. 94–132, 207–60.

29 It was the US defeat in Indo-China (in which the USSR played a major role) that helped transform the international system, which, along with a new wave of revolutionary upheaval in the Third World, the 'arc of crises', saw the boldest projection of Soviet international power in the Cold War. See Halliday, *Making of the Second Cold War*.

30 However, the United States had been hostile in thought and deed towards the new Soviet state, in its military intervention in support of anti-Bolshevik forces after

1917, and did not establish relations with it until the mid-1930s. See A. Mayer, *The Politics and Diplomacy of Peacemaking: Containment and Counterrevolution at Versailles, 1918–1919* (London: Weidenfeld & Nicolson, 1968).

31 Horowitz, *Imperialism and Revolution*, p. 73, cites 20 examples of US military intervention between 1900 and 1917. See also W. A. Williams, *The Tragedy of American Diplomacy* (New York: Dell Publishing Co., 1972).

32 See J. Ruggie, *Constructing World Polity: Essays on International Institutionalization* (London: Routledge, 1998), pp. 72–5.

33 This vision and its institutionalization prevailed up until the early 1970s. But with domestic changes in the United States (partly caused by the economic and political burden of Vietnam) and wider changes in the international capitalist order, a new institutionalization of American power was required and with it a new set of economic and political relations with Europe.

34 However, though autonomous in terms of the rationale for economic decisions and their consequences, the 'regime' within which economic activity took place (i.e. managed exchange rates, convertibility of the dollar) was a state creation. See E. A. Brett, *The World Economy since the War: The Politics of Uneven Development* (Basingstoke: Macmillan, 1985); P. Armstrong, A. Glyn and J. Harrison, *Capitalism Since 1945* (Oxford: Basil Blackwell, 1991).

35 Thus, as Pollard, *Economic Security*, pp. 69–70, highlights, postwar negotiations over the new international economic arrangements allowed the United States to press Britain to remove barriers to trade and greater access for American goods within British-controlled markets.

36 See Brett, *World Economy since the War*, pp. 80–102; Armstrong, *Capitalism since 1945*, pp. 1–113; Maier, 'Politics of Productivity'.

37 Because of the coercive–authoritarian nature of Soviet politics, particularly in the Stalin period after 1945, a hostile and militarized international environment provided a valuable justification for that coercion in the USSR and Eastern Europe, notably with the worries over a rearmed West Germany. See Kaldor, *Imaginary War*, pp. 49–76.

38 According to Nove, *Economic History*, p. 274, armaments production accounted for 52 per cent of national income in 1942, the highest reached anywhere by any state.

39 This was seen in the fact that Soviet support for its allies and its attempts to secure influence in other states was largely confined to arms exports. Soviet arms agreements with non-communist Third World states were worth a total of US$70,000 million, whereas economic aid amounted to less than one-third of this amount (see Dibb, *Soviet Union*, p. 43). The export of weapons was a significant aspect of military competition, but the development and deployment of military power by the USSR itself, as reflected in the impact of the launch of Sputnik 1 in the late 1950s, followed by the subsequent attempt to place nuclear missiles in Cuba, were important elements in the escalation of strategic competition with the United States. Moreover, the deployment of SS-20 intermediate-range nuclear missiles in 1976–77 was a major factor that contributed to the end of the détente (G. Roberts, *The Soviet Union in World Politics: Coexistence, Revolution and Cold War, 1945–1991* (London: Routledge, 1991), p. 77.

40 See R. Craig Nation, *Black Earth Red Star: A History of Soviet Security Policy, 1917–1991* (New York: Columbia University Press, 1992); Holloway, *Soviet Union and the Arms Race*.

41 Kaldor, *Imaginary War*, pp. 131–7, focuses on the strains on the Soviet bloc economies through being organized around militarized production. Whereas the demands of war can justify militarized production and the acceptance of the

problems that go with it: shortages of consumer goods, hierarchical and coercive social relations, and general economic hardship, it would be difficult to maintain political legitimacy if such conditions prevailed for a long period of time or in the absence of war. Although we may not need to accept Kaldor's assertion about the degree to which the Soviet bloc economies were organized for war production, her argument about the strains on the social order of it are convincing. Thus, by accepting the logic of international military competition, the USSR and its allies exposed their economies to greater military production than otherwise would have been the case, which served to strain further the relations between people and the ruling authorities in these states.

42 In absolute terms this was obviously not the case. In Eastern Europe there were recognized areas of authority of non-state institutions, such as the Roman Catholic Church in Poland.

43 Local communist parties were an adjunct to this, but were usually identified directly with the USSR, thus undermining their domestic political position, and largely because of this, communist parties conformed to Soviet strategy which involved the cultivation of links with the state in question. See Jones, 'Soviet Allies in Europe'.

44 Kramer, 'Ideology and the Cold War', pp. 548–9.

45 Ibid. Whereas 'deviancy' in NATO could go as far as not only accommodating markedly different conceptions of economic good but also the 'freedom' of states to leave it. Moreover, when Britain and France clashed with the United States over the Suez crisis in 1956, there was no anxiety that the United States would enforce its will through force.

46 For discussions on this point see J. Hough, *The Struggle for the Third World: Soviet Debates and American Options* (Washington, DC: Brookings Institution, 1985); E. Valkeneir, *The Soviet Union and the Third World: An Economic Bind* (New York: Praeger, 1983).

47 See Dibb, *Soviet Union*, pp. 189–90.

48 See Binns, *Russia*; P. Binns and M. Gonzales, 'Cuba, Castro and Socialism', *International Socialism*, 82 (spring 1980), pp. 1–35.

49 The 1960s, particularly after the Cuban missile crisis, saw substantial increases in Soviet military spending. Figures given in the *SIPRI Yearbook 1968/9*, pp. 200–1 show that Soviet military spending increased from US$22 billion in 1960 to US$33 billion in 1963 up to US$40 billion in 1968. Cited in Halliday, *Making of the Second Cold War*, p. 59.

50 Lenin quoted in Armstrong, *Revolution and World Order*, p. 138.

51 The over-reliance on military power also had the tendency to raise fears in many parts of the world, and which were not confined to the West, about Soviet military ambitions, especially after the intervention in Afghanistan. See Dibb, *Soviet Union*, pp. 194–5.

52 In all, the United States used its strategic-nuclear advantage against the USSR in 19 international crises after 1945. See Halliday, *Making of the Second Cold War*, pp. 50; Davis, 'Nuclear Imperialism', pp. 35–64; Ellsberg, 'Call to Mutiny', pp. i–xxviii.

53 See Kramer, 'Ideology and the Cold War', pp. 541–4.

54 The USSR, and Stalin in particular, were condemned for their failure adequately to support the Spanish Republic and thus the undermining of the Spanish Revolution. What this argument overlooks, however, is that the Spanish Republic was defeated by superior military force, supported by external Fascist powers. What might have saved it was a greater Soviet military intervention, but this would have entailed not only greater Stalinist influence in Spain, but also a militarized

revolution, something that many critics of Soviet policy would not have coun-
tenanced. Thus, it was Soviet military weakness that prevented it from supporting
the Spanish Republic more fully. Moreover, it was this inferiority that directed
Soviet attempts to limit the scope and radicalism of the Revolution and thus avoid
antagonizing France and Britain.

55 I. Deutscher, *The Great Contest: Russia and the West* (London: Oxford University
Press, 1960).

56 One of the first costs of these explicitly coercive 'economic' relations was the
Yugoslav split from the Soviet bloc in 1948. See Kramer, 'Ideology and the Cold
War', p. 556.

57 J. Lévesque, *The USSR and the Cuban Revolution: Soviet Ideological and Strategical
Perspectives, 1959–77* (New York: Praeger, 1978); H. Dinerstein, *The Making of a
Missile Crisis: October 1962* (Baltimore, MD: Johns Hopkins University Press,
1976).

58 This was also to be facilitated by supporting pro-Soviet elements within the Cuban
leadership, such as Aníbal Escalante, who was later accused of being a 'Soviet
stooge' and imprisoned. Also, more significantly, the USSR pressured/encouraged
the Cuban political leadership to organize itself according to the Soviet model of
the CPSU, which it began to do from the early 1970s onwards. See Lévesque, *USSR*.

59 Even more significant was the decision to rearm the newly created Federal Republic
of Germany, and permit it to join NATO in 1955.

60 By the 1980s the Soviet share of world trade was still less than 4 per cent and mainly
concentrated in oil exports. Its foreign aid programme was comparable with the
combined programmes of the Netherlands, Belgium, Norway and Denmark, while
the Third World carried out less than 4 per cent of its trade with the Soviet bloc.
Dibb, *Soviet Union*, pp. 216–20.

5

Social Revolution and the Cold War

The two preceding chapters on the state and military power and the Cold War have sought to conceptualize these terms from a wider historical and social context. In doing so, the argument they put forward is that the Cold War needs to be seen as reflecting an antagonism between two different forms of politics founded on specific class-based sets of social relations. This chapter will complete the theoretical framework of the book before Part II provides a more historically registered exposition of the theoretical discussions. Through an analysis of social revolution this chapter will centre on the principal social dynamic within the Cold War, the expansion and transformation of capitalist social relations and their political contestation. The Cold War was inclusive of the transformation of the international capitalist system in terms of political forms (sovereign states) and the corresponding mode of accumulation. Indeed, the core of the antagonism between the superpowers did not only rest on their respective internal social features, but also on how and why each superpower *form* of politics conducted relations with those states that had sought their own revolutionary sociopolitical transformation.

Social revolution as a form of rapid, violent and structural social and political transformation, involving class-based forms of political agency, has not been widely discussed in the literature of the Cold War. This chapter will seek to address what is obviously a major oversight. Social revolution, it will be argued, exposes a number of fissures in international relations at the level of the state as a particular institutionalization of politics and the way in which it relates to the wider social formation through the social relations of socioeconomic production. Social revolutions see a rupture and transformation at both levels: the state is reconstituted by a new form of political agency that is located within a distinct *class* constituency, and the newly defined/institutionalized state, through mass mobilization and the sponsoring of social struggle, effects a transformation in the social relationship between what constitutes 'politics' and 'economics,' and between the domestic and the international.

The revolutionary transformation of the state directly relates to the discussion in Chapter 3 on the nature of the politics of the state in the Cold War. Social revolution, alongside the agency of the Soviet state in the form of the Red Army and the organs of the bureaucratic Party-state, was the principal means for the political contestation of the 'states system' and the social fabric that it rested on. Moreover, social revolution not only led to new, alternative relations of social and material production and politics, but also to a new definition of military power, as suggested in Chapter 4. Finally, social revolution exposed the tensions and contradictions within capitalist social relations, in their expansion and transformation during the Cold War under US leadership.[1] It was this, the attempted political contestation and overthrow of capitalist politics and the response to it – political, economic and military – that directly involved the superpowers as reflections of distinct political forms, that crystallized the conflict that was the Cold War.[2]

The organization of the chapter revolves around the core assumptions of those scholars who have tried to explain the Cold War in terms of the impact of social revolution on world politics. These scholars have tended to be those working within the Marxist tradition,[3] some of whom are associated with American Cold War Revisionism,[4] and non-Marxists who have tended to downplay the international significance of domestic revolutionary change. Whereas the former have tried to explain social revolution as a response to capitalist penetration and exploitation, they have differed in their analysis of the international consequences of revolution and the responses of the superpowers. The latter, on the other hand, have tended to avoid dwelling on the class or social uniqueness of the transformative effects of revolution, seeing them more in terms of a generalized form of modernization.[5] Finally, liberals have focused on rejecting American (militarized) hostility to revolutions,[6] by arguing that it was possible to reach a political accommodation with revolutions, thus downplaying the assumption that revolutions *a priori* have challenged American objectives.

The chapter begins with those non-Marxist scholars of social revolution and is followed by an examination of Marxist-based approaches. The third and final section of the chapter will develop the criticism put forward in the second section and reconstruct a Marxist-based understanding of the nature and role of social revolution in the Cold War.

Non-Marxist Approaches to Social Revolution and the Cold War

Social revolution, as noted earlier, has been a phenomenon largely marginalized or ignored in International Relations.[7] This has also been the case in Cold War scholarship. This needs some qualification because although revolution has been recognized as leading to international instability in traditional Cold War theory, it has not *in itself* been seen as the major causal dynamic of the Cold War.[8]

Liberal theory, like Marxism, adopts an explicitly 'normative' position on social revolution, seeing revolution in terms of particular local eruptions of political violence that are explicable in terms of the repressive nature of a state or its lack of legitimacy. However, what is more significant for the Cold War is that revolutionary change is not inherently hostile to the existing international social or political order, and despite the rhetoric of revolutionaries, in essence revolutions did *not* have to be a source of international conflict.[9] Because of this appreciation of revolutions, liberals attempt to distinguish the internal revolution and its consequences from the international. Revolutions occur in particular societies and should be seen in this light.

This being the case, liberals have been preoccupied with a critique of the foreign policy responses of established states to revolution and the suggested alternatives to them; the ways to create a modus vivendi with revolutions.[10] Such assumptions are associated with the liberal fringe of American Cold War Revisionism, in particular the work of Richard Barnet and Walter LaFeber. Revolutions themselves were not a threat to the international system. They only became a threat when they were pushed into hostility with neighbouring states and great powers through the *exaggerated* perceived threat that revolutions posed. Thus, like many Realists, liberals tend to suggest that the international impact of revolution is limited. They only acquire significance through the hostile reactions of outside powers that, in effect, provoke the revolutionaries into extremist positions instead of a search for common ground.

In many respects there is an element of truth in such arguments; notably in the actual choice and execution of US foreign policy: some revolutionaries, especially those in former colonial territories, or those fighting anti-colonial wars, have been drawn to American anti-colonialism.[11] A specific example concerns Gamal Abd al-Nasser, the Egyptian leader. His prime political and ideological goals in the 1950s were the removal of the Anglo-French colonial presence in the Middle East and following this, Arab unity under Egyptian hegemony. Nasser turned to the West and in particular the United States for military and economic aid after seizing power. He was not successful and thus sought arms elsewhere. The only other source was the Soviet bloc. The infamous 'Czech arms deal' in 1955 was enough to alienate the United States, and led to their subsequent withdrawal from funding the construction of the Aswan dam. Again Nasser turned to the Soviet Union, and an alliance ensued.

Although these points shed some light on the relationship between revolutionary states and the Cold War, they all overlook the fact that in all of the instances of *social* revolution, and even in those without a class-based revolution from below, as in the case of Egypt, where there was a radical nationalist regime, all conflicted with the international *capitalist* nature of American/Western social and political forms. All of the revolutions were concerned with expropriating foreign-controlled parts of their economies, and this activity also extended to the expulsion of the foreign presence and halting their interference in domestic affairs. This also, but to a lesser degree, applied to the Soviet Union as well.[12] Inevitably and consistently the rhetoric of revolutionaries did correspond to actions as foreign, usually Western, property, was confiscated and foreign activity was outlawed or severely limited. To argue that such developments could be avoided or 'worked around' is to miss the point about what a revolution actually is. Furthermore, all the revolutions in question inherently had a project of 'exporting' revolution. The revolutionary project was based on the destabilizing of neighbours if not the overthrow of the regimes in power.[13] This was something that was at the heart of the revolutionary project, which although confounded by the political–territorial limitations of states, was always based on ideological concepts located in an internationalism that sought to transcend the territorial and political limitations of states, but never succeeded.[14] This situation was prevalent in the Cold War not only in the instances of the newly created revolutionary regimes in Cuba or Vietnam, which either provided assistance or were directly involved in the attempts at the export of revolution, but also in the case of the Soviet Union.[15] The history of the Soviet role *was* contradictory, reflecting shifting priorities and fluctuations of Soviet interests and the opportunities that developments in international relations offered. Yet throughout its existence, even up until the final days of the Gorbachev leadership, the Soviet Union did convey an element of revolutionary internationalism, offering military and economic aid to a number of revolutionary states in the Third World.[16] Thus, the liberal argument concerning the political hostility of revolutions or the lack of it, and the ability to overcome this, does not hold. Revolutions were in essence political threats to the existing international order and to the internal structures of other states.

The second feature of non-Marxist approaches to revolutionary change concerns the socioeconomic dimension of revolutionary transformations in the Third World. For a number of scholars who have addressed either the Cold War or the social and economic development of the Third World, revolutionary transformation was merely a variant of modernization. It was an attempt at rapidly catching up with the more advanced West, based on a different method, but with the same aim.[17] Revolutionary or Communist modernization was not something that sought to transcend, or form a distinct social alternative to, the Western defined experience of what it was to be 'modern', but sought actually to realize it. The Soviet Union was the supreme example of a model for the emergent world through communist revolution:

> What Russia sought to achieve by communism, and what the underdeveloped countries are trying to achieve by reliving the Russian experience, is the status of a Western society, a powerful, wealthy, and modern state.[18]

This understanding of what it meant to be 'modern' pointed to the attempts by states to break from traditional social and political patterns of organization to avoid subservience or even colonization by more advanced states (the West), as in the case of 'Meiji' Japan and the flawed attempts of the Ottoman Empire and Egypt in the nineteenth century.[19] Soviet socialism, and the social revolutions in China, Vietnam, Cuba and elsewhere all figured within this conceptual understanding of what it meant to be modern. Thus social revolution in the Third World was fundamentally no different from the modernization or the development of the states of Western Europe.[20]

Such an understanding potentially provides a cogent critique of the Cold War, and in particular the American response to social revolution. Social revolution and its ensuing project of redefining the state, and using a bureaucratic state to orchestrate the destruction of traditional, pre-capitalist patterns of socioeconomic organization and production, was to be welcomed as something 'progressive'. The state was the instrument because of the weakness or non-existence of a 'progressive' bourgeois class which could lead economic development. The vehicle was social revolution because existing elite(s) were not only repressive and corrupt, they were also an obstacle to socioeconomic development and political change.[21]

The substance of such developments is not very different from the Western experience of the development of national consciousness in political communities and the emergence of the state. Nationalism is the fundamental force or form of political agency here, not communism.[22] Communism or socialism was an extreme form of state-induced nationalism, whereby the state sought to remove foreign interference and protect the development of the national political economy. The Soviet Union was important only because it provided an historic example of this process and a particular method of state–bureaucratic modernization. And as already mentioned, because of American–Western hostility, the Soviets filled the vacuum of external influence and provided political and military support against American hostility. Class as a form of agency represented within a movement or a vanguard party is dismissed, as intellectuals are identified as the principal revolutionary agents.[23] And the consequences of social change within the Third World were not seen in class terms (i.e. the replacement of one ruling class with another), but rather as the centralization of state power by a party movement led by intellectuals using a nationalist-based ideology.[24]

How this linked to international relations and the Cold War in particular has already been alluded to. First, there was what was wrongly perceived as a hostile response from the United States, which served to create a conflict when one was not necessary. Second, there was the fact that American hostility amounted to a withdrawal of American influence and external (economic) support for any programme of change, which provided an opportunity for the Soviet Union to secure influence by offering economic support to the new regime. For scholars taking this view, such actions disqualified any beneficial American involvement with the 'radical' regime and led to an almost complete cut-off in influence with the government concerned. Thus, international conflict arose out of a situation that did not warrant it.

This understanding of social change and the problems of socio-economic development in the Third World, however, is not without its problems. First, such a theory has a flawed understanding of the history of modernization or what is usually termed 'modernity' itself, in the sense that it fails properly to historicize or ground the capitalist state form in any genuine historical or class context. Clearly the peculiar form of 'state' that is capitalism is not something that is either natural or inevitable. It is something that emerged and was created by a particular form of human social agency. The organization of the economy and polity, the relative separation of the spheres of politics in the state and the economy in capitalist expropriation is the classical form associated with Western modernity. If this social form was created by an historical process of political and social conflict, we must be very careful about applying this to the particular social forms of the Third World, most of which were already under, and emerged as political entities (colonies) through, Western political and economic dominance and exploitation.

Thus, the nature of social relations that developed in the non-European world were such that they were imbued in many ways, racial, social and economic, with the structural legacy of imperialism and exploitation that destroyed the possibility of taking the 'Western path' to modernity. The fact that the social, economic and political tasks that they confronted were all the greater and in an international context all the more difficult, ensured that 'modernization' and state formation were bound to be more tortuous and problematic, but also qualitatively different.[25] The most important point, however, is that 'modernization theory' leaves out subjective human political agency. Thus, what characterized the Third World states was a 'bastardized' incorporation into the world market, where each individual society was integrated differently according to local conditions and the changing nature of the world market and the states system.[26] What this meant was that not only did the social and political content of the inter-national order change (from imperialism to liberal free trade and democ-racy in the postwar era), but also the nature of social transformation in each colonial/Third World state created the social conditions (or not) and the political agents and organizations for sociopolitical transforma-tion, which in one instance might be led by communists promoting revolutionary change and in another by the military and a 'moderate' or reactionary politics. Finally, it was the impact of internationally derived crisis, particularly the Second World War, that was to provide the structural context for human agency and the contingent nature of the possibilities of revolutionary social transformation.

The second problem with 'modernization theory' is that it tends to read history backwards. The West is the final outcome of modernization; it is the end of the modernization project and it is what all states want to realize. This is a classic case of 'reading back' into history from what has happened in a number of dominant states. The advanced capitalist states went through a particular process of evolution and reached a stage where, to all intents and purposes, and through social theory as much as in actual politics, they defined what it was, or was meant, to be modern, or what characterized 'modernity', and the rest of the world was merely following in one way or another this inevitable path. If Marx can be accused of being teleological, so can this understanding, for it plainly misrepresents the distinct conceptual break that 1917 and social revolution provided. In one sense it ignores the profound problems and consequences of Western imperialism and the expansion of capitalism to a global stage. It does this by avoiding the issue raised by the fact that very few states have been able to break the bond of poverty, exploitation and political vulnerability. It applies a general rule to a situation that clearly confounds such a rule. In doing this it misunderstands the import of social revolution, which was about restructuring the productive forces in a society and through this redefining the state.

It was not, then, the case that revolutionary parties ended up as the historical substitutes for the absent or weak bourgeoisie, rather that the social and political edifice constructed by social revolution was premised on the combination of a self-conscious and planned ideological vision, anchored within a specific class constituency. This not only facilitated rapid and intense programmes of transformation, but gave the products of such changes a peculiar and unique social character, not without contradictions. These features and their contradictions had domestic and international repercussions in the social relationship between state and society and in the nature of their relationship with the wider international system, premised, as they were, on an economic 'decoupling' from the capitalist world market.

These approaches to social revolution and the Cold War, then, point to particular areas of investigation but fail to grasp fully the nature or context of social revolution in the Cold War. They do not refute or undermine the social essence of social revolution; in fact they tend to neglect this. They fail to historicize the concept or understand the particular form of agency involved, and they fail to recognize the genuine and real, *inevitable* political conflict and hostility that revolutions created for international relations.

Marxist Approaches to Social Revolution and the Cold War

Of all the theoretical traditions that were identified in Chapter 1, Historical Materialism is the one that has sought an explanation of the Cold War through a focus on social revolution. In this regard the work of Isaac Deutscher, Fred Halliday and scholars associated with American Cold War Revisionism will be critically discussed in terms of how they understand social revolution and relate it to the Cold War.

American Revisionism

In the case of the American Revisionists, the analysis of the Cold War was a means of giving a radical interpretation of American history and foreign policy. Though obviously having roots in forms of Marxist economic analysis, the principal focus was an understanding of the postwar role of the United States in international relations that reached a point of crisis during the Vietnam War. It was this conflict and American involvement that provided an intellectual and radical political space within which to critique US foreign policy as the source of the Cold War and to *blame* the policies of the United States for the Cold War.[27]

The impact of social revolution in the Cold War was, principally, a relationship between revolutionary states and the United States and its foreign policy. Thus, presidential national security doctrines, beginning with the Truman Doctrine, were responses to revolutionary threats that had a global reach not reducible to the Soviet Union.[28] Although the main point of conflict in the Cold War era was that between the United States and revolutionary states, this conflict was global because it derived from the contradictions of the international hegemony of American capitalism.[29] Such an understanding drew on the work of William Appleman Williams[30] and other radical historians who located the Cold War in the dynamic of American capitalism that faced potential stagnation if it did not expand beyond its borders after the Second World War.[31] This being the case, the conflict was with not only revolutionary forces but also the closed colonies of the Western European powers.[32] The explanatory formula derives from the domestic contradictions of American capitalist-accumulation and the necessity for American capital to have access to foreign markets, denied them by revolutionary and colonial political barriers. American power thus was not just about counter-revolution, but also about the destruction of the international power of its capitalist competitors.

The focus of American Revisionism, then, is US imperialism and the international challenges to it, and not US–Soviet antagonism. Thus, the Soviet Union neither was a threat to the United States, nor did it support international revolution.[33] Not only do the American Revisionists identify the Cold War as being a conflict, in Horowitz's words, between 'imperial-ism and revolution' rather than between the United States and the USSR, but they suggest that this conflict predates the postwar era. Thus, American Revisionists show how the United States consistently intervened using military power against social disorder and the perceived revolutionary threats to international sociopolitical order in the Western hemisphere. A Cold War existed in the Western hemisphere prior to 1945, and the source of this was the dynamic of social revolution and the hostility towards American political and economic dominance in the region. Although not in formal colonial relationships, American influence in many Latin American states and American hostility to outside interference in the region closely resembled a set of quasi-colonial relationships. Thus, the political conflicts that concerned the United States in the inter-war period, exemplified by the revolutionary crisis in Cuba in the early 1930s, confirm a continuity to American international relations.

The Soviet Union was *not* a significant actor, and its role in social revo-lution, be it support, example, or facilitation, was considered marginal or problematic. The Soviet Union presented a problem, primarily, because of the internal nature of the Soviet Union. In many respects it was seen as 'counter-revolutionary' or a kind of 'imperial' power, most notably in the episodes of the invasion of Hungary in 1956 and of Czechoslovakia in 1968. American Revisionists, however, were concerned to highlight the greater 'evil' or to lay blame for the origins of the Cold War at the door of American capitalism. The United States was the predatory and expan-sionist power both against revolutionary regimes and its Western capital-ist rivals, whereas the USSR was primarily concerned with domestic issues.

This account of social revolution and the Cold War has a lot to offer, particularly in identifying the locus of the Cold War in the revolutionary response to the contradictions of capitalism. However, there are a number of difficulties. First is the identification of capitalism with American hegemony. Postwar capitalism has indeed been shaped by the absolute and then relative American dominance. However, in this focus on one par-ticular state, and on the tensions between this and other capitalist states, the Revisionists obscure the common fears and the policies to contain radical nationalisms and communism of all the major capitalist powers. Thus, the United States provided massive military support to the French in Indo-China in the war against the Viet Minh. Moreover, it was not just the United States that directly intervened against social revolution, but also the other capitalist powers. Therefore, if the Cold War was about 'imperial-ism and revolution', then it went beyond US imperialism, and also witnessed cooperation rather than conflict between the major capitalist powers.

The other main point of contention is the role of the Soviet Union, or lack of one, in the Cold War. For the Revisionists, the Cold War was about the outbreak of social revolution in the Third World, but these developments were separate from the conflict between the United States and the Soviet Union. Furthermore, the United States was a counter-revolutionary power even before the USSR existed. This point presents a problem because it tends to overlook the particular historical–social context of the Cold War, in that revolutions in the Third World were located within a context that was already defined by the theory and practice of Bolshevism, as manifested in the USSR. Finally, although we need to qualify the Soviet role, we should be clear that despite the contradictions and the propaganda, the Soviet Union, as Fred Halliday has suggested, did act with a degree of consistency to support revolutionary states. Without this 'progressive' Soviet role the outcome of a number of these revolutions would have been less clear-cut and their existence much more problematic.

Isaac Deutscher

The second major theorization of the Cold War and social revolution is associated with the work of Isaac Deutscher. Deutscher argued that post-war international relations was dominated by two main features. The first was Western hostility towards the USSR and revolution. For Deutscher this was misplaced, because the USSR was not a political–military threat to Western Europe or the United States and, more importantly, its foreign policy was primarily concerned with assisting *domestic* consolidation over anything else.[34] The Western depiction of the USSR as an aggressive revolutionary state was, then, the 'myth' of the Cold War. The second feature was what Deutscher termed the 'Great Contest'. This was the international socioeconomic competition between the material potential and productive power of capitalism and communism. It was Deutscher's belief that because of the contradictions of capitalism and its proneness to periodic economic crisis, the inherent superiority of socialized production over private– capitalist production would permit the USSR to surpass the economic and material achievements of Western capitalism.[35]

Within this conception he saw the potential for a progressive role for the USSR in international relations, especially in economic competition with the West.[36] However, he was also clear that under Stalin international communism had been seriously weakened.[37] Deutscher was not willing to go along with American Revisionism so far as to ignore or marginalize any 'progressive' Soviet role in world politics, especially with respect to revolution in the Third World, but neither was he willing fully to endorse the Soviet Union as 'progressive'. His position was equivocal, and exposed the contradictory position of the Soviet Union, on the one hand cautionary in its direct relationship with the United States, but in other respects supportive of revolutionary change. This was a situation he could not fully reconcile.[38] For him, the Soviet Union was an opportunist power, and the cause of the Cold War lay in ideological hostility between the superpowers,[39] increased by the currency of social revolution in the Third World, but essentially it was about American containment of social revolution, and not the inherently revolutionary threat of Soviet expansionism.[40]

For Deutscher, Stalin and the Soviet Union pursued the two goals of realizing the material basis of a politically controlled mode of production and a reduced security threat, which was secured by the buffer zone of Eastern Europe.[41] These objectives were achieved by the time of Stalin's death, and because of this the Cold War and Soviet international relations were subordinated to what Deutscher termed 'the Great Contest', the *internal* goal of 'outproducing' Western capitalism.[42] Deutscher, then, fore-closed his analysis of the linkage between the expansion of international communism through social revolution and the international presence of the Soviet Union. Indeed, he even went further, to suggest that in some instances the Soviet Union did more to hinder the successful expansion of international communism than did the counter-revolutionary policies of the United States.[43] Because the Soviet Union wanted to avoid a military conflict with the stronger United States, and because its priority was always internal consolidation and development of its productive forces, the actual competition with the West was limited to the level of production.[44]

Deutscher's work, though persuasive and insightful, contains a number of unresolved tensions that problematize his understanding of the relationship between social revolution and the Cold War. The first is how Deutscher understands the USSR's relationship with revolution and revo-lutionary states. Although he did recognize the importance of the Soviet Union for the potential success of social revolution,[45] he had problems in explaining why the Soviet Union did support and help sustain revolu-tionary movements and states. The argument that the Soviet Union's support for particular revolutionary movements and states for a *raison d'état*, or its own internal consolidation, or to control and manipulate such movements, fails to provide an adequate explanation as to why, following the logic suggested, the Soviet Union supported movements and regimes that actually undermined what could be identified as aspects of Soviet *raison d'état*. Thus, Deutscher cannot provide a consistent explanation as to why, in a number of historical instances, the Soviet Union intervened to support international revolutions when it could not have been sure of controlling them, and when such interventions served to jeopardize the relationship with the United States, other than like some other Marxists, reducing this behaviour to domestic politics. Moreover, to understand this[46] in terms of the need for the USSR to be seen to support international revolution, although it did not want to, does not provide an adequate Marxist explanation.

The source of this problem lies in Deutscher's failure to put forward a developed theory of the form of Soviet international relations. This is partly related to his conceptualization of the Cold War as a 'contest' confined to competition in material production between East and West. Although he is correct to stress the impact of Soviet internal material goals (and the impact they had on social relations within the USSR), he fails to link this to the means with which the Soviet Union sought to realize its international relations and 'expand'. The problem, then, was how the economic relations of the USSR could be considered a currency of international relations when they were inseparable from the Soviet state. Because Soviet economic strength and success was directly tied to the Soviet state, its international expansion necessitated a corresponding direct political expansion as well. Yet, this, as history after 1945 highlighted, required territorial expansion, something which the USSR could not risk.

The second concern with Deutscher's analysis is his expectation that capitalist crisis would not only provide a possibility for radical transformation in the advanced capitalist states towards socialized production, but that the obvious success of the Soviet model of socialized production would make this even more likely. Deutscher remained wedded to Trotsky's theory of 'uneven and combined development and permanent revolution'[47] manifested in the impact of capitalist social relations in the Third World. Deutscher follows the imminent teleology of Trotsky's theory, by assuming that the contradictions of capitalist expansion will serve to weaken metropolitan capitalism through revolutionary upheavals in the Third World, and that the Soviet Union will take advantage of the 'paradox of backwardness' to overtake the United States.[48] His failure to conceptualize the specificity of the American era of capitalism, and particularly the successes of class compromises in the Western metropoles that altered the form of capitalist social relations, led him to adopt a position that had a 'productivist' orientation. Indeed, his analysis of the Soviet Union and the 'socialist bloc' ended up falling into the same trap that he had accused Stalinism of falling into. Deutscher fails to recognize that, from the beginning, Bolshevism was based on the contradictions between a theory of productive forces and social relations. Its history highlights the unwinding of this contradiction, where not only did the objective of (rapid) productive growth (i.e. the attempt to catch up with and overtake the West in terms of material development) fail, but the coercive and hierarchical methods employed in the 'command economy' to achieve this goal also undermined the social basis of communism. Class antagonism, ultimately, is the explanatory source here, and it was this, alongside the geopolitical limits imposed by American power, that determined the outcome of the Soviet project.

Fred Halliday

Halliday offers one of the most insightful theorizations of the Cold War and revolution by suggesting that social revolution in the Third World was an aspect of international conflict that involved the superpowers in social conflict as 'systemic' actors.[49] To put it simply, the United States and the Soviet Union were different states, based on different constitutive political and economic values. One acted to support one form of 'systemic values', identified with liberal-democratic capitalism, while the other sought to support a different form of constituent values based on communist revolution. The Cold War, then, was about this struggle between two different types of state projected on to world politics, and derived from the different political and economic constituencies of each superpower.[50] And we cannot fully understand the occurrence of revolution unless we can understand the Soviet Union as a particular kind of state that contested American international hegemony, and sought to support those states that were anti-American and anti-capitalist.[51]

Halliday's work is characterized by a distinction between his work on the Cold War and that on social revolution, which is most clearly reflected in his later understanding of international conflict in terms of 'homogeneity and heterogeneity'. Using these concepts he attempts to set out international conflict in terms of an international society distinguished by a distinct set of norms

> shared by different societies, which are promoted by inter-state competition. This is based neither on inter-state nor on transnational models, but on the assumption of inter-societal and inter-state homology.[52]

Thus, international relations has a tendency to produce homogeneity in the internal constituent norms (in terms of both state and society) of the members of international society. And it is international pressures which are responsible for compelling states to conform to a particular kind of internal arrangement.[53] Revolutionary states are important within this conceptualization of the international in that they are attempts to overcome these pressures to conform. Revolutions represent a crisis in the internal and international social order because the seizure of state power produces a radical transformation in state–society relations which creates a heterogeneous international system whereby rival forms of internal norms compete to homogenize the other.

There is obviously some truth in this. The Soviet Union was characterized by internal norms different from those of the United States, and through political hegemony and forms of international activity sought to expand the social space of 'socialism', in conflict with capitalism. However, on two crucial points this understanding of international relations and the place of revolution within it is problematic. First, how can this conceptualization explain the *occurrence* of social revolution? If the operation of international relations is about the compulsion of states to conform to a particular political, economic and cultural configuration, then how can these same processes of compulsion be responsible for helping to create a crisis which has an outcome of revolution and the transformation of a state in direct contravention of the existing and dominant international norms? The only way of resolving this is to understand social revolution in terms of 'catching up', as a crisis that results in structural transformation, which seeks to transform a state so it can more adequately compete with its international competitors. Halliday suggests as much with his citing of scholars associated with Historical Sociology, Otto Hintze, Michael Mann and Theda Skocpol. Thus, the concept of homogenization appears to have a Neo-Weberian predisposition where modernity or modernization is the goal, and the logic of international competition dictates this end. Such an understanding of revolution underestimates the *class* nature of the transformation that they engender. Social revolution is a response to a class crisis, which obviously implicates the state as a defender of particular class interests and the manager of class antagonisms. It is in the crisis engendered by the international expansion of capitalism and the contradictions this creates for particular types of state that lead to a breakdown in the arrangement of class relations that sows the seeds of revolution.[54] Thus, the crises of those states that succumbed to revolution were fundamentally related to the contradictory impact of capitalist social relations at a particular conjuncture and within a specific domestic class structure. The state in this respect was important as being a *relation* of production, a facilitative regime–institution that managed, or in the case of a revolutionary crisis, failed effectively to manage, the existing social order on behalf of capitalist accumulation.

Homogenization, then, tends to understand social revolution in terms of inter-state competition[55] whereby the state is subject to external pressure and its reaction to this pressure leads to an internal social crisis. Such an analysis, however, does not adequately acknowledge the class nature, which is international, but relates ultimately to the transformation of class relations within a revolutionary state. If Halliday embraces the Skocpol thesis then he must downplay social conflict for political–state conflict. In doing so, homogeneity or heterogeneity, as the outcome of revolutions, becomes a form of modernization or development, rather than a class-based phenomenon.

Halliday's model is dependent on a notion of international competition, which seasons his notion of the Cold War as 'inter-systemic conflict'. This competition in the realms of political, economic and military affairs assumes a degree of symmetry between the constituents involved in this competition (for all intents and purposes the Soviet Union and the United

States), and in the form and logic of that competition. In one sphere, the nature of competition was quite apparent, and it fitted the orthodox understanding of international relations and the explanation of the Cold War. The arms race, and in particular the strategic and nuclear arms race, provided a potentially devastating currency of competition. However, as argued in Chapter 4, such a currency of competition is insufficient for the conceptualization of the Cold War, and indeed, does not fully reflect Halliday's focus. Halliday points to a combination of competitive logics from ideas to the production of consumer goods. What he does not do is place them within an overall configuration, and neither does he argue that we need to distinguish the qualitatively *different* logics present within each system. However, in terms of the nature of revolution, and the conflict of revolutionary social formations with the existing capitalist social forms, what separated them was the distinctly different ways of organizing the reproduction of social life. For the latter, the society *and* state are based and dependent on a particular set of class relations that facilitates a logic determined by the accumulation of profit. Capitalist states exist within a self-perpetuating system of profit and expansion. It is this which drives economic growth, resource depletion, the organization of the economy and society, and the strategic role of the state as the guarantor and facilitator of a particular kind of class relationship. We can even see the state as 'autonomous' in these terms, not in the sense of 'in and for itself' *à la* Skocpol,[56] but in the sense of the logic of capitalist accumulation.

The reconfiguration of social relations within the newly constructed social structures of the revolutionary state not only ends up destroying the class power of the previous regime, but also institutionalizes a new social logic for the reproduction of social life, based on the sanction of the bureaucratic Party-state. The dynamic that governed these states was no longer their place within the international capitalist division of labour, but the internal compulsion of social transformation, and how this conditioned relations with other states in the international system. Whereas in the past this international relationship was both 'inter-state' and 'inter-societal', it was now about explicitly political relations.

Thus, inter-state or geopolitical conflict between revolutionary and non-revolutionary states was founded on the social antagonism between different forms of politics. It was more the case of the uneven and combined nature of capitalist expansion, which was contingent on social processes within states and how this conditioned geopolitical outcomes, rather than the distinction between interest and ideology, inter-systemic and/or inter-state conflict, that characterized the international relations of social revolution in the Cold War. Thus, how the revolutionary state was internally constituted also contributed to modifying the properties of the international system, which was also to have an impact on the character of other states. Inter-state conflict was the outcome of social revolution, then, not only because of the structural imperative of the international system but also because these states were internally constituted in a way that foreclosed alternative currencies of international politics.

Revolutions, then, do not just produce greater state autonomy from society, rather, they virtually eliminate it, because what previously demarcated one from the other is dissolved. By attempting to characterize social revolution as international heterogeneity Halliday ends up having to detach the internal social transformation from its international consequences, when in fact, revolutions not only rupture the state–society relationship but also the domestic–international relationship. Revolutionary ruptures were a product of the uneven expansion of capitalism effecting changes that ended up demolishing these distinctions and thus provoking militarized conflict.

The Marxist-informed approaches to social revolution and the Cold War discussed in this section highlight a number of important features of the Cold War: for American Revisionists, these are the counter-revolutionary posture and hostility of the United States; for Isaac Deutscher, the problematic nature of social revolution in 'backward' states and the internally derived inconsistencies in Soviet support for international revolution; and finally, for Fred Halliday, the role of revolution in the Cold War conflict and the competing global projects of the USSR and the United States. However, all are also problematic: the Revisionists for their neglect of the USSR as an antagonist in the Cold War; Deutscher for his differentiation between economic and political conflict; and Halliday in his tendency to disperse political motive either to ideology or to interest, and his imposition of a quasi-Realist geopolitical logic on the international relations of revolutionary states. In the following section I shall try to offer a Marxist-based alternative perspective on the relationship between social revolution and the Cold War.

Social Revolution as the Dynamic of the Cold War

The importance of social revolution to a theory of the Cold War lies in the fact that it was this type of sociopolitical change that provided the dynamic of the Cold War. As David Horowitz has correctly asserted:

> The very term 'cold war' may be a misleading description, for unlike its prototype, this 'war' has no locality in terms of geopolitical space … its *contested* areas are themselves shifting and non-delimitable.[57]

More specifically, revolutionary sociopolitical transformation was defining of the Cold War for the following reasons. First, the changes, internal and external, that they engendered were based on a contestation of the existing social order, a social order that was not only marked by the consequences of uneven and combined capitalist development (as will be shown in Cuba and Vietnam in particular), but also *international* capitalist development, which infused domestic social relations with a strong 'foreign' accent. Thus, the political agents and organs of social revolution were founded on class-based mobilizations that reflected the unique historical and social legacy of each society's incorporation into the capitalist world market, and the uneven nature of that 'integration'.

Secondly, the contestation of the international capitalist order, first imperialist and then American-defined, had outcomes that saw attempts by revolutionary states to renegotiate not only the domestic social relationship between rule/authority and socioeconomic production, but also the international relationship between the revolutionary state and the international system, which amounted to the construction of an alternative form of international order. Thus, not only were international relations between states domestically constituted by social revolution different, but they also, in effect, amounted to a different kind of international order characterized by the absence of any relations between non-state or private sources of politics.

Thirdly, the process of revolutionary contestation and transformation directly impinged on the hostility between the major capitalist powers and the USSR. In the period up to the Second World War this primarily concerned the European capitalist powers and their colonial possessions. Nationalist and communist movements in the colonies were directly linked to Moscow through Comintern, and not only challenged colonial power, but provided the foundations for the subsequent overthrow of colonial rule. These challenges and their links with the USSR were obviously undermined by the USSR's preoccupation with its own national security in the late 1920s, but, nevertheless, the role of communist parties in Europe (Spain in 1936–39 and Germany until 1933) tied the USSR to internal challenges to the ruling orders in Europe as well as further afield.

The transformation in the international capitalist order after 1945 with American hegemonic ascendancy, shifted the orientation of the challenge to the international order. Challenges to imperialism and colonial power were merged with and, ultimately, replaced by challenges to the new American-drafted international order. With the Truman Doctrine, NSC-68 and subsequent executive (presidential national security doctrines) responses to international crisis, the United States not only replaced the European great powers as the architect of the postwar international order, but also had the most to lose by challenges to it, which necessitated not only containment but also counter-revolution. The axis of systemic hostility had, then, shifted from that between the USSR and the European capitalist powers to that between the United States and the USSR. This was highlighted in the division of Europe, but it quickly spread to the non-European world. Whereas the prewar period had not witnessed any successful social revolutions, the postwar era saw revolution, in a number of instances, merge with decolonization. Thus, not only did the eruption of social revolutions challenge American international order and American capitalist power, but they also provided the means for an expansion of Soviet international power. Thus, what had been 'imminent' and thwarted in the period after 1917, exploded in the postwar era as a number of the new states that emerged out of the conjunctural crisis of war[58] were 'blessed' with communist 'revolutionary paternity'. Finally, the central importance of these episodes of social revolution not only saw 'bilateral' relations of revolutionary 'solidarity' and, conversely, counter-revolutionary hostility involving either superpower, but they also conditioned the *direct* relationship between the United States and the USSR. As Halliday has rightly maintained, the consequences of social revolution *always* provoked Cold War crises between the superpowers, the most obvious and dangerous being that of Cuba in late 1962.

In the remaining part of this chapter, I will discuss these aspects of the relationship between social revolution and the Cold War with reference to Third World revolution and the Cuban and Vietnamese revolutions in particular, which are the focus of Part II.

Revolutionary Consequences of Capitalist Development

The social revolutions in the Third World that punctuated postwar world politics reflected the outcomes of the uneven and combined nature of capitalist development. Capitalist development created social and political structures (state and economy) that in a number of cases reduced the possibility of independent local capitalist development, leaving the way open for revolutionary communists (or nationalists) to determine the anti-imperialist struggle and subsequent sociopolitical transformation in a number of states, Cuba and Vietnam being the most critical.

The way in which colonies were incorporated into the international capitalist order was such that social structures were created that stunted the possibility of indigenous capitalist development, *while at the same time* promoting intense exposure to the rigours of the world market in other sectors of the economy. It was in these sectors, primarily sugar and tobacco in Cuba, rice and rubber in Vietnam, that Vietnam and Cuba were capitalist, and it was through the social relations that developed in these areas of production that the defining social antagonism emerged that was not only one between direct producers or workers and capitalists, but an international one about the international control of the state and how this mediated the exposure of the domestic economy to the fluctuations in the world market. Thus, the outcomes of capitalist development in Cuba, Vietnam and elsewhere saw particular domestic contradictions that were ultimately resolved within distinct international contexts.

The Cuban Revolution

In the case of Cuba, the contradictions centred on the pervasive American stranglehold on the Cuban economy, itself based on sugar exports to the United States, which structured economic development, and meant that Cuban capitalist development was effectively determined by its subordinate relationship with the United States. After independence the 1902 Reciprocal Trade Agreement regulated 'economic' relations between Cuba and the United States. This agreement was heavily weighted towards American economic needs, principally the import from Cuba of crude sugar, rather than refined sugar, and also reduced import duties for American goods entering Cuba.[59] The 1934 Reciprocal Trade Agreement, which followed in the wake of the Cuban abrogation of the Platt Amendment, saw a continuation of American capitalist penetration of Cuba, and the latter's dependency on the United States. The 1934 Jones-Costigan Act served to limit American imports of refined sugar, and reduced it to a maximum of 22 per cent of overall Cuban sugar imports. This went hand in hand with the 'export' of Cuban manufacturing capacity to the United States especially in tobacco, and high import tariffs on Cuban manufactured imports, which actually helped encourage Cuban manufacturing capital to move to the United States.[60] The American dominance of the Cuban sugar economy was but part of a pervasive domination of the wider economy and social relations. By the 1950s, 40 per cent of raw sugar production, 23 per cent of non-sugar production, 90 per cent of telephone and electrical services, and 50 per cent of public railways were all American-owned.[61] The American dominance of the economy also prevented the development of other local resources, such as nickel, to which American companies controlled access.

The pervasive power of American 'economic' relations over 'independent' Cuba was matched by an intrusive political presence that might justify the description of Cuba as a kind of neo-colonial state. The expulsion of the Spanish in 1898 was quickly followed by the US drafting of Cuba's independent constitution, finalized in the 1901 Treaty of Paris with Spain. The American presence was, however, more visible in the 1902 Platt Amendment to the Cuban constitution that established a legal right of US intervention in Cuban domestic affairs if and when the US thought that Cuban constitutional democracy was threatened, or if and when developments within Cuba threatened to undermine American interests.[62]

Thus, in both state and economy, Cuba was dominated by the United States. Economic development was conditional on the United States, and the scope for indigenous interests to predominate in Cuba was severely curtailed by the possibility of US intervention.[63] It was in such a structural context that the social order faced a serious social and political challenge in the early 1930s that was to be resuscitated in the 1959 revolution. The 'revolutionary crisis' that preceded Batista's coup d'état of 1934 emerged out of an economic crisis precipitated by the Great Depression. This not only exposed the nature of Cuban capitalist development, but its subordinate dependence on the United States. Thus, in 1930 the United States passed the Smoot-Hawley Act which increased the excise duty on Cuban sugar. Following this, the Cuban share of the US market declined from 49.4 per cent in 1930 to 25.3 per cent in 1933; sugar production fell by 60 per cent and exports by 80 per cent.[64] The economic crisis was compounded by the weaknesses and failings of Cuba's political institutions witnessed in the attempts by the President, Gerardo Machado, illegally to extend his term of office, along with his sponsoring violent attacks against the organized left. Machado's machinations had alienated not only the organized working class but also sections of the middle class. The conjuncture of the early 1930s, then, saw an international spark to a domestic political and economic crisis which provoked the communist-led CNOC (Confederación Nacional de Obreros de Cuba) to organize a general strike in August 1933.[65] By the end of September 1933, workers had seized control of 36 sugar mills, establishing 'soviets', accounting for over 30 per cent of total sugar production.[66] It was in this context of a serious threat not only to the capitalist social order in Cuba, but also to the American presence in Cuba, that the United States intervened in the guise of the US Assistant Secretary of State, Sumner Welles, who, when he could not engineer a moderate replacement for Machado who would have middle-class support, finally ended up acquiescing to the Batista coup in 1933 that ensured an end to the 'Red threat'.

The Batista coup quelled the communist and revolutionary threat for the time being, but it did not resolve the deeper structural problems that dominated Cuban development. Despite Batista's exit to Miami in the 1940s and the return of a 'constitutional order', Cuba continued to be characterized by distorted and uneven capitalist development[67] and weak political institutions, such that political 'order' required continued regular military interventions and severe political repression combined with 'terrorism' against the state.[68] The emergence in the 1950s of a radical nationalist movement led by Fidel Castro, the 'Movement of 26 July', was symptomatic of these contradictions and of the urgent need for a radical transformation of the sociopolitical order. Clearly, the traditional ruling class and political parties had failed to establish a viable political order in Cuba, tied as they were not only to weak local political institutions and corruption, but also to an overbearing foreign presence that had, by the 1950s, expanded into real estate and tourism, but was still dominated by the class relations of sugar production.[69] What was also significant for the revolutionary outcome in Cuba was the role of the Cuban Communist Party (PCC). It was communist cadres that had initiated the revolutionary disturbances of the early 1930s, and though the Party itself remained either passive or tied to the state after winning a number of socioeconomic concessions for organized labour in the 1940s, its strength within the Cuban working class was to be of crucial significance in the subsequent direction of the revolution after January 1959.

The weakness of the state, combined with the rapid alienation of all sections of the population due to the incompetence and brutality of Batista's army's struggle against the Fidelistas, ensured the collapse of the regime by late 1958. It was not the case that the guerrilla struggle had defeated the regime, rather, it had shown the regime for what it was: corrupt, inefficient, brutal and fragile. The irony in all this was the American role in Batista's downfall. In a case of *déjà vu*, just as the United States had intervened using Welles in 1933 to ensure an 'adequate' replacement for Machado, so they intervened, but less directly so, in 1958 by withdrawing diplomatic support for Batista and trusting that the national cross-class coalition government that replaced him in early 1959 on the back of a widespread popular mobilization against the regime would be amenable to American objectives.

By 1959, then, the 'liberal-democratic' and capitalist episode of Cuban development had exhausted itself and reached a dead end. This allowed for the seizure of power by radical-nationalists who quickly identified with a class-based political constituency. With this alliance, based on the control of Cuba's political institutions by radical nationalists, backed by communist cadres and other militants in the Cuban working class, and alongside the urgent political objective of independent national political and economic development, a conflict with the United States quickly developed. This was because the principal class and political contradiction was not one between the Cuban working class and Cuban capital, but rather an imperialist one between the Cuban *people* and the United States. It was this relationship, a product of Cuba's 'independent' capitalist development, and its transformation that was the focus of the revolution. The central tasks that the revolutionary government set itself rested on securing Cuban national control of the economy to ensure that economic development met the needs of Cuban people rather than foreign capital, and that independent political institutions were freed from the tentacles of American interference and weak local foundation.[70] In effect, both of these objectives required the eviction of American power and the construction of a radically new sociopolitical order in Cuba that challenged American power and ended up threatening wider American interests in the region.

The transformation was achieved through domestic class mobilizations in support of the radical sections of the newly formed revolutionary government. The support of the working class and the PCC was crucial in this respect, and their support was secured through instituting revolutionary decrees that sought to redress many of the material and social grievances of this constituency. There were land and property expropriations, rent reductions, subsidies introduced on basic goods and wage rises.[71] Alongside these 'policies from above'[72] to win over a class constituency, the regime, with the collaboration of the apparatus of the PCC, set out to build an organizational structure that would institutionalize the regime, and cement its legitimacy within the working class.

The Vietnamese revolution

The revolutionary consequences of capitalist development in Vietnam, though historically and sociologically distinct, shared a number of similarities with Cuba and the outcome of the Cold War. Whereas Cuban state formation and economic development was marked by a determining American 'neo-colonial' influence, however, Vietnam's was through the legacy of French colonial rule. French colonial power took upon itself not only the economical and commercial exploitation of Vietnam, principally its indigenous crops, rice and rubber, but also its political unification. However, what characterized the uprooting of this traditional Indo-Chinese society and its brutal journey to modernity was its uneven nature. Thus, French colonial rule reflected an uneasy relationship between the modernity of the French colonial state and capitalist social relations of exploitation that destroyed traditional forms of political authority and undermined indigenous forms of material production, and the persistence of pre-capitalist forms of agricultural cultivation and petty-commodity production.

The impact and substance of French colonial rule, then, was uneven and varied in character. Politically, French rule was 'parcellized', in the sense that what became the constituent parts of the Democratic Republic of Vietnam (DRV – North Vietnam) were in fact protectorates rather than a formal colony. Cochinchina in the south was a formal French colony and locus of French power. It was also the most capitalistically advanced and penetrated. And it was here in the areas of French colonial domination of rice and rubber production for the world market that private property and capitalist social relations were most developed. This area became the 'rice basket', producing sufficient rice to make Vietnam one of the world's largest exporters of rice.[73] This contrasted with the north, where the traditional institutions of the family and village and more traditional forms of material reproduction persisted.[74]

With the political and economic transformation wrought by French colonialism, increasingly large numbers of local people became subject to the demands of the capitalist world market and its fluctuations. Agriculture was transformed, particularly in rice cultivation and in rubber plantations developed by French capital. The expropriation of fertile agricultural land by French capitalists ushered in an upheaval in the social relations of the countryside. Subsistence peasant cultivation was squeezed and many peasants were transformed into a rural proletariat or wage labourers in mines, plantations and other forms of emerging commodity production, and land ownership was concentrated in the hands of French capitalists and indigenous landlords subservient to the colonial state. This was clear from the French transformation of the rural economy. Increases in taxation, punitive rates of interest on loans, and the general 'monetization' of the rural economy represented particularly in the French monopolies on salt and other necessities (which peasants had to pay for in cash) highlighted the French and commodified nature of the transformation and the alienation of many peasants.[75] Moreover, the destruction of traditional social relations and institutions (villages and families) was also directly political in the sense that it was carried out with the legal sanction of the state, and sometimes involved direct violence, with peasants being 'press ganged' into the social relations of wage labour.

Labour conditions were horrific, leading to a high labour turnover because of deaths, injuries and desertions. This meant that the working class was never stable in size, and its ranks were constantly being depleted and replenished. It also meant however, that, one, the effects of 'proletarianization' were much wider than figures might suggest,[76] and, two, that workers continued to have links with the peasantry which meant that the militancy of workers could be adopted and emulated by peasants in their struggles with landlords. In this sense capitalist contradictions and class struggle existed in contexts where capitalist social relations were not always visible.

Thus, although the working class appeared numerically very small,[77] as a percentage of the population of Indo-China, the transformation in social relations derived from the incorporation of Indo-China into the French colonial system was enough to set in motion the collapse of the existing social structure and indigenous political order. This transformation and the role of the embryonic working class was important, because this new class was in a political and strategic position within the political economy of Indo-China such that its potential influence and confrontation with international capital was a crucial factor in the colonial political economy. Strategically, it was exposed to the deepest contradiction in the colony, at the nexus of the internal class structure and the international relations of that structure which was mediated through the French colonial state. Capitalist social relations of production in this respect did not appear separate from direct political authority. Economic exploitation was intrinsically linked with the French colonial state.

The emerging contradictions, then, were not seen in purely national terms, but rather were identified with the international presence of French capital, and because of this, sections of the working class began to organize and struggle against this relationship. Thus, why Vietnamese national liberation was combined with communist-led socialist transformation was that French colonial rule exposed workers to the twin contradiction of economic exploitation and political repression, which was seized upon by the Communist Party. Economic improvement could only come about through political national liberation, and it was the Communist Party that was the only political force in Vietnam that not only identified these objectives but also actively sought to achieve them.

The consequences of capitalist transformation in the form of class formation and class struggle first became apparent in the 1920s, when a number of strikes were organized in French-owned enterprises. This upsurge in class struggle and the development of a more sophisticated and pronounced form of struggle led to the founding in 1925 of the Thanh Nien or 'Revolutionary Youth League of Vietnam'. This was a direct consequence of the level of exploitation in French capitalist enterprises and the agitational activity of communists which ultimately led to the founding of the Communist Party in 1930.[78] These developments coalesced to produce a communist-led anti-colonial movement that, although officially following a 'Comintern line' of a national patriotic cross-class alliance against imperialism, was located in the agency of the peasantry and the working class.[79] The activists and cadres of the Party were drawn from a wide section of the populace, and although the membership of the Party was not dominated by workers or peasants, but rather by intellectuals and the petty bourgeoisie, the power or effectiveness of the Party rested on its ability to mobilize the support of these class constituencies.

The increasing internationalization of the political economy of Indo-China exposed the colonial institutions and the emerging working class to these contradictions in their daily lives. This was exemplified by the Great Depression in the early 1930s, which had a particularly severe impact on the export of rice and other commodities produced in French Indo-China. In three years rice and rubber prices fell by over 80 per cent compared with their pre-Depression value, and the overall value of these exports fell by over half between 1929 and 1931.[80] What followed was economic retrenchment and belt-tightening. Workers suffered massive pay cuts and unemployment, with nearly 40 per cent of wage labour having lost their jobs by 1934. In the countryside, landlords squeezed peasants through higher rents and taxes, which saw the abandonment of over half a million hectares of cultivable land and increased widespread poverty.[81] The consequences of the Depression, then, amounted to a reduction in rice (and other goods) production and prices, which served severely to undermine the livelihoods of many indigènes. Capitalist investment was reduced, and this served to weaken further the possibility of the emergence of a local-national bourgeois class that could campaign for political change and ensure a gradual transformation of French rule. Instead, economic stagnation and political repression strangled any hopes of internal political change from within the realms of imperial rule.

The 1930s, then, saw a consolidation of the Party and the development of its cadre network throughout Vietnam. Its support base among workers and peasants was developed through strike mobilizations, which culminated in the 1930–31 revolt throughout Cochinchina, Annam and Tonkin. Although this revolt was uncoordinated, and not nationally organized, it managed to test severely French colonial power. As Hunh Kim Khánh has stated:

> From 1 May 1930 until the summer of 1931 there were few days without some sort of political agitation – worker strikes, peasant demonstrations, sabotage, assassinations of government officials, and dissemination of communist leaflets ... Starting with a joint worker–peasant action ... on 1 May 1930, unrest quickly spread to outlying rural areas of the Nghe Tinh region ... Before long these peaceful demonstrations became armed struggles. A general disintegration of the administrative machinery followed, and by August 1930 several village and district officials had sided with the peasant rebels ... In early September 1930, 'Red Villages' sometimes called 'soviets' were established in several rural districts of Nghe An.[82]

This communist-led insurrection was effectively suppressed by the French authorities, thus exposing the relative weakness of Vietnamese communism. It was to be a new and more significant international conjuncture that proved to be decisive for French rule and the possibility of revolutionary change. With the elimination of French political and military power through Japanese occupation, the Communist Party took advantage of the situation to consolidate its position and make preparations for a seizure of power at the end of the war. Moreover its position within wider Vietnamese society was strengthened through its organization of an anti-Japanese Patriotic Front, like that organized by Mao Zedong in China.[83]

What characterized politics in French Indo-China was that colonial rule and socioeconomic transformation had ended up seriously weakening if not destroying the power of the traditional ruling class. The ruling entity that replaced the fragmented power of the monarchy was French imperial capital. The indigenous elements had no economic or political power base from which to force themselves into the French colonial state or develop an indigenous capitalist class. This was part of the wider process of the internal transformation of the political economy and class structure. The French presence not only saw the direct exploitation of former peasants and the socialization of increasing numbers of Indo-Chinese into the rigours of capitalist social relations, but also the development of a new indigenous landlord class that was ultimately dependent on the colonial state.[84] This colonial transformation produced an indigenous class structure that was shaped within and limited by the colonial state-economy, the principal features being the 'bastardized proletarianization' of the Indo-Chinese poor, and the lack of an autonomous national capitalist class.

This being the case, and this being partly explained by the contradictory nature of French colonial rule, it was the fledgling workers' movement that was to become the source of political and revolutionary transformation. However, this was not purely internally contrived. The development of the workers' movement in colonial Indo-China was inextricably tied up with international developments, primarily production for the world market. This was compounded by the development of the international workers' movement as manifested in communist parties and by the emergence of the Soviet Union and its international revolutionary arm, Comintern. Thus the social and material transformation of Indo-China wrought by French colonialism was itself conditioned by the rigours of the international capitalist system, both in terms of the fluctuations in the world market, and in the form of inter-state conflict, most importantly the approach of war in the mid- to late 1930s. In addition to this, a product of these broader developments which came increasingly to determine the politics of Indo-China–Vietnam was the political project of the Indo-Chinese–Vietnamese Communist Party.

The emergence of a revolutionary conjuncture within Vietnam, then, emerged from within the colonial episode, as it was situated internationally. This conjuncture was mediated by the significance of specific forms of political agency. Although strikes, riots, and periodic property seizures or attacks on it weakened the colonial state and the accumulative drives of colonial capital, these acts of rebellion and alienation did not in themselves challenge colonial and capitalist rule. Only a direct contestation of the form of political rule, an assault on the apparatus of coercion and administrative control, could challenge colonial power. Because of the stunted development, weakness and most of all coercive dependence of the indigenous upper class on the colonial ruling class, there was no effective 'natural' constituency for genuine political contestation. As Gareth Porter has suggested, this political situation, that is, the lack of the independent basis of the local upper class in Vietnam, classically a local-national bourgeoisie, meant that the local landlord class was dependent for its own exploitation of the peasantry on the coercive power of the colonial state:

> the absence of an independent commercial or industrial bourgeoisie and the survival of a land tenure system that allowed a land-owning class to maintain power over the peasantry discouraged a political evolution towards liberalism. Meanwhile the abuses of a bourgeois democratic colonial power made it easy for an anti-capitalist revolutionary movement to discount the possibility of genuine liberalism for the masses under capitalism.[85]

Thus contestation was most acute at the site of production–exploitation and this provided the basis for a political agency that would mediate, within a crisis, between the status quo and change. And this was more pronounced because the outlet for a 'liberal politics' was reduced due to the inability of the traditional or local landlord class to separate political rights from economic exploitation. There was a quid pro quo with the colonial regime: the maintenance or acceptance of French political domination in return for the French guarantee of the social relations in the countryside, which ultimately removed any material impetus for political change.[86]

The absence of any indigenous political alternative allowed Vietnamese communists to take advantage of the power vacuum in August 1945 with the Japanese surrender, after prior military capitulation of French power in 1941. With the return of the French, war ensued between the Viet Minh, who were greatly helped by the Chinese communist victory in 1949. By 1954 the French had been routed, indicated by the humiliation of Dien Bien Phu, and with France suing for a negotiated exit, the Viet Minh were effectively a state in waiting. Partition, under the 1954 Geneva Accords, resulted in the establishment of a state in the north, the DRV, under Communist control. The south, what became the short-lived Republic of Vietnam (RV), continued to bear the social and political contradictions that had dominated French Indo-China. Whereas communist national liberation struggle had focused on a national class mobilization to force a French withdrawal, the struggle for the south now involved the larger and more dangerous task of removing American power in South Vietnam. Thus the Cold War saw a transformation from a communist revolutionary contestation of French imperial capital to a contestation of American international order.[87]

American attempts to construct a new capitalist state in South Vietnam confronted the social legacy of French colonial rule and the revolutionary war. Thus, access and control of land was the defining social and political issue that the corrupt, inefficient and brutal South Vietnamese state, although pressed by their American backers to deal with it, never properly addressed, and it provided a key source of peasant mobilization for the National Liberation Front (NLF) with the renewal of revolutionary guerrilla war in 1960. The periodic bouts of land reform under both Ngo Dinh Diem and Nguyen Van Thieu failed either to alleviate poverty and the alienation of the bulk of the peasantry or to develop the basis of a capitalist agriculture.[88] Instead, not only were peasants increasingly caught up in the violence of the insurgency, but also, because of the 'reforms', many peasants were driven through poverty and lack of land to migrate to urban areas that could barely cope with the massive influx of people from the countryside.

The Vietnamese Revolution was, then, a product of French colonial capitalist development, notably socioeconomic transformation that created the class agency for the eventual overthrow of French power, which in turn was fundamentally mediated by the wider and longer-term incorporation of Vietnam into the international capitalist market, and the crisis of the Second World War and its consequences. The conflict between communist revolutionaries, dedicated to political and economic, national and international, revolutionary transformation, and French imperial capital was a cold war, in the sense that the conflict was centred on a crisis within the structures of capitalist development based on a form of political (class) agency dedicated to a revolutionary sociopolitical transformation. Moreover, it was a cold war in that revolutionary success rested on a transformation of international order as much as domestic order. Whereas the struggle started within a French and imperialist context, after the Second World War French attempts to maintain power and determine the future of Vietnam required American economic and military support as the United States sought to support French counter-revolution as a means of containing communism and securing its vision of the postwar international order. This ended with French defeat, which was strongly influenced by communist success in China. Vietnam, then, became a front of the Cold War between capitalist and communist visions of domestic and international order.

Conclusions: The Cold War as Social Revolution

Social revolution was one response to the crises in sociopolitical order that confronted many states in the Third World in the postwar era. The alternatives to communist revolution largely consisted of military dictatorships, with or without direct US/Western support, and forms of radical–nationalist regime where communist parties were either subordinate to a nationalist leadership (as in Indonesia until 1965) or exterminated (as in Egypt and Iraq and in Indonesia after 1965). In both of these cases, the states that emerged fluctuated in their hostility and conflict with the American-led international order, but did not fundamentally break with that order in the way in which communist revolutions did.

The political, ideological and organizational model that emerged out of the 1917 Bolshevik Revolution spurred its application elsewhere in the postwar era. What characterized the Cold War, then, was the existence of what E. H. Carr identified as a global professional class of revolutionaries.[89] Communist revolutionary agency was obviously inspired by the October Revolution, but just as Lenin and the Bolsheviks emerged out of the structures and contradictions of Russian capitalist development, so the *differentia specifica* of the Third World revolutionary struggles in Latin America, Asia and Africa emerged out of each one's unique experience of externally enforced domestic socioeconomic transformation.

In this sense, revolution was embryonic within capitalism, yet its 'delivery' was not always assured. While social revolution was successful in Cuba and Vietnam, it was contained and destroyed in Korea, Indonesia, Chile and elsewhere. Revolutionary conjunctures were products of the outcomes of the crises induced by uneven capitalist development, thus although they emerged from within the structures of imperialist capitalist development, their resolution was consequent on the crisis of imperialism and the restructuring of international capitalism under an American hegemonic order. With the weakness of the European colonial powers brought about by the burden and destruction of war, and the fact that the challenges to many of their possessions were led by communist parties with a vision of national liberation very different from that envisaged by the colonial powers and the United States, international conflict with the United States, the new architect and guarantor of the international capital-ist order, was inevitable.

The revolutionary challenge was not just about the impact of domestic transformation in Cuba, Vietnam and elsewhere, but the fact that these transformations also consisted of a redefinition of the international system. This had more than regional consequences, because all revolu-tionary states, even those states not led by communist parties, could look to the USSR and/or China for international support, and both Communist powers were keen to expand their international interests through establish-ing relations and influence in such states. This was never a smooth process as the intensity of doctrinal and political conflict within the international communist movement, notably the Sino-Soviet split and their descent into military confrontation by the late 1960s, highlighted. However, it was precisely these types of conflict, derived as they were from the relations between communist revolutionary states, that are suggestive of a type of international order different from that between liberal-democratic capitalist states.

The dynamic of the Cold War, then, was class-based social revolution. It was this, alongside the persistence of the Soviet strategic challenge to American capitalist power, that provided the momentum of the Cold War and also its resolution. Beyond direct Soviet expansion based on the external projection of military power, which risked nuclear war, the only way in which international capitalist order could be challenged was through its local contestation and overthrow within the weaker, more fragile links of that order. These turned out to be states in the Third World rather than the more advanced capitalist states of Europe. Because of the geopolitical constraints imposed on the projection of Soviet power, social revolution was the only means through which the Soviet system could expand. It was this that ensured continued Soviet support for international revolution until the mid-1980s.

The outcomes of revolutionary transformation, just as much as they contributed to the dynamic of the Cold War by inducing international crises, were also determined by the Cold War. The shape of post-revolutionary transformation, indeed, *how* the revolutionary seizure of power was to extend to the construction of a new form of politics and social relations, was decided by the *interaction and conflict* between revolution and the responses of the international system. Thus, the objectives of social revolution, just as was the case in the USSR after 1917, only *materialized* through the process of conflict with the international system.

The single factor that was ultimately determining in this regard was military power. Military power was a necessary factor in *all* revolutions, despite its different qualities in Cuba and Vietnam. Military power was also defining in consolidating and completing revolutionary change, both in terms of domestic politics, and more significantly in the international context of the defeat of American-backed counter-revolution in the Cuban Bay of Pigs incident in April 1961, and the North Vietnamese victory in 1975 in the long war with the United States and its RV ally that had started in 1960. What was crucial in both of these episodes was the part played by the strategic Cold War involving the two dominant global powers, the United States and the USSR, that not only transformed the consequences of domestic revolutionary change, but also ultimately determined the quality of it. Indeed, military power succeeded in defending the gains of social revolution, but by largely constituting the domestic politics of revolutionary states, also fundamentally weakened them in the longer term.

NOTES

1 The location of social revolution in the Third World highlights the wider impact of developments in the non-European world on Western capitalism in the postwar era. In one area, energy, there was a critical dependence on oil and gas resources from the Third World, and the oil price 'hikes' of the 1970s, involving the Arab-dominated Organization of the Petroleum Exporting Countries (OPEC), highlighted the ability of Third World producers to spark a major crisis in the major capitalist economies that played an important part in the destabilization and unravelling of the postwar boom. Moreover, it was the fact that this economic tool had been used for political reasons by Arab states to press the West and, in particular, the United States, to help resolve the conflict in the Middle East after Israel's capture of Arab lands in the 1967 Six-Day War. This importance was also highlighted in the late 1960s and early 1970s with the burden on the American economy created by its military intervention in Indo-China, which also contributed to the inability of the American economy and its finances to 'fund' global economic expansion. The result was an end to the Bretton Woods system of exchange rate management, which presaged a major economic recession in the West in the 1970s.
2 This shares a similar perspective to that of Halliday, *Making of the Second Cold War*, p. 33, who asserts:

the very social interests embodied in the leading capitalist and communist states are present, in a fluid and conflicting manner, in third countries; the result is that the clash of the two blocs is constantly reanimated and sustained by developments in these states that may be supporters or allies of one or other bloc.

3 See the following works by I. Deutscher: *Russia, China and the West*, ed. Fred Halliday (Harmondsworth: Penguin, 1970); *Great Contest*; *Ironies of History*; *Unfinished Revolution*; *Marxism, Wars and Revolutions: Essays From Four Decades* (London: Verso, 1984).

4 Specifically, G. Alperovitz, *Cold War Essays* (Garden City, NJ: Anchor Books, 1970); D. Horowitz, *From Yalta to Vietnam: American Foreign Policy in the Cold War* (Harmondsworth: Penguin, 1967); idem, *Imperialism*; idem (ed.), *Containment and Revolution: Western Policy Towards Social Revolution, 1917 to Vietnam* (London: Anthony Blond, 1967); W. A. Williams, *The Tragedy of American Diplomacy* (New York: Dell Publishing, 1972); G. Kolko, *Confronting the Third World: United States Foreign Policy, 1945-1980* (New York: Pantheon Books, 1988).

5 See W. W. Rostow, *The Stages of Economic Growth: A Non-Communist Manifesto* (Cambridge: Cambridge University Press, 1971); S. Huntington, *Political Order in Changing Societies* (New Haven, CT: Yale University Press, 1968); C. Black and T. Thornton (eds), *Communism and Revolution: The Strategic Uses of Political Violence* (Princeton, NJ: Princeton University Press, 1971); J. Kautsky, *Communism and the Politics of Development: Persistent Myths and Changing Behaviour* (New York: John Wiley and Sons, 1968); J. Kautsky (ed.), *Political Change in Underdeveloped Countries: Nationalism and Communism* (New York: Robert E. Krieger, 1976); B. Kiernan, *The United States, Communism and the Emergent World* (Bloomington: Indiana University Press, 1972).

6 R. Barnet, *Intervention and Revolution: The United States in the Third World*, revised edn (New York: New American Library, 1980); R. Lowenthal, *Model or Ally. The Communist Powers and the Developing Countries* (New York: Oxford University Press, 1977); W. LaFeber, *America, Russia, and the Cold War, 1945–1992*, 7th edn (New York: McGraw-Hill, 1993); R. Feinberg, *The Intemperate Zone. The Third World Challenge to US Foreign Policy* (New York: W. W. Norton, 1974).

7 For two very good exceptions see Armstrong, *Revolution and World Order*, and Halliday, *Revolution and World Politics*.

8 Thus, many Cold War Realists, such as Kennan, *Nuclear Delusion*, pp. xx–xxi, and H. Morgenthau, *Vietnam and the United States* (Washington: Public Affairs Press, 1965), were critical of US foreign policy responses to social revolution, most notably during US intervention in South Vietnam in the 1960s, because they did not regard these developments as a threat to US strategic interests.

9 See Barnet, *Intervention*, p. 20; Lowenthal, *Model or Ally*, pp. 256–7; LaFeber, *America, Russia, and the Cold War*, p. 171; Feinberg, *Intemperate Zone*, pp. 1–9.

10 This also relates to the problem of (mis)perception in foreign policy and how the chaos and turmoil of revolutionary change can make it very difficult for states to identify the genuine policy of the revolution, beyond the rhetoric to appease the masses. See Jervis, *Misperception*.

11 Thus, Vietnam's revolutionary proclamation of August 1945 drew some of its wording from the American declaration of independence, and the United States supported non-communist Indonesian nationalists' calls for independence against Dutch colonial power.

12 This related more to direct political interference (rather than to economic property), through local communists loyal to Moscow or Beijing who, in Egypt, Iraq, Syria and Indonesia, were persecuted and murdered. Even in communist-

ruled states such as China and Cuba, both leaderships were concerned to maintain political autonomy by purging party-state structures of those too closely identified with Moscow. See G. White *et al.* (eds), *Revolutionary Socialist Developments in the Third World* (Brighton: Wheatsheaf, 1983), pp. 5–6.

13 Thus Nasser's international objectives of 'Pan-Arabism' rested on expelling Western influence in the Middle East, which necessitated a direct involvement in the affairs of neighbouring states, particularly the pro-Western Hashemite monarchies tied to the 1954 Baghdad Pact. The instability that followed contributed to US intervention in Lebanon in 1958 and the pronouncement of the Eisenhower Doctrine.

14 See Halliday's excellent survey of revolutionary internationalism in *Revolution and World Politics*, pp. 94–132.

15 Ibid., pp. 196–206.

16 See Halliday, *From Kabul to Managua*, pp. 128–9.

17 See Black, *Communism and Revolution*, pp. 3–25, 431; Kiernan, *United States*; Huntington, *Political Order*. Such a perspective informs the work of Skocpol, *States and Social Revolutions*, who tends to under-emphasize the impact of socioeconomic and class transformation on the nature of the state, and exaggerates the logic of traditional inter-state conflict as the outcome of social revolution.

18 Kiernan, *United States*, p. 6.

19 For a comparative analysis, see the seminal work of B. Moore, *The Social Origins of Dictatorship and Development: Lord and Peasant in the Making of the Modern World* (London: Penguin Books, 1967).

20 Kiernan, *United States*, pp. 8–18, 35–57.

21 See Kautsky, *Communism*, pp. 93–6, 101; idem, *Political Change*, pp. 20–1.

22 Kautsky, *Communism*.

23 See M. Watnick, 'The Appeal of Communism to the Peoples of the Underdeveloped Areas', in S. M. Lipset and R. Bendix (eds), *Class Status, and Power: Social Stratifications in Comparative Perspective*, 2nd edn (London: Routledge & Kegan Paul, 1967), p. 428–36. For a Marxist critique of this position and a restatement of the class basis of social revolution and its project see J. Petras, 'Socialist Revolutions and their Class Components', *New Left Review*, 111 (September–October 1978), pp. 37–64.

24 See Kautsky, *Communism*, pp. 7–57; Huntington, *Political Order*.

25 Indeed, as E. Hobsbawm, *The Age of Extremes: The Short Twentieth Century, 1914–1991* (London: Michael Joseph, 1994), has argued, capitalism was 'saved' by the alternative vision and realization of revolutionary communist modernity, in the form of the use of state planning, limits on capital and concessions to the working class that not only 'civilized' the rule of capital but reduced the threat and impact of crisis.

26 In many respects, the nature of both were conditioned by social struggles in the metropoles, in terms of demands for democratic rights and economic redistribution, which also had an effect on the quality of the relationship with the colonies.

27 See Horowitz, *From Yalta to Vietnam*, p. 19.

28 Horowitz, *Containment*, p. 10; Horowitz, *Imperialism*, p. 94.

29 The contradictions related to the global quest for markets and raw materials and how this necessitated an aggressive foreign policy, but also how the militarized nature of the economy led to the emergence of a military–industrial complex. See D. Horowitz (ed.), *Corporations and the Cold War* (New York: Monthly Review Press, 1969); G. Kolko, *The Roots of American Foreign Policy: An Analysis of Power and Purpose* (Boston, MA: Beacon Press, 1969).

30 See Williams, *Tragedy of American Diplomacy*, pp. 15, 229–69; W. A. Williams (ed.),

From Colony to Empire: Essays in the History of American Foreign Relations (New York: John Wiley, 1972).

31 See Horowitz, *Imperialism*, pp. 71–88, 238–40.

32 See Kolko, *Confronting the Third World*, pp. 33–75; Alperovitz, *Cold War Essays*, pp. 14, 86.

33 See Horowitz, From *Yalta to Vietnam*, p. 401.

34 Deutscher, *Great Contest*, pp. 54–5; *Ironies of History*, p. 154; *Unfinished Revolution*, p. 68.

35 Deutscher, *Great Contest*, pp. 52–74, *Ironies of History*, pp. 55–8.

36 Deutscher, *Great Contest*, p. 59.

37 Deutscher, *Ironies of History*, pp. 55–6.

38 Ibid., pp. 147–63; Deutscher, *Unfinished Revolution, passim*.

39 See Deutscher, *Marxism, Wars and Revolutions*, pp. 72–87.

40 See Deutscher, *Great Contest*, pp. 54–7.

41 Deutscher, *Ironies of History*, p. 52; *Russia, China and the West*, pp. 192–3.

42 His understanding of capitalism, particularly its proneness to periodic 'economic' crises, led him to assume that the Soviet Union could outproduce the leading capitalist states and win over the masses of the world with its example of economic efficiency and productivity alone. See *Unfinished Revolution*, pp. 52–70; *Russia, China and the West*, pp. 67, 197; *Great Contest, passim*.

43 *Unfinished Revolution*, p. 154; *Marxism, Wars and Revolutions*, p. 78.

44 *Russia, China and the West*, pp. 22–67.

45 *Unfinished Revolution*, p. 155; *Marxism, Wars and Revolutions*, p. 201.

46 As Deutscher does in *Unfinished Revolution*, pp. 155–6.

47 L. Trotsky, *The Permanent Revolution* and *Results and Prospects* (London: New Park Publications, 1962 [1930, 1906]).

48 Deutscher, *Unfinished Revolution*, pp. 55–6.

49 See Halliday, *Rethinking International Relations*, pp. 170–80; *Revolution and World Politics*, pp. 143–55.

50 Halliday, *Rethinking International Relations*, p. 175.

51 See Halliday, *Making of the Second Cold War*, pp. 97–104, *Revolution and World Politics*, pp. 108–9, 49–50.

52 See Halliday, *Rethinking International Relations*, p. 94.

53 Ibid., p. 95.

54 See the work of M. Löwy, *The Politics of Combined and Uneven Development: The Theory of Permanent Revolution* (London: Verso, 1981); and J. Petras, J. Morley, M. DeWitt and Eugene Havens (eds), *Class, State and Power in the Third World* (London: Zed Books, 1981); J. Petras, *Critical Perspectives on Imperialism and Social Class in the Third World* (New York: Monthly Review Press, 1978).

55 Skocpol, *States and Social Revolutions*, provides the best example of this.

56 For a discussion and critique of Skocpol's position see P. Cammack, 'Bringing the State Back In?' *British Journal of Political Science*, 19, 2 (April 1989), pp. 261–90; and R. Miliband, 'State Power and Class Interests', *New Left Review*, 138 (March–April 1983), pp. 57–68.

57 Horowitz, *Containment and Revolution*, p. 9 (emphasis added).

58 See E. Mandel, *The Meaning of the Second World War* (London: Verso, 1986).

59 See P. Ruffin, *Capitalism and Socialism in Cuba: A Study of Dependency, Development and Underdevelopment* (London: Macmillan, 1990), p. 57.

60 See J. O'Connor, 'Cuba: Its Political Economy', in R. Bonachea and N. Valdés (eds), *Cuba in Revolution* (Garden City, NJ: Anchor Books, 1972), pp. 54–69.

61 US Department of Commerce figures cited in D. Wood, 'The Long Revolution: Class Relations and Political Conflict in Cuba, 1868–1968', *Science and Society:*

An Independent Journal of Marxism, 34, 1 (spring 1970), p. 17.

62 M. Pérez-Stable, *The Cuban Revolution: Origins, Course and Legacy* (New York: Oxford University Press, 1999), pp. 14–31.

63 The US intervened on numerous occasions between 1906 and 1909 and 1917 and 1922, and was a major factor in the coup d'état by Batista in 1934 that ended the communist-initiated revolutionary disturbances of the preceding months.

64 L. Pérez, *Cuba and the United States: Ties of Singular Intimacy* (Athens, GA: University of Georgia Press, 1990), p. 181.

65 See H. Thomas, *Cuba or the Pursuit of Freedom* (London: Eyre & Spottiswoode, 1971), p. 615.

66 Pérez, *Cuba and the United States*, p. 195.

67 Thus, by the 1950s the Cuban economy continued to be dependent on sugar production, which contributed to 80 per cent of exports and 25 per cent of national income, yet actual production was 0.5 million tonnes lower than it had been in 1925. Thus vast areas of productive land lay uncultivated and wasted. Moreover, the need to pay for food imports, which made up 25 per cent of food consumption in 1958, led to a rapid dwindling of foreign currency reserves. See R. Blackburn, 'Prologue to the Cuban Revolution', *New Left Review*, 21 (October 1963), pp. 61–2; S. Farber, *Revolution and Reaction in Cuba, 1933–1960: A Political Sociology from Machado to Castro* (Middletown, CT: Wesleyan University Press, 1976), pp. 153–6.

68 Farber, *Revolution and Reaction*, pp. 176–84; Pérez-Stable, *Cuban Revolution*, pp. 52–60.

69 Although this had stunted Cuban socioeconomic development under the 'capitalist regime', it facilitated post-revolutionary class transformation in the countryside. Rural class relations were not dominated by a large peasantry, but rather landless, property-less wage-earners. Class relations in the countryside, then, were capitalist in terms of a large rural proletariat who wanted access to the means of production, but not in terms of land ownership that tends to characterize a 'peasant outlook', but through job security (the blight of seasonal/temporary labour), higher wages and other social and material benefits, like education and health care. See S. Mintz, 'Foreword', in R. Guerra y Sánchez, *Sugar and Society in the Caribbean: An Economic History of Cuban Agriculture* (New Haven, CT: Yale University Press, 1964), pp. xi–xliv.

70 The Fidelistas were well aware of the need for strong domestic and armed support, particularly in view of the crushing of the Arbenz government in Guatemala in 1954 by a US-backed coup.

71 As Blackburn, 'Prologue to the Cuban Revolution', pp. 18–23, has stated:

> Within six months of the entry into Havana, a radical Agrarian reform was realised. Within twenty months nearly all US property in Cuba was expropriated. Within twenty-two months the vast majority of Cuban firms were expropriated.

> Moreover, within the first year of the revolution the government had engineered, with the cooperation of the Cuban working class, a redistribution from the propertied classes to working people of more than 15 per cent of national income. See Wood, 'Long Revolution', p. 30.

72 Although the regime initiated these acts, there was some mass participation both in their being called for and in their implementation. Many of the land expropriations were demanded and/or welcomed by the rural proletariat. See R. Blackburn, 'Class Forces in the Cuban Revolution: A Reply to Peter Binns and Mike Gonzales', *International Socialism*, 9 (summer 1980), pp. 86–8.

73 M. Murray, *The Development of Capitalism in Colonial Indo-China* (Los Angeles:

University of California Press, 1980), pp. 428–44.

74 N. Wiegersma, *Vietnam: Peasant Land, Peasant Revolution. Patriarchy and Collectivity in the Rural Economy* (London: Macmillan, 1988), pp. 19–21, 67–86.

75 See G. Kolko, *Vietnam: Anatomy of a War, 1940–1975* (London: Allen & Unwin, 1986), p. 14; K. Post, *Revolution, Socialism and Nationalism in Viet Nam*, Vol. I, *An Interrupted Revolution* (Aldershot: Dartmouth Publishing, 1989) pp. 33–4.

76 E. Wolf, *Peasant Wars of the Twentieth Century* (New York: Harper & Row, 1969), p. 169.

77 For figures see Kolko, *Vietnam*, pp. 16–17; Post, *Revolution*, I, pp. 28–30.

78 Murray, *Development of Capitalism*, pp. 363–5; W. Duiker, 'The Red Soviets of Nghe Tinh: An Early Communist Rebellion in Vietnam', *Journal of Southeast Asian Studies*, 4, 2 (September 1973), pp. 186–98.

79 Thus, the Stalinist *diktaks* of the Comintern which had been so costly for the Chinese Communist Party were formally accepted and executed by the Vietnamese. However, in practice, primarily because of the pressing concerns for the USSR relating to events in Europe, the Vietnamese were quite flexible in their approach to developing the Indo-Chinese revolution, even to the point of sharing a slate with a Trotskyite faction in local elections for the Saigon legislature in 1935. See W. Duiker, *The Communist Road to Power in Vietnam*, 2nd edn (Boulder, CO: Westview Press, 1996), p. 56.

80 Murray, *Development of Capitalism*, p. 201.

81 Ibid., p. 464.

82 H. Kim Khánh, *Vietnamese Communism, 1925–45* (Ithaca, NY: Cornell University Press, 1982), pp. 152–4.

83 Duiker, *Communist Road to Power*, p. 72.

84 See Kolko, *Vietnam*, pp. 14–15.

85 G. Porter, *Vietnam: The Politics of Bureaucratic Socialism* (Ithaca, NY: Cornell University Press, 1993), p. 5.

86 Ibid., p. 6.

87 Initially this focused on the fundamental problems that confronted the RV, securing political order. Thus, early American aid to South Vietnam was heavily weighted towards the creation of a military capacity that would allow Diem to eliminate any threats to his regime, ethnic or class-based, left over from the Franco-Viet Minh war and then the construction of an army for internal policing and external defence, with the US concerned not to see a repeat of the events in Korea in 1950. Of US aid between 55.5 per cent and 73 per cent was military in nature. See Post, *Revolution*, I, pp. 244–5.

88 After 1965 South Vietnam became a net importer of rice for the first time. See Kolko, *Vietnam*, p. 226. Moreover, the impact of war destroyed the social basis of agrarian production. Agricultural productivity collapsed because not only was the soil ruined by napalm and toxic defoliants, but thousands of peasants fled to the cities, thus reducing the labour supply and creating a greater food demand in urban areas which could not be met through internal production. See Wiegersma, *Vietnam*, pp. 175–97.

89 E. H. Carr, *The October Revolution: Before and After* (New York: Alfred Knopf, 1969), pp. 8–9.

PART II:
HISTORY

6

The International Relations of the USSR in the Cold War

Thus far I have sought to put forward a theoretical argument that, using a historical materialist-based approach, IR theory might reconceptualize the Cold War as a conflict between differently constituted states, epitomized by the United States and the USSR, based on the relationship between the formal and coercive authority of the state and the realm of social and material production. The relationship between these two spheres of human action rested on specific kinds of social relations, which, put simply, were conditioned by the way in which people were socially organized to produce, and what role politics and, in particular, the directly coercive and militarized nature of that politics, played in this process of production and in the management of the overall social order.

The argument in Part I, then, was that power and politics are socially constituted according to the way in which social relations are organized. The conceptual distinction offered derived from Marx's categories of 'politics' and 'economics' and the way in which political processes and outcomes are consequent on the nature of the relationship between the formal and coercive power of the state and the informal and privatized power of economic production and exchange. It was also argued that the relationship between 'rule' and 'production' conditioned the role of coercive and military power in the domestic politics of states, such that the existence of a non-state sphere of politics based on the social relations of capitalist production and exchange within *advanced* capitalist states tended to produce a politics *less* determined by coercive and military power. Finally, social revolution was a product of a crisis within developing capitalist or 'backward' states that had been incorporated into the capitalist world economy through imperialism, where a social and political crisis erupted out of the international weakness of the state that was a product of an uneven and conflict-ridden set of social structures unable to contain class antagonisms.

It is the concern of this chapter and Chapter 7 to relate the preceding theoretical discussion of the state, military power and social revolution to a more historically orientated understanding of the international relations of the superpowers with the Cuban and Vietnamese revolutions, the point being to see how far the theoretical framework put forward offers a useful perspective in terms of understanding the relationship between the Cold

War and social revolution. The Cuban and Vietnamese revolutions were, arguably, defining of the Cold War in the sense that they exposed, both from within and internationally, the themes raised in the preceding theoretical discussion. These revolutionary conjunctures emerged within the context of the uneven international expansion of capitalist social relations and the contradictory impact this had on Cuba and Vietnam. Moreover, not only did these revolutions emerge within an international capitalist context; they were also largely *determined* by that international conjuncture. Revolutionary crises saw the transformation of the state and the emergence of new currencies of domestic and international relations, which were reflected in the realm of the economy and military power. However, what is most important for the argument put forward here is that these revolutions contributed directly to the Cold War by challenging capitalist rule and US power and serving as forms of expansion for Soviet-type socialism.

The issue of revolutions and the international impact on them is at the heart of an understanding of the Cold War. The developments within Cuba and Vietnam were greatly influenced by the hostility and/or support from either superpower. This and the following chapter will examine the nature of each superpower's relationship with each revolution. Applying the foregoing analysis will, I hope, bring out the distinctive nature of Soviet and American international relations, and the possibilities and limitations of each that contributed to the Cold War acquiring its particular character.

The International Relations of the Soviet Union and Social Revolution

The Soviet Union was characterized by international relations that related directly with other states in the international system, politically and economically, coordinated by the Party-state apparatus and with non-ruling communist parties.[1] Unlike its direct physical presence in Eastern Europe, the Soviet Union had to rely on local revolutionary leaderships in other states. Soviet relations, however, were conditioned not only by the perceived goals in the bilateral relations with each revolutionary state, but also by the debates and struggles within the CPSU, the ideological confrontation with China and,[2] most importantly, the conflict with the United States, and the way in which Soviet relations with revolutionary states affected this. As argued in Part I, the USSR was confined to a 'politics of expansion' through social revolution or direct political 'occupation'. Revolutions were important, then, because they were potential sources for augmenting Soviet political and strategic power in the Cold War. In this sense, although the internal politics of the USSR determined the *form* of Soviet international relations, with respect to *substance* Cuba, Vietnam and other revolutionary states were important as internationally derived sources for augmenting Soviet strategic power. Objectively, the possibility of placing nuclear missiles in Cuba and securing a US withdrawal from South Vietnam were issues that would influence Soviet domestic politics, but were not reducible to it.

The central point to be made, then, is that Soviet international relations were limited to a form of relations based on a politics confined to the organs and currency of the Party-state. While this provided an ideological and political link with the other revolutionary states, the Soviet Union's inability to relate to these revolutions in other ways served to limit the forms and impact of its influence. Because of the inability to secure a direct physical and political presence in Cuba and Vietnam, the Soviets were limited to relying on local communist leaderships. This relationship, though secured through ideological unity and hostility to and from the United States, also exposed the tensions within and between revolutionary states.[3] Soviet pressure and influence was politically transparent because it was confined to only one currency of international relations. Moreover, the constricting and then elimination of non-state sources of social and political autonomy and power within Cuba and Vietnam, with the abolition of the institutions and patterns of capitalist economic activity and the suppression of rival centres of authority, religious, cultural and political, effectively cut off the possibilities of cultivating relationships, influence and institutions that might serve as an alternative channel for external influence. Cultivating influence was confined to the higher bureaucracy of the Party-state, be it through economic aid or military support.

Thus, despite providing important advantages, especially in terms of political controls and channels of authority, the nature of the Soviet Union's influence also had significant disadvantages. The most important of these was that the Soviet Union could only foster a politics through the local revolutionary leadership. Following this the Soviet Union was identified with the local revolutionary leadership, although its ability to influence it was not always successful. Moreover, the domestic politics of revolutionary states, including the USSR, was greatly influenced by and extremely sensitive to developments in the relations between revolutionary states. Thus, in the relations between the USSR, China, Cuba and North Vietnam Soviet leaders were concerned to ensure not only that their allies kept in line with Soviet ideological and international objectives, but also that these relations did not undermine the internal political and ideological authority of the leadership within the upper echelons of the CPSU.

External developments could be used and manipulated by contending factions within the Soviet leadership to gain advantage over rivals, as occurred in the 1953–56 post-Stalin succession over policy towards the German Democratic Republic (GDR – East Germany).[4] While in this case external events were manipulated for domestic political advantage, conflicts between different revolutionary states, derived from internal–external linkages between the leaderships and the ideological positions of different factions within each revolutionary leadership, were also involved. The emergence of the Sino-Soviet split reflected this, with the speeches made by Mao Zedong during his visit to the USSR in November 1957 having many similarities to the anti-'peaceful coexistence' ideas and policies of the 'anti-Party group' of Kaganovich, Molotov and others in the leadership of the CPSU, whose plot to overthrow Khrushchev had only recently been defeated.[5]

The influence of international developments on the domestic politics of revolutionary states was such that the Sino-Soviet split could be seen to be an outcome of not only the conflicting international positions of the USSR and China on imperialism, but also a product of the domestic political preoccupations of each leadership. Thus, as much as Khrushchev's policy of de-Stalinization was about Soviet domestic politics it had profound consequences for other leaderships in Eastern Europe and also, more importantly, China. Therefore, Khrushchev's concern to redefine socialism in the USSR was to have profound consequences for other socialist states. As Westad has shown, basing his observations on recently accessed documents, Mao saw Khrushchev's 'secret speech' of 1956 denouncing Stalin as an opportunity to consolidate his own power within the leadership of China by distancing himself and the Chinese Communist Party (CCP) from the CPSU. This was done by pursuing economic policies (the 'Great Leap Forward') at odds with the official Soviet line, which were used as a test of loyalty to his leadership. Thus, Mao's domestic political authority was tied to an ideological line antagonistic to that of the CPSU.[6]

Because of the inability of the Soviet Union directly to control events in these states, its relationships with other revolutionary states were characterized by opportunism and danger. Despite the ideological and political sympathies, because of its nature and internal problems the Soviet Union was concerned to avoid political commitments that threatened to problematize its own physical security and its principal political–ideological objective, the rapid augmenting of its material-base and productive forces so as to enable it eventually to surpass the achievements of capitalism. However, these objectives also had to be compatible with its internationalist commitments and, in particular, the maintenance of its position of dominance within the socialist camp, which was threatened by the possibility of other revolutionary states developing closer relations with China. Moreover, this was not just a case of combating Chinese taunts of weakness and betrayal and growing Chinese international influence in the Third World, but also reinforcing the security of the leadership position of incumbents in the Kremlin. Whereas successes in consolidating and bringing other revolutionary states into the Soviet bloc were a means of strengthening a Soviet leader's domestic political position, failure could have serious consequences. This was most evident with Khrushchev, whose unsuccessful attempts to deal with Berlin through threats and sabre-rattling and the humiliating climb-down over Cuba in 1962 (all part of his doctrine of 'peaceful coexistence') played a significant part in his removal in 1964.

However, the USSR's most important concern was how its relations with and, particularly, its political and military commitments to revolutionary states, might lead to a direct conflict with the United States. It was this concern that haunted its relations with all revolutionary states and exposed the problem of the extent to which the USSR could secure strategic advantage through an alliance with revolutionary states yet not put itself at risk of direct nuclear conflict with the United States. This was most crucially exposed over Cuba in 1962. However, it was also seen in the inability of the USSR to secure a resolution of the 'Berlin/German Problem' to its complete satisfaction in 1960–61,[7] and in the relationship between the USSR and China over the latter's objective of 'liberating' Taiwan during the 1958 Taiwan Straits crisis.[8] What it highlighted, and this must have been in the minds of the Soviet leadership and of Khrushchev in particular in late 1962,[9] was that the USSR could not afford to risk its own security with that of other revolutionary states whose domestic and international objectives were not always in accordance with those of the USSR.[10] However, this concern to limit its military entanglements with other revolutionary states undermined its ability to determine events within these states, as the absence of a military commitment tended to correspond to a weakening of political influence.

Revolutions posed both threats and opportunities for the Soviet Union. The threat derived from a revolutionary form of international relations that identified itself with the Bolshevik Revolution, but was not directly led or controlled by the CPSU or the Red Army. This not only served to bring into question the ideological and political legitimacy of the Soviet Union within the international communist movement that could exploit fissures within the CPSU leadership, but it also problematized the wider international position of the Soviet Union, particularly its relations with the advanced capitalist states, especially the United States. Revolutions exposed the fundamental contradiction of the Soviet Union, a form of politics born of social revolution that had reduced the revolutionary potential of the Soviet Union internally through the silencing of any alternative currents of politics, yet which proclaimed itself to be the vanguard of the international revolution, and had prioritized internal material development and the establishment of a powerful coercive state over all other political goals. Revolutions tested whether the Soviet Union was true to its ideology, particularly when they jeopardized its international position by threatening to create crisis situations that would engulf it along with other states.

The opportunities derived from revolutions served, potentially, to consolidate political rule within the Soviet Union, both within the Party-state apparatus as it related to the rest of society and within the particular leadership faction in the ruling apparatus. Revolutions also undermined international capitalism and the international power of the United States. Cuba and Vietnam reflected this par excellence. Indeed, because of the limited nature of Soviet international relations, revolutions were the *only* means of an extra-territorial proliferation of the Soviet social form. Without direct physical control, as in Eastern Europe and Mongolia, the Soviet social form only spread through social revolution. Moreover, because of the mixed experience of the Soviet Union in the post-Stalin era with a number of Third World states (something that was to persist throughout the international history of the USSR), revolutions led by communist parties provided the only means by which the Soviet Union could secure stable and long-term goals based on Communist Party-state control and the social transformation premised on the abrogation of capital-ist social relations and political forms. In the many instances where the Soviet Union had relations with non-communist/revolutionary political leaderships, as in Algeria, Egypt, India, Indonesia and others, because of the limited ability to influence and manipulate events in these countries, pro-Soviet tendencies were vulnerable to removal and the eviction of Soviet influence. Without communist party leadership or, as in the case of Cuba, a proto-communist leadership, the Soviet Union had no guarantee that it could secure and maintain a long-term influence in a country. With communist leadership, although the Soviet influence was not quite direct, because it was based on a specific kind of internal social and political trans-formation, it made it difficult if not nigh impossible for alternative political leaderships to emerge. As long as the Soviets could maintain good relations with other Party-states, then, Soviet influence would be preserved. Though even here, as the Sino-Soviet dispute highlights, ideological and political symmetry based on social transformation did not ensure international political solidarity.

Cuba

Soviet relations with Cuba reflected many of the tensions outlined above. These included the relationship between Soviet policy towards Cuba and the internal position of not only the Party-state in the USSR, but also the position of the leading faction within the CPSU. This situation was also linked to the wider relations with the international communist movement; particularly the problems associated with the Sino-Soviet split and national liberation/revolutionary movements in the Third World. Finally, the Soviet–Cuban relationship was a major factor in the US–Soviet relationship, provoking a crisis that brought the world to the brink of nuclear war in October–November 1962. Thus, while providing a major opportunity for Soviet penetration of Latin America, an area in which, prior to the Cuban revolution, the Soviet Union appeared to have had scant intellectual, political or economic interest,[11] as the 1962 Cuban missile crisis emphasized, it also offered grave dangers.

One of the most important features of the Cuban revolution, which has marked all social revolutions, was the unique local nature of the revolution. Indeed, the Cuban revolution was *sui generis*[12] in that it had not had any significant Soviet involvement until Castro had fully secured himself in power by the early 1960s and sought Soviet aid. The Cuban revolution, then, was not only geographically distinct (i.e. it took place in what the Soviets had always understood as 'America's backyard'), but also organizationally, ideologically and politically distinct. This is important because for a long period of Soviet relations with Cuba it was the distinctiveness of the Cuban revolution, in all its forms, that was of major importance not only in terms of the USSR's relationship with Cuba, but also of how the Soviet Union should relate to other national liberation movements in the Third World that were not led by communist parties. This was of particular concern at the time as Soviet authority was already being undermined and challenged from within the international communist movement through the Sino-Soviet split, and the actuality of Cuba seemed to justify Chinese attacks on Khrushchev's policy of 'peaceful coexistence'. These concerns were aired in different official publications in the USSR, and were reflected in their initially lukewarm and inconsistent responses to the Cuban revolution with it being described as 'national democratic', 'revolutionary democratic', and 'socialist'. It was not until April 1962 that the Soviet Union finally began to acknowledge, consistently, that Cuba was socialist.[13]

Thus it was not just a concern to avoid provoking the United States by 'recognizing' Cuba as socialist, but rather a more complex triangular relationship between the USSR and Cuba, China and the United States. In the case of the first, the Cuban Communist Party (PCC) had not led the revolution and was in a subordinate position within Cuba. Moreover, until 1962 Castro's overall strategy for the future direction of the revolution was not completely clear. With respect to China, the Soviet leadership wanted to prevent any further splits in the international communist movement. Therefore it was concerned as to how far it should publicly support Cuba, yet well aware that not to show support would further fuel Chinese attacks and the possibility of a new independent revolution joining the Chinese camp. Finally, the USSR was involved with the United States in a number of disputes over the status of Berlin and developments within Laos, which were bound to be influenced by what happened in Cuba, and whether or not the United States would blame these on Moscow.

Central to Soviet policy was the concern to ensure ideological and political unity under Soviet international leadership while maintaining an international momentum that could undermine American–imperialist power. Thus, at the core of Soviet policy towards Cuba were the goals of consolidating the revolution and using Cuba as a kind of 'revolutionary bridgehead' for the penetration of Latin America, and in doing so secure Cuba, ideologically, politically and militarily within the Soviet-dominated international communist movement. This was to ensure not only the expansion of the Soviet bloc system, and thus strengthen the world 'correlation of forces' in favour of socialism, but also to reduce the potential for a Cuban-induced confrontation between the superpowers over Cuba and also an undermining of wider Soviet goals (diplomatic and economic) in the region.

The support for Cuba was a delicate matter, then, for the Soviet leadership, in that it potentially offered not only an opportunity to rebut Chinese claims of passivity, weakness and ideological treachery, but also a means of expanding the international communist movement under Soviet leadership and challenging US power in its own backyard. However, it also posed significant risks. Would too eager and premature support provoke conflict within Cuba as the revolutionary coalition split at the prospect of Soviet influence? Would it also provoke a crushing US military intervention which the USSR could do little to forestall? Finally, would support for Cuba end up undermining wider Soviet interests where negotiation with the United States was preferable, as over Berlin, or, even more importantly, as with the crisis between the United States and China over Taiwan in 1958, would support for a revolution that the Soviet Union could not direct end by dragging the USSR into a direct military–nuclear conflict with the United States?

Soviet policy towards Cuba, and why that policy was to lead to the Cuban missile crisis of October–November 1962, was a product of the linkages between internal and external politics based on the form of Soviet international relations and how it could best effectively realize its dual aims of securing Cuba within the Soviet bloc and undermining US strategic power. The deployment of nuclear weapons by Khrushchev came at a crucial conjuncture with respect to his leadership position within the USSR and the international communist movement, his relations with the West and the escalating hostility between the United States and Cuba. The withdrawal of Soviet nuclear weapons not only exposed the USSR to a diplomatic humiliation, but also revealed its inability to secure Cuba fully into the *political and ideological discipline* of the Soviet bloc. Thus throughout the 1960s Cuba continued to advocate and practice a revolutionary strategy at odds with the official Soviet line. At times this was detrimental to Soviet interests, with Cuba sponsoring non-communist revolutionary groups in Latin America and beyond that were opposed to local communist parties loyal to the Soviet doctrine of 'peaceful coexistence', basing their strategy on armed struggle.[14]

The Soviet form of politics provided the framework for Soviet–Cuban relations in the sense of the exact form that Soviet relations took, and in the consequent interests those relations were meant to serve. Soviet international relations were meant to secure the realization of not only Soviet international goals, but also internal ones. This was particularly the case during the sometimes turbulent leadership of Khrushchev. These internal concerns were not just about the political and economic situation within the USSR and the authority of the Khrushchev leadership, but also about how far the growing conflict with China further challenged Khrushchev's internal authority. Primarily, however, the concern was for the problems associated with Soviet economic development and the need for an improvement, particularly if Khrushchev's policy of 'peaceful co-existence', which was based on economic rather than military competition and conflict with the West, was to be achievable. For this to be so, the Soviet objectives over the status of Berlin and an armaments agreement that would allow the USSR to reduce its overall military capacity would have to have been accomplished. Yet from a position of relative strategic weakness, despite the success of the successful inter-continental ballistic missile (ICBM) test in August 1957 and then the launch of Sputnik I the following October, this was unlikely.[15] Indeed, it seems that it was the combination of internal political–economic problems alongside the challenges of continued US 'arrogance' based on strategic superiority (despite the rhetoric of a 'missile gap' by US presidential candidate John Kennedy in 1959), and the combined ideological challenges of China and Cuba, that pushed Khrushchev publicly to utter threats of nuclear support for Cuba in July 1960.[16]

However, Khrushchev's concerns about Soviet domestic economic development were complicated by the USSR's leadership of the international communist movement, to the point that internal economic development could not come at the expense of losing revolutionary allies in the Third World through their overthrow by the United States or their forming an alliance with China. Indeed, the international context became increasingly important for Khrushchev, particularly when his domestic economic reforms began to flounder,[17] contradicting his promise of 'the reaching of communism' in the near future at the 22nd Congress of the CPSU in 1961.[18] Internal problems, however, could be compensated for by external success. The Cuban revolution and the possibilities this opened up for his leadership and for the Soviet bloc were an opportunity to secure an international success that would compensate for the continuing problems of productive development within the Soviet Union,[19] and also for the political conflicts with the Chinese and his rivals in the Party-state machine.[20] Cuba, then, could play a decisive role, not only in securing the position of a faction of the CPSU, but also in posing a direct challenge to US strategic power which offered the possibility of squeezing concessions out of the United States.

The nature of Soviet politics, then, problematized the internal stability of the regime, since not only was it subject to external pressure from the United States, but the leadership also had to contend with attacks from China and the domestic problems of meeting the socioeconomic expectations of Soviet people. The problems and opportunities that confronted Khrushchev were similar in form to those that faced Lenin and Stalin. However, the qualitative difference that Khrushchev had to deal with, unlike his predecessors, was that if war occurred with capitalist states it would, in all likelihood, lead to nuclear war, and that the management of the conflict with the West was complicated by the successful expansion of international communist revolution.

The growing internal economic problems and the 'festering sore' of the conflict with China, alongside the apparent failure of the USSR to force concessions out of the United States, notably over Berlin,[21] made Cuba an even greater issue for the Khrushchev leadership than it might otherwise have been, and with domestic as well as strategic importance. Thus, the success of Sputnik I and increased revolutionary activity in the Third World were expected to succeed in pressuring the United States to agree to Soviet terms over Berlin and a wider acceptance of the strategic power of the USSR; this would, in effect, have allowed the USSR to focus more resources on internal economic development while maintaining a political challenge to American global supremacy. It was the evident failure of this, and the continued American contempt for Soviet threats evidenced by the continuation of U-2 surveillance flights over Soviet airspace, that threatened to destroy the doctrine of 'peaceful coexistence'.

However, we should not see Soviet relations with Cuba purely as being the consequence of failures in other aspects of Soviet policy, because this suggests a too simplistic quid pro quo. Instead, Soviet relations were both cautious and strident, reflecting the brittleness of Soviet power and its exposure to 'nuclear blackmail' and military containment.[22] Thus it was not the case that initial Soviet support for Cuba was hesitant because of Khrushchev's fear of jeopardizing the possibility of securing a concession from the Americans over the future status of Berlin.[23] Rather, Khrushchev overruled his colleagues and agreed to sanction a Cuban request to purchase military equipment from Poland in September 1959 *in spite of* the ongoing prospect of talks over Berlin.[24] Although this was done through third parties and the use of 'shell companies' to avoid provoking the United States, this was a Cuban as much as a Soviet initiative. The more radical elements within the Cuban leadership were as wary as the Soviets in trying to avoid providing a pretext for hostile American intervention against the revolution. Well aware of what the United States had engineered in

Guatemala in 1954, early Cuban contact with the Soviet Union was made through 'back channels' and instead of direct visits to communist countries, contacts were made with Soviet bloc diplomats in third countries.[25] Raúl Castro, Ernesto 'Che' Guevara and others in the Cuban leadership were not only concerned to avoid, at least early on in the revolution, a direct provocation of the United States; they also needed to ensure that their activities did not undermine Fidel Castro and the revolution as a whole by making a premature public declaration of friendship with the USSR.

Support for Cuba, then, continued alongside Soviet attempts to negotiate agreements with the United States. The relationship intensified as American hostility towards Cuba increased and as the prospect for securing agreements with the United States disappeared.[26] Support for Cuba, then, continued alongside Soviet attempts to negotiate agreements with the United States. The relationship intensified as US hostility towards Cuba increased and as the prospect for securing agreements with the US disappeared. However, the primary dynamic of the Soviet–Cuban relationship derived from developments within Cuba and, in particular, how far the increasingly socialist direction of the Revolution was likely to provoke a hostile/military response from the United States, and if this occurred, what the USSR could, in practical terms (especially because of the geographical problems of supporting Cuba, thousands of miles away), do about it.

The growing Soviet commitment to Cuba was thus highly problematic and dangerous, and was to lead to the decision to place nuclear missiles on the island (codenamed 'Operation Anadyr') in May 1962 and to the crisis that brought the superpowers to the brink of nuclear war. It was a product of the contradictions in the relationship between Cuba and the USSR which stemmed from the growing militancy of the Cuban revolution and its policy of promoting armed struggle as the means to promote revolution in Latin America. Such a policy looked increasingly likely to provide a pretext for an American invasion, particularly after the United States managed to gain the support of the Organization of American States (OAS) in isolating Cuba. Thus, it was not only the internal direction of the revolution, but, more importantly, its international bearing that seemed to be both provoking the United States and directly challenging the 'peaceful coexistence' policy of orthodox communist parties following the official line of Cuba's new great power ally, the USSR. As things stood before 1962, Cuba was pursuing its own path, but at the risk of dragging the USSR into a confrontation with the United States. To save the revolution 'from itself' the Soviets had to secure greater influence in Havana, so as to influence the revolution's *domestic and foreign policy* thus ensuring its survival, a victory for the Khrushchev leadership against its enemies inside and outside the CPSU, and a strengthening of the strategic position of the USSR vis-à-vis the United States.

The deployment of nuclear missiles in autumn 1962 came after a period of growing Soviet and PCC influence in Cuba, as relations with the United States increased in tension.[27] This was seen in the increase in KGB involvement in managing Cuban security and in the greater dependence of the Castroites on the leading cadres of the PCC. The objective of PCC/Soviet influence was to consolidate the revolution in Cuba by removing any non-communist elements from the leadership and redirecting the revolution's international goals[28] so that they conformed with Soviet policy, thus incorporating Cuba into a broader Latin American strategy associated with orthodox communist parties. In this sense, the PCC was an instrument of Soviet foreign policy in not only influencing the Castro leadership, but also, as its influence expanded (along with Soviet involvement, political, military and economic), as a possible vehicle through which to limit the leadership autonomy of Castro by institutionalizing the revolution according to a form of the Soviet model.[29]

However, as long as Castro maintained individual leadership and autonomy in decision-making it was very difficult to provide an internal institutional limit to his policy. Castro was aware of this, and was keen to preserve his autonomy even after the merger of the Movement of 26th July in October 1965 with the PCC and the creation of a Central Committee.[30] He was also wary of possible institutional limitations on his and the Cuban revolution's autonomy. Although there is no clear evidence that the Soviet leadership encouraged the dissident Aníbal Escalante in the early 1960s, they would have benefited had Escalante's attempts to increase PCC influence over Castro proved successful.[31] Escalante sought not only to increase PCC influence over Castro but also to strengthen Soviet policy–ideological positions. Thus there was a significant tension between the Cuban leadership and its sponsoring of armed revolution in Latin America and the PCC/Soviet line on Third World revolution. This was seen in the fact that although the Cubans asked for more Soviet military assistance in terms of personnel and matériel after April 1961, they continued to maintain guerrilla training camps independent of any Soviet involvement. Moreover, they were very hostile to what they perceived to be encroachments in October 1961, when Soviet military officers wanted to open a station for the recruitment of Cuban trainees in Cuba that appeared to be outside Cuban control.[32]

The Escalante affair exposed not only cracks within the Cuban revolution but also, more gravely for Moscow, fractures in Castro's relationship with the USSR, which highlighted Khrushchev's fears that the USSR could 'lose' Cuba to Chinese influence, since the words and deeds of both China and Cuba (the former in south-east Asia, the latter in Latin America) contradicted the doctrine of 'peaceful coexistence' and emphasized military power in revolutionary struggle, which would have had profoundly damaging consequences domestically and internationally for the USSR. Escalante's arrest in 1961 was soon followed by news reaching Moscow that the conflict between Castro and the 'micro-faction' of the PCC led by

Escalante was about not only strategy for the revolution in Cuba but also international policy, with Escalante supporting the criticisms of regional communist parties (following Moscow's line) of the inappropriateness of Castro's policy towards revolutionary struggle in the region.

The fall of Escalante was followed by the increasing importance of Che Guevara and what the Soviets and their PCC allies saw as pro-Chinese elements within the revolution.[33] The problem, as suggested above, was that the increasing militancy of the Cubans under Che Guevara's influence, whether or not this signalled a move towards Peking, would only serve to heighten the prospect of a US military intervention against Cuba, with the adverse consequences of this for Moscow. The options in such a scenario were to stand by Cuba and meet its revolutionary internationalist commitments, which would have risked a direct conflict with the United States,[34] or to stand aside and be guilty of allowing a revolutionary ally to be overthrown, with all the consequent ideological and political condemnation, along with the collapse of Soviet standing in the Third World.[35]

Soviet attempts to institutionalize the revolution from both within Cuba and without did not, at least initially, prove successful.[36] Moreover, they exposed the limitations of Soviet policy. And because not only was Castro aware of Soviet objectives but also he had his own ideas about international revolution, fissures emerged.[37] Castro and Cuba obviously needed Soviet military and economic support, but to avoid a dependence that would bring an end to Cuban autonomy (particularly pertinent for Castro during and after the missile crisis), Castro identified the necessity of cultivating autonomous non-communist party revolutionary movements that would look to Havana and not Moscow for guidance and support. The emergence of a difference in both strategy and organizational form simmered in Soviet–Cuban relations, highlighted first by Castro's speech of February 1962, known as 'The Second Declaration of Havana', on the need to encourage revolution in Latin America and beyond which directly challenged Soviet policy. These differences surfaced in the compromise statement on armed struggle in the Latin American revolution at the December 1964 Havana Conference of communist parties and were explicit in the January 1966 Tri-continental Conference of communist parties in Havana and the meeting of the Latin American Solidarity Organization (LASO) in August 1967. This meeting was dominated by non-communist revolutionary organizations with a separate Cuban-led organization (LASO) which was very critical of the Soviet position on armed struggle, and also Soviet links with national–bourgeois regimes in the region.[38]

The failure to engineer a 'Sovietization' of the Cuban revolution, through the channels of increasing PCC influence over Castro along with increased Soviet involvement in security matters and military support, meant that that not only did Cuba appear to be heading towards a military confrontation with the United States, but also, from the advice of the PCC and the observations of the KGB in Cuba, the Cubans appeared to be pursuing an autonomous policy that was the practical manifestation of Chinese rather than Soviet doctrine regarding Third World revolution. However, the greatest concern was that if things continued to develop as they had done since 1960, then it looked likely that the United States would attempt to destroy the revolution by force.

Castro and the Cuban leadership were increasingly concerned with the American threat, with the watershed of the April 1961 invasion signalling that Washington was willing to use military force to extinguish the revolution.[39] This was not a case of opportunism; rather Castro knew that the regime's external and internal security would be improved by a Soviet military guarantee. Moreover, with the evidence from Playa Girón (the 'Bay of Pigs' episode in 1961) and the sabotage of the *La Coubre*, and with the internal dynamic of socioeconomic transformation, reflected in the wave of expropriations of Cuban and foreign (largely American) capital and the regime's anchorage in the Cuban working class and the increasing influence of the PCC, it was clear that Castro would have no problem with convincing the Cuban people of the reality of the 'Yankee threat'. For the Soviets, however, a military guarantee was highly problematic, because there was little practical possibility of this being realized in a place in a different hemisphere less than 100 miles from the United States and in time to prevent expected further US military interventions.

Yet a form of Soviet military guarantee was agreed by the Kremlin to ensure that the Soviets would be able not only to defend Cuba from US attack, thus securing the revolution, but also, by effectively incorporating the Cuban revolution into the Soviet bloc and its *discipline*, to provide the *political* means with which to guarantee Cuba's pursuit of an international path in line with the Soviet Union and its allies in the region. Through this, Khrushchev and the Soviet leadership not only would have 'saved' the Cuban revolution, thus restating the USSR's claim to global power and respect, but also would have achieved a political–ideological victory over opponents within the CPSU and the wider international communist movement, thus strengthening the doctrine of 'peaceful coexistence'. Finally, the expectation of a *fait accompli*, in that the Soviets hoped to have fully installed the missiles and support forces before the United States would know about or be able to prevent it, would have insured not only a significant strengthening of the USSR's strategic position vis-à-vis the United States, but also the expectation that it would also have forced the United States to move towards accepting Soviet interests in a number of disputes between the two superpowers.[40]

The decision to install missiles in Cuba, however, was to have major political significance, in that through the de facto incorporation of Cuba into the Soviet bloc, not only would it be secured from external attack, but also it would create a political relationship in which it was expected the Soviet Union would be predominant.[41] There was also the real possibility that this would serve directly to affect the United States–USSR strategic equation to the benefit of the latter, making it more likely that the United States would temper its international hostility not only towards the USSR but also towards many Third World states, and move towards an acceptance of Soviet power. At a stroke, then, the successful deployment of missiles was expected to achieve the consolidation of the Soviet bloc through the incorporation of a successful revolution, and also a more direct consequence, the levelling of Soviet strategic power with that of the United States. As Jacques Lévesque remarked:

> Thus, it was rather to terminate the permanent state of uncertainty and insecurity surrounding Cuba and eventually to consolidate its membership in the socialist camp that a stable means of defence seemed to be imperative ... Khrushchev attempted to achieve a *fait accompli* over nuclear missiles in Cuba ... once there and ready there was little the US could do.[42]

Nuclear missiles, then, became the *means* by which the Soviet Union could formally expand the socialist camp. Although the Soviet Union at this moment, and subsequently, provided massive economic aid to Cuba, culminating in the incorporation of Cuba into the socialist economic bloc, the Council of Mutual Economic Assistance (CMEA) in July 1972, because of the nature of the situation, this military means was the only one by which to secure Cuba from external attack, and also to lock it into the *discipline* of the Soviet bloc. It was the partial failure of this policy, due to the forthright US response and the brinkmanship of the United States, that for the Soviet Union meant the worst of both worlds. Although Khrushchev had secured a form of commitment on the part of the United Stated not to invade Cuba, because he had failed fully to secure Cuba politically within the Soviet bloc in the style of the states of Eastern Europe, Soviet political problems with Cuba persisted. The removal of the missiles, then, also saw the removal from Cuba of a significant Soviet political presence, and thus allowed an increasing space for Castro's autonomy.

Towards the end of the crisis the USSR in November 1962 took decisions about the future and security of Cuba without any real Cuban involvement.[43] This, understandably, infuriated Castro, yet it followed the tensions between the Kremlin and its forces in Cuba and the Cuban leadership during the crisis, when actions by Cuban forces to defend the island, as in the shooting down of an American surveillance aircraft in October 1962, gravely concerned the Soviets, since they feared that Cuba would provoke the United States into military action and that grave consequences for the USSR would inevitably follow. Thus, while the Soviet commitment was seen as an act of solidarity with the Cuban people and their struggle within Cuba and beyond, it was in fact more than this: with Soviet involvement came Soviet discipline and inevitable limits on what Cuba could do.

Khrushchev's decision to use the installation of nuclear missiles to meet his objective was, then, a partial failure. Although the revolution was saved, Cuba was still not subject to the discipline and doctrine of the Soviet bloc. Castro felt humiliated, angry and vulnerable, in that Cuba was left without any formal public Soviet military guarantee akin to the Warsaw Pact,[44] a situation which spurred Cuba, at least for the rest of the 1960s, to follow its own domestic and international path. Despite the massive amounts of Soviet economic and military aid to Cuba after the missile crisis,[45] Cuba continued to maintain political and ideological autonomy whereby its policies in the region for the rest of the 1960s clashed with and sometimes undermined Soviet positions. Soviet policy in the limited success of October–November 1962 had put it in a position where it was financing and arming a revolution that in many respects sought to undermine its (the USSR's) perceived interests, particularly in Latin America.

Soviet policy towards the Latin American revolution most acutely exposed the contradictions of its policy towards Cuba. This was conditioned by Soviet concerns to avoid a confrontation like that in late 1962, or, if one were to occur again, at least it would be when the USSR was militarily prepared for it. This being the case, the USSR sought to reduce international tension and concentrate on cultivating formal links with which to secure for itself economic and political benefits and weaken the 'imperialist chain'. Such a policy was even less consistent than that of its support for Cuba. As had been the case with its other formal ventures with *capitalist* states, because of the nature of its sociopolitical system, the Soviet Union was very limited in developing *political* relations with the non-communist states of Latin America. Such a policy also necessitated moderation or even the sidelining of local communist parties. Indeed, Soviet overtures rested on a trade deficit where it ended up importing more from Latin American states than it exported to them.[46] Moreover, developments like the 1969 Andean Pact and the more substantial period of anti-imperialist politics in Chile between 1970 and 1973 did not lead to any significant and long-term increase in Soviet power in the region. With the military overthrow of the Allende government in September 1973, it was not until the Nicaraguan revolution of 1979 that the revolutionary left secured a substantial change in the balance of forces in favour of the USSR.

Soviet relations with Cuba, then, reflected the tensions of a form of politics that was premised on a specific kind of social and material development combined with its external objectives as the leading force within the international communist movement, which fostered a specific type of international relations. Such relations were characterized by the necessity to ensure internal defence (of the revolution and its political-form outcome), and an external policy that facilitated internal economic growth, which secured the ascendancy of the Party-state leadership. Cuba provided a case where the expectation of a kind of military and economic dependence on its part on the USSR would allow the Soviet Union to maximize the political gains from the undermining of American imperialism in Latin America, and increase the international power of the USSR, thus assisting its internal development. The outcome instead reflected a relationship of tensions, whereby Soviet policy of using the revolution as a base for Soviet penetration of the region for its own internal and external goals was contested by the separate goals of Cuba. As long as the revolutionary conjuncture in the region provided an opportunity for guerrilla struggle Cuba would continue to maximize its international autonomy. When this had dissipated (by the late 1960s, but it was rekindled again in the late 1970s), Cuban and Soviet interests became more compatible.

The Soviet form of international relations, then, rested on a limited capacity either to direct Cuba or to influence the wider Latin American scene. Because of its limited political form, confined to the economic and military instruments of the Party-state, the Soviet Union could not detach itself from Cuba and have a fully autonomous relationship with Latin America. Because revolutions were the only means by which the Soviet social and political form could expand (beyond a direct Soviet military–political presence), the Soviet Union was limited to not allowing Cuba to detach itself from the Soviet bloc, and, barring direct political control, this could only be achieved through economic and military inducements, and encouragement for a Soviet-style institutionalization of the revolution. The failure of the Soviet Union to 'expand' (i.e. for capitalist social relations to be overthrown and a revolutionary dictatorship led by a communist party to be installed) in its relations with other Latin American states reflected the limitations of the Soviet form of international relations in offering a 'politics of expansion'.

Vietnam

Soviet relations with Vietnam brought to the surface many of the issues and problems identified with its relations with Cuba that highlighted the nature of its particular form of international relations, and the problems it had in relating to other revolutionary states. However, in two crucial ways the situation was fundamentally different. First, from the early 1960s onwards the United States began a direct military intervention in south-east Asia that escalated from 1965 to the commitment of combat troops that peaked in 1968 at over half a million. Whereas Soviet policy had largely focused on *preventing* US military action against Cuba after 1959, in Indo-China Soviet policy centred on *containing* the escalation of US military power, yet without provoking a direct military conflict with the United States. The second major difference was the impact of Chinese involvement in Vietnam and the region after its successful 1949 communist revolution.[47] Whereas the Chinese had been an indirect ideological presence in Cuba, although enough to worry the Soviet leadership, they were directly involved in the affairs of Indo-China after 1949, at one point, between 1965 and 1973, having over 300,000 troops in North Vietnam.[48] This physical presence was paralleled by similar ideological convictions over the notion of a 'people's war' and the strong political links forged between the two communist parties from the 1930s onwards and, in particular, after 1949 when Chinese military support was crucial to Viet Minh military successes against the French.

The closeness of Sino-Vietnamese relations contrasted with the more distant Soviet relations with the Vietnamese up until the 1954 Geneva conference. As in the Cuban case Soviet involvement in the origins of the Vietnamese revolution was minimal if at all. The Soviet Union under Stalin premised its international relations on autarchic development and the prevention of military conquest from the West. Despite the ideological links of Comintern, the Vietnamese, because of their geographical and political distance and the strategic preoccupations of the USSR, were able to manage a relatively autonomous strategy in Indo-China until the Second World War.[49] Thus, the seizure of power by the Viet Minh in August 1945 and the subsequent war with the French did not see any significant Soviet involvement.

What then were the principal concerns of the Soviet Union towards Vietnam? The most important was to limit and prevent the escalation of US military involvement in south-east Asia generally, and in Indo-China particularly, and through this consolidate the revolution within the discipline and organization of the Soviet bloc. This was partially achieved in 1954 with the Geneva Agreement, when the Vietnamese leadership acceded to joint Soviet and Chinese pressure to agree to a temporary partition of Vietnam, which was to be resolved by an internationally supervised set of elections within two years to unify the country. However, although the Soviets had been a party to the agreement and were important in pressing the Vietnamese to make concessions, because China had a more direct and historical influence in the region, the USSR was in some senses a secondary influence. With the emergence of the Sino-Soviet split that became public by 1960 with the withdrawal of nearly all Soviet advisers from China and the publication of the 'Long Live Leninism' article in *Renmin Ribao* in April 1960 that contained a veiled attack on Khrushchev's supposed 'revisionism',[50] the preponderance of Chinese influence in south-east Asia was now seen as a threat to Soviet interests. This, combined with an escalation of conflict within Vietnam, marked by an increase in US military involvement, meant that the need to ensure greater Soviet influence in Vietnam suddenly became urgent.

Vietnam became a central issue in Soviet international relations, then, with the increase in US military involvement in the early 1960s, something that the Geneva Agreement had explicitly sought to avoid,[51] and the fact that this was a consequence of political developments within Vietnam, North and South. In the latter it was a product of the intensification of the anti-communist terror of the Diem regime, and in the former the shift in policy from an acceptance of the Geneva Agreement that had been violated by both the United States and the Diem regime in South Vietnam to one of unification through armed struggle.[52] While the shifting terrain of international relations forced a reappraisal of Soviet policy towards Vietnam, domestic developments within the USSR, which came in 1964 with the removal of Khrushchev and his replacement by the Brezhnev–Kosygin leadership, also marked change. The fear of a loss of influence in the region to greater Chinese involvement, which appeared to be the case as the North Vietnamese adopted a more aggressive posture towards the South, combined with increased US military intervention and the possible consequences of this, especially after the humiliation over Cuba, led the new Soviet leadership to decide to improve relations with the Vietnamese. This was regarded as a means of eclipsing China's influence, and its tendency of 'reckless adventurism',[53] and also to ensure that the Vietnamese leadership would be subject to Soviet 'discipline' in its conduct of the war.[54]

Soviet relations with Vietnam were conditioned, as they were with respect to Cuba, by wider international developments, most notably the level of US military escalation and the continuing influence of the Chinese over the Vietnamese leadership. What the Vietnamese revolution reflected was an internal dynamic, powered by the attempts at 'socialist construction' in the North and the level of sociopolitical conflict in the South, that was heavily influenced by international relations. Just as the August revolution emerged out of a local political vacuum brought about by the Japanese surrender in August 1945 (and the prior defeat of French colonial power by the Japanese in 1941) that permitted the Vietnamese Workers' Party to seize power, so the development of the revolution was determined by international events, from the return of French military forces in 1946, to Chinese support after 1949, and the involvement of the United States after Korea in 1954. Finally, the situation of the Vietnamese communists after 1954 was largely down to the combined international pressure of their respective allies in Moscow and Peking. And though many in the leadership were angry with the concessions forced upon them by their allies at Geneva, it was far from clear how, without continued support, particularly from China, they would have been able to withstand the US military escalation and intervention which was threatened if they had not agreed to Geneva.

Thus, the autonomy of the Vietnamese was limited, particularly in a material sense after 1954 with the need to build socialism from a very underdeveloped socioeconomic base.[55] The Vietnamese were, then, reliant on their communist allies for economic aid and later, as war intensified with the United States, for sophisticated military equipment. However, because of the obligation of Moscow to support a fellow communist state, and also because of the continuing polemics within the international communist movement, especially after the 1962 Cuban missile crisis, and the significant Chinese influence in Hanoi,[56] Vietnam, despite its dependence on external support, was not and did not become a pawn of either communist ally.[57] What the revolution and the Vietnam War did do was provide another major crisis point in the Cold War, when communist expansion provoked US military intervention, thus locating the internal politics of the Vietnamese revolution right in the heart of the international political and strategic conflict between the superpowers.

Two things stand out from the Soviet relationship with the Vietnamese revolution. First, the fact that as the war went on from the early 1960s and intensified in the late 1960s, with North Vietnamese forces taking an increasingly dominant role in the struggle over southern-based guerrillas, Soviet military and economic aid also became more important, eventually eclipsing Chinese support. Secondly, not only was Soviet aid related to developments in the Soviet–Chinese–Vietnamese 'triangle', it was also sensitive to the nature and level of US military intervention. Thus, although the Soviets did pursue a policy of pressing their Vietnamese allies to negotiate with the United States as a means of reducing not only military tension between Hanoi and Washington but also political tension between the United States and the USSR,[58] they did not abandon their communist allies to diplomacy. Rather they maintained a military commitment until the final stages of the war, despite the fact that the Vietnamese remained very defensive about their independence, and did not always inform the Soviets of their military decisions.[59]

Thus, by the end of the 1950s Beijing provided about 60 per cent and Moscow 30 per cent of socialist aid to North Vietnam.[60] Indeed not until after 1965, that is, after the introduction of US combat troops and the beginning of 'Operation Rolling Thunder', did Soviet support significantly increase.[61] For example Gaiduk,[62] citing US intelligence sources, states that in May 1965 (after the commencement of 'Operation Rolling Thunder') the Soviets delivered 100 armoured personnel carriers (essential for mobile offensive warfare) and 15 MiG 15/17 fighter aircraft. Gaiduk also claims, this time drawing on Soviet sources, that overall Soviet aid to the DRV/ Vietnamese revolution grew steadily between 1965 and 1968 (the period of most intense US military involvement in Indo-China):

Moscow sent to North Vietnam industrial and telecommunications equipment ... trucks, medical supplies, machine tools, iron ore, and non-ferrous metals (for war production) ... By 1967 overall socialist aid to the DRV accounted for approximately 1.5 billion Roubles ... Moscow's share was 36.8% ... as the years passed Soviet assistance grew to over 50%, and in 1968 accounted for 524 million Roubles.[63]

Not surprisingly, considering Chinese policy on the previous occasion that the United States threatened military escalation over Vietnam, China began after 1965 to encourage Hanoi to reduce military tension. By 1968, with Mao Zedong preoccupied with the Cultural Revolution in China, although the threat of American imperialism in Asia continued to be manipulated for the purposes of domestic political struggles, the Chinese were in fact reducing their support for the Vietnamese and modifying their aim to unify Vietnam through force of arms,[64] which ultimately rested on defeating the United States. Such a prospect not only concerned Mao because of the continued threat of US military power to China, but also the potential future ideological–political threat to the whole of south-east Asia of a victorious Vietnam allied to the USSR.[65]

Just as the USSR had been concerned with the prospect of a Sino-Vietnamese alliance, so the Chinese, by the latter half of the 1960s, were worried about the increasing closeness between Moscow and Hanoi, and the increasing Soviet military involvement in Vietnam. Indeed, because of these concerns Chinese policy towards Vietnam went through a volte-face. The Chinese had been willing to support the Vietnamese in the earlier part of the decade in their attempts to unite their country through force of arms, but this was before the massive escalation in US military involvement after 1965, and before the increase in Soviet support for Hanoi. With the dramatically altered circumstances of the late 1960s, the Chinese were now concerned to see the war come to an end, to remove the US military presence and to reduce Hanoi's dependence on the USSR. The ideological and strategic circumstances of the late 1960s were a reversal of the situation earlier. The early part of the decade was a time for China's radical critique of Khrushchev's policy of 'peaceful coexistence' and its emphasis on the necessity of armed struggle, yet by the end of the decade the consequences of this policy had helped unleash US military power in the region and led to a corresponding increase in Soviet regional influence. By 1968–69 the situation was almost critical, with China in the middle of the chaos of Mao's Cultural Revolution, armed clashes with Soviet troops on the northern border and intensified US bombing over Vietnam coming perilously close to Chinese territory.

The levels of Soviet (military) aid corresponded to the nature and intensity of the war, with the provision of mainly defensive equipment to the

DRV to allow it to resist US air power and included the dispatch of nearly 3,000 Soviet military personnel to train the Vietnamese. With this the Vietnamese airforce effectively doubled in size. With the gradual withdrawal of American land forces after 1968, the Soviets began to provide the DRV with heavy armour which was of crucial significance in the final stages of the war.[66] The conclusion of the Vietnamese revolution and victory for the communists did not come through an uprising led by the NLF (National Front for the Liberation of Vietnam) in the South. Rather, the *coup de grâce* in April 1975 came through the armed forces of the DRV, supplied and supported by the USSR. Thus Soviet military technology helped limit the military damage caused by US firepower and ultimately provided much of the logistical and organizational support that facilitated the rout of the RV's army after the US military withdrawal.

As with Cuba in Latin America, Soviet policy towards Vietnam and south-east Asia was concerned not only with Vietnam but also with how to consolidate the Vietnamese revolution, incorporate it into the Soviet bloc, and use it as a base from which to cultivate wider anti-imperialist relationships in the region, thus not only reducing American and British power in the area, but also interfering (indirectly) in the principal American regional goal, the postwar development of Japan as a regional power. In this respect Vietnam was to be a potential asset in the region, especially as a counter to Chinese revolutionary designs in the area and the ways in which these differed from Soviet concerns. However, Soviet policy towards Vietnam was characterized by a contradiction. On the one hand was the desire to expand Soviet influence in the region, thus diminishing imperialist power, and to secure concessions from the West by facilitating Vietnamese links with other non-communist and non-aligned states in the region (for example Cambodia, Laos and Indonesia, and possibly even subverting the pro-Western dictatorship in Thailand and elsewhere). On the other hand, however, its involvement in the conflict had led to the massive commitment of US military power with the effect of seriously undermining the possibilities of extending links with anti-imperialist groups.

Soviet policy, then, was concerned to influence decisions in Hanoi as a way not only of influencing the 'construction of socialism' in the DRV, but also of directing regional policy by limiting Chinese room for political manoeuvre and autonomy and by fostering a 'revolutionary' policy that would consolidate 'socialist' gains and prevent a major US military involvement in the region. However, the contradictions in these objectives emerged from the way in which the USSR sought to realize these goals and the instruments it used. For the most part, the situation in Indo-China was beyond its control because the North Vietnamese were committed to unification through force, and, for most of the period of the war, until the early 1970s anyway, they could continue to rely on at least some support from Beijing, thus avoiding a complete dependence on Moscow.

The USSR sought to increase its influence over the DRV through increased aid, principally military equipment.[67] Through this the USSR expected the Vietnamese to open up not only to greater external-fraternal advice and influence over the conduct of the war with an increased Soviet political–military presence within Vietnam, but also to an increase in inter-Party links and the encouragement of pro-Soviet elements within the Vietnamese Workers' Party by the purging of pro-Chinese elements. However, like Cuba's, the Vietnamese communists were committed to national unification, and despite an increase in Soviet military influence this did not correspond with an expansion of Soviet political influence. What it did do, however, was alter the international-strategic dimension of the war. Alongside Chinese support, the USSR foreclosed channels of escalation by the United States that in all likelihood would have led to a US military victory.[68] Thus the USSR was directly associated with the strategy of Hanoi, though it could not control it, and because of this the USSR contributed to *containing* the strategic consequences of the war while at the same time *amplifying* the international and strategic aspects of the revolution and war by being a presence in the DRV and providing it with political and military support.

The only means by which the USSR could have effectively increased its influence over Hanoi would have been to increase its military presence in the DRV and thus its influence over the war as a whole. Therefore, attempts by the Soviet Union to secure greater leverage over Hanoi required greater political influence, which could only come through a bigger political–military presence within the Vietnamese Party-state. Through this, the Soviets would then have been able to influence strategy towards the war, yet such a presence, in all probability, would have only served to increase further American hostility to the regime in Hanoi and to undermine wider Soviet interests that rested on the reduction in this hostility.

This not only would have been a major problem with respect to what the American response would have been to such developments, but also would have provoked major friction within the socialist camp, particularly in relations with the Chinese. As Ralph Smith has argued, the role of military power in the socialist revolution and the struggle against imperialism was a major theme in the ideological disputes that surfaced in Sino-Soviet relations after 1956 that had a direct bearing on Soviet relations with the DRV. The role of military power, particularly nuclear weapons, was a source of Soviet political advantage and dominance in its relations with China. For China, nuclear weapons were a potential means of ensuring political autonomy to underline its ideological, social and economic autonomy, emphasized by the Great Leap Forward, with respect to both the USSR and the United States.

One of the central issues was that of military cooperation between socialist countries 'in an age of increasingly complex technology and continuing confrontation with the West'.[69] This issue provided both a major source of conflict between the triad of the USSR, China and the DRV, but also, for the Soviets, the principal political means with which to determine events in Vietnam. However, a tension existed between the Soviet Union increasing its military involvement in the war, and from this, extending its political control, and the way in which this might provoke the United States into a more offensive strategy.[70] Again, as Smith suggests:

> From an ideological point of view, however, there was a certain danger in extending the sphere of military collaboration beyond the group of countries that could be held together ideologically ... Russians may have been afraid of a situation where Yugoslavia and China might collaborate with one another independently of the *discipline* of the Warsaw Treaty Organization, and that may explain Soviet willingness to enter into a technical argument with Peking in October 1957 ... one of [the Warsaw Treaty's] provisions was to provide the Chinese with nuclear weapons technology.[71]

Soviet political–military guarantees, as with Cuba, only came with direct Soviet military control of the means of that guarantee and thus a severe limitation on the political autonomy of the country concerned, China or Vietnam. Indeed, an increase in Soviet involvement in the Vietnam War would have come at the cost of direct Soviet interference in Chinese internal affairs, something that the majority of the CCP leadership would not tolerate. Soviet military proposals of April 1965 suggested as much.[72] After Kosygin's visit to Hanoi in February 1965 and the subsequent US military escalation, the Soviets proposed to China a policy for 'united action' against the United States. This proposal included allowing Soviet forces and weapons to have transit rights through China, the use of airfields and the stationing of Soviet personnel there, a free air corridor over China to facilitate the supply of the DRV, and finally talks between the leaders of the three communist powers to decide on future strategy. Not surprisingly the proposal for 'united action' was quickly rejected by Beijing.[73]

Equally, North Vietnam was concerned to maintain its autonomy vis-à-vis China and the USSR, knowing full well that Chinese offers of more extended military assistance would have come at a political cost.[74] The Soviets, then, sought to use military power not only to assist the DRV/NLF against US military attack, but also to secure political concessions with which to help determine policy in Vietnam. However, even this aspect of Soviet relations was not free from tensions. To have involved itself more directly in the revolutionary war would have potentially exposed the

Soviets to direct military conflict with the United States, something which, post-Cuban missile crisis, they were very concerned to avoid. Thus, the policy that was settled on was to ensure that the DRV could withstand American military power and remain autonomous, separate from Chinese political influence.

In pursuing such a path the Soviet Union maintained some influence on the DRV, and ensured, in the long term, the support of an ally in the region with which to counter China, and act as a means to facilitate international relations alternative to the American-dominated SEATO (South-East Asia Treaty Organization).[75] This was not all. In terms of the conflict with the United States, and the realization of the successful 'war of liberation' with the collapse of the RV in 1975, Soviet aid, because it was limited to a particular form, helped maintain and consolidate the DRV state as a more autonomous political form, which the RV manifestly was not, and because of this, when the form of American support changed, it collapsed.

Soviet international relations with the Vietnamese revolution, then, helped realize a successful war of national liberation and contributed to the biggest military–political defeat for the US during the Cold War. This was at a relatively small cost.[76] Soviet military involvement ensured that the DRV could maintain the strategic and political offensive despite being heavily bombed, and also limited, ultimately (alongside the Chinese conventional military threat), the possibility of a US political victory through military power. Soviet militarization at the strategic and conventional level served to undermine US military omnipotence post-Cuban missile crisis. The ability of the USSR to manage to maintain a strategic influence in Vietnam, which in the long run helped to ensure a US military defeat, appeared to reflect that the United States, for a number of reasons, had finally recognized the strategic–military weight of the USSR, and acted accordingly. Victory in Vietnam served to undermine US and Chinese power in south-east Asia. It also seemed to reinforce the Soviet form of an international relations of expansion whereby the Soviet Union would consolidate and expand internationally through the successful transformation of social relations by means of social revolution, premised on Soviet strategic and political protection. The international vanguard of the USSR had appeared to be realized in the successful conclusion of the Vietnamese revolution.

However, because of the nature and form of the 'extra-territorial expansion' of the Soviet Union, which resulted in Vietnam, like Cuba, joining the CMEA and then signing a defence agreement with the USSR,[77] although the Soviet Union led this bloc and subjected it to its political discipline, the internal strains on the USSR proved to be very costly. The Soviet Union was concerned to prevent Vietnam from having too great autonomy, because that would prevent the USSR from securing the maximum amount of political–strategic advantage vis-à-vis the United States. However, the political–economic costs of maintaining such a disciplined system that rested on directly political links meant that the USSR had over-extended itself as a form of political rule. This served to exacerbate the existing economic tensions within the Soviet Union and Soviet bloc, mainly over the course of economic reform (and how this related to links with the West), which was problematized by the political edifice that the USSR had constructed in the Cold War. Political equated to economic links, and thus economic reform when it came (under Mikhail Gorbachev) saw the eventual severing of the political and thus economic link. The Soviet Union's difficulties in resolving its internal economic problems were recognized as being compounded by its international relations. The successes of the past highlighted the limitations and the burdens of the present.

Conclusions

This chapter has sought to provide an historically focused sketch of the international relations of the USSR in its relations with the Cuban and Vietnamese revolutions. In doing so, the principal objective has been to show how the Soviet Union sought to influence and determine political outcomes in these revolutions. The source of this influence in the international relations of the USSR lay in the social constitution of its form of politics. The preceding analysis has shown how the internal social constitution of the USSR conditioned its international relations.

The abolition of the sphere of privatized production (and politics) in the USSR limited international relations to the organs of the Party-state, and the 'politics of expansion' to specific forms of political agency: either the Red Army or social revolution. Because of this form of international expansion the Soviet Union was *dependent* on social revolution for a *means* of political expansion, but also threatened by it. The threat derived from the potential impact international social revolution had on the internal social relations and form of political rule in the USSR, and also from how social revolution and the relations with Cuba and Vietnam threatened to undermine the strategic policy vis-à-vis the United States. The Soviet Union attempted to consolidate social revolution in Cuba and Vietnam within the Soviet bloc to ensure an augmenting of political power within the USSR and the wider international communist movement, but also as a means with which to undermine American imperialism. The undermining of American imperialism through social revolution offered the USSR access to regions otherwise off-limits, and in so doing challenged the global logic of American capital. Thus it was hoped that these developments would lead to both material and political benefits from a more globally orientated Soviet international relations, and from possibilities of forcing through armaments reductions with the United States.

However, instead of securing political extensions of the Soviet bloc that would undermine American and Western power, the increased international role of the USSR actually increased the tensions and thus fissures within the USSR. Internal material development, while becoming increasingly reliant on international relations, became more problematic, as the Soviet Union had to contend not only with the fissures within the socialist camp, but also with the material and political costs of links with other revolutionary states. The coalescence of the 'political' and 'economic' in its international relations facilitated close relationships with social revolutions, but because of the lack of an autonomous agency and currency of relations, made the political commitment to these 'states' much more costly from the wider perspective of the Cold War. The inability to cultivate alternative forms of relations obviously determined the substance of these relations, but more importantly limited the USSR to an international relations that was limited to the political–military sphere. Thus, the Soviet Union was hesitant because it did not want to provoke a stronger US military response, something that the USSR could not reciprocate. This not only determined the need to make revolutions politically and militarily strong in themselves, but also determined the wider relations of the USSR to the point that *all* of the major crises of the Cold War, from the 1946 Soviet occupation of northern Iran and the 1948 Berlin Blockade to the 1962 Cuban missile crisis and the war in Vietnam, involved international conflict derived from the Soviet form of international relations.

NOTES

1 As will become clearer in this chapter, the Soviet Union did not limit itself to cultivating international relations only with like-minded states and movements. From its inception it sought to expand diplomatic and economic links with capitalist states for its internal development and external security. This diversification was seen as a means to limit the possibility of attack and also to increase its chances of survival should war occur. As Trotsky claimed in 1925:

> The more multiform our international relations, the more difficult it will be ... for our possible enemies to break them. And ... even if [war or blockade] ... were to come about, we should still be much stronger than we would have been under a 'self-sufficient' and consequently belated development.

Quoted in E. Krippendorff, 'Revolutionary Foreign Policy in a Capitalist Environment', in E. Jahn (ed.), *Soviet Foreign Policy: Its Social and Economic Conditions* (London: Allison & Busby, 1978), p. 32.

2 This became centred for both the CPSU and other communist parties, notably the Chinese, on the policy of 'peaceful coexistence' outlined by Khrushchev in his 'secret speech' to the 20th Party Congress in 1956. In this Khrushchev introduced the argument that economic competition with the West would be decisive, that war

between socialist and imperialist states was not inevitable (and should be avoided), and finally the possibility of alternate, non-violent roads to socialism based on the growing strength of national liberation movements throughout the world. See G. Roberts, *The Soviet Union in World Politics: Coexistence, Revolution and Cold War, 1945–1991* (London: Routledge, 1999), pp. 42–60.

3 See O. A. Westad (ed.), *Brothers in Arms: The Rise and Fall of the Sino-Soviet Alliance, 1945–63* (Stanford: Stanford University Press, 1998), and 'Mao on Sino-Soviet Relations: Conversations with the Soviet Ambassador', *Cold War International History Project Bulletin*, 6–7 (winter 1995–96), pp. 157, 164–8; for analyses of such relations between the USSR and China and the breakdown of the Sino-Soviet alliance.

4 See M. Kramer, 'The Early Post-Stalin Succession Struggle and Upheavals in East-Central Europe: Internal–External Linkages in Soviet Policy Making', *Journal of Cold War Studies*, 1, 3 (fall 1999), pp. 60–1.

5 Westad, *Brothers in Arms*, p. 20. This situation was reversed in 1964, well into the Sino-Soviet split, when a number of leading Soviet figures encouraged senior Chinese communists on a visit to the USSR to remove Mao Zedong as Chinese leader. See Q. Zhai, 'Beijing and the Vietnam Conflict, 1964–65: New Evidence', *Cold War International History Project Bulletin*, 6–7 (winter 1995–96), pp. 233–50.

6 Westad, *Brothers in Arms*, pp. 20–2. See also O. A. Westad and C. Jian (eds), '77 Conversations Between Chinese and Foreign Leaders on the Wars in Indochina', *Cold War International History Project Working Papers*, 22 (May 1998).

7 This problem had reached a peak by the late 1950s with East Germany, having lost 1.2 million people through exodus to West Germany via Berlin, being close to approaching economic collapse. To prevent this the Soviet and East German authorities had to deal with East Germany's economic problems, but also the outlet providing access to West Berlin. An economic solution was not possible as Kosygin, then head of the Soviet state economic planning authority, Gosplan, informed Khrushchev that the USSR could barely meet the demands of its own people at that time and therefore would not be able to meet Ulbricht's pleas for more meat and food for the people of East Germany. The other option used of threatening Western access to West Berlin by a unilateral treaty with East Germany threatened either war or, more probably, economic sanctions against the whole Soviet bloc, which would not only have further weakened East Germany, but would have exposed the whole of Soviet-controlled Eastern Europe to the fate of East Germany, thus extending the crisis to the whole of the bloc. The construction of the Berlin Wall in August 1961 'resolved' the crisis, at least in the sense that it stemmed the population loss and contained the problem without risking war or an economic blockade by the West. See V. Zubok, 'Document Two: Khrushchev's Secret Speech on the Berlin Crisis, August 1961', *Cold War International History Project Bulletin*, 1 (spring 1992), pp. 58–61; V. Zubok and C. Pleshakov, *Inside the Kremlin's Cold War: From Stalin to Khrushchev* (Cambridge, MA: Harvard University Press, 1996), pp. 248–58.

8 This threatened to provoke US military intervention and the possibility of direct military conflict with the United States, because the 1950 Sino-Soviet Treaty would have obliged the USSR to intervene in support of China.

9 Mao's reckless attitude towards nuclear weapons was followed by Castro in a letter he sent to Khrushchev during the Cuban missile crisis, where he appeared to advocate nuclear war with a pre-emptive strike on the United States. See J. Hershberg, 'New Evidence on the Cuban Missile Crisis: More Documents from the Russian Archives', *Cold War International History Project Bulletin*, 8–9 (winter 1996–97), pp. 270–338.

10 See Zubok, *Inside the Kremlin's Cold War*, pp. 221–32; V. Zubok, 'Khrushchev's Nuclear Promise to Beijing During the 1958 Crisis', *Cold War International History Project Bulletin*, 6–7 (winter 1995–96), pp. 219, 226–7.

11 See N. Miller, *Soviet Relations with Latin America* (Cambridge: Cambridge University Press, 1989).

12 For analyses of the Cuban revolution see Wood, 'Long Revolution'; Blackburn, 'Prologue to the Cuban Revolution'; Farber, *Revolution and Reaction*; Pérez-Stable, *Cuban Revolution*.

13 See Lévesque, *USSR*, p. 30; Y. Pavlov, *Soviet–Cuban Alliance: 1959–1991* (Miami, FL: North-South Centre Press/University of Miami Press, 1994), pp. 11–23.

14 P. Brenner and J. Blight, 'Cuba 1962. The Crisis and Cuban-Soviet Relations: Fidel Castro's 1968 Speech', *Cold War International History Project Bulletin*, 5 (spring 1995), pp. 81–5.

15 See Miller, *Soviet Relations*, pp. 58–9 and Zubok, *Inside the Kremlin's Cold War*, pp. 184–5.

16 This also came after Khrushchev had been informed by the KGB in June 1960 of intelligence that suggested that elements within the US Defense Department (Pentagon) wanted to launch a pre-emptive strike on the USSR. See A. Fursenko and T. Naftali, *'One Hell of a Gamble': Khrushchev, Castro, Kennedy and the Cuban Missile Crisis, 1958–1964* (London: John Murray, 1997), pp. 51–2.

17 Khrushchev's successes in the mid-1950s in boosting agricultural production, raising the grain yield by almost 50 per cent, fortified his political position. However, after 1958 agricultural production moved towards stagnation and into crisis. Several seasons of falling yields due to over-intensive farming and the lack of economic inducements to productivity culminated in the drought of 1963 which was a political disaster for Khrushchev. See K. Nelson, *The Making of Détente: Soviet–American Relations in the Shadow of Vietnam* (Baltimore, MD: Johns Hopkins University Press, 1995), pp. 28–9.

18 J. Lévesque, *The USSR and the Cuban Revolution: Soviet Ideological and Strategic Perspectives, 1959–1977* (New York: Praeger, 1978), p. 87.

19 These problems boiled over in the spring of 1962 just months before the crisis in the Caribbean, with Khrushchev's announcement of the doubling of prices for meat, sausages and butter being met by major civil unrest. The most serious disturbances took place in Novocherkassk in southern Russia, where the army had to be deployed to restore order and where dozens were killed. The threat of further disturbances was taken so seriously by the Soviet leadership that in July Khrushchev ordered the KGB to mobilize its reserves for possible future riots on a large scale. See B. Gidwitz, 'Labour Unrest in the Soviet Union', *Problems of Communism*, 31, 6 (November–December 1982), pp. 25–42, and Zubok, *Inside the Kremlin's Cold War*, pp. 262–5.

20 For extended discussion of this see K. S. Karol, *Guerrillas in Power: The Course of the Cuban Revolution* (London: Jonathan Cape, 1971), pp. 204–7.

21 Despite a number of threats and ultimatums from 1958, Khrushchev was no nearer a resolution to Berlin, and by 1961 East Germany's regime was in crisis. Yet, even when the Soviets further increased the level of threat by demanding that the United States sign a finalized peace treaty within six months of June 1961 or face the prospect of losing Western access to West Berlin, Kennedy responded by stating that the United States would go to war if necessary to save West Berlin. See Roberts, *Soviet Union*, pp. 49–51.

22 As Roberts, *Soviet Union*, pp. 58–60, has highlighted, Khrushchev made a number of statements threatening the use of nuclear weapons before 1962, at the height of the Suez crisis in 1956 in support of Nasser after the Anglo-French attack, in

support of China in 1954 and 1958, and over Berlin in October 1961. However, none of these threats could be seen to have succeeded in deterring the United States, mainly because the United States continued to have a strategic-nuclear superiority over the USSR, and also because the prospect of triggering nuclear war, in the final analysis, would have been too great a risk.

23 As suggested by H. Dinerstein, *The Making of a Missile Crisis: October 1962* (Baltimore, MD: Johns Hopkins University Press, 1976), p. 60.

24 Fursenko and Naftali, *'One Hell of a Gamble'*, pp. 21–4.

25 Ibid., p. 26.

26 These other areas of concern obviously reflected Soviet interests but, as in the case of the status of Berlin, were also of concern to other communist leaderships/states. Thus, it was Ulbricht, the East German leader, who pushed the Soviets to pursue a more aggressive policy over Berlin, that would force the Americans to make concessions, knowing full well that if the situation continued the regime was likely to implode. See V. Zubok, 'Document Two'.

27 This derived from the apparent sabotage in Havana harbour in March 1960 of the Belgian freighter *La Coubre*, carrying an arms shipment, that the Cubans blamed on the CIA, and escalated towards a state of war when the US-backed exiles invaded in April 1961.

28 Fursenko and Naftali, *'One Hell of a Gamble'*, pp. 61–70.

29 For an analysis that treats the Cuban regime as essentially a Soviet type of 'state capitalism', see P. Binns and M. Gonzales, 'Cuba, Castro and Socialism', *International Socialism*, 2, 8 (spring 1980), pp. 1–35, and for a critical response to this see Blackburn, 'Class Forces in the Cuban Revolution'.

30 A. Suarez, *Cuba: Castroism and Communism, 1959–1966* (Cambridge, MA: The MIT Press, 1967), pp. 226–7.

31 See Y. Pavlov, *The Soviet–Cuban Alliance: 1959–1991* (Miami: North–South Center Press/University of Miami Press, 1994), pp. 84–9.

32 Fursenko and Naftali, *'One Hell of a Gamble'*, pp. 140–1.

33 Ibid., pp. 163–9.

34 Though logistically, because of the distance from the USSR, there would have been little that the USSR could do to prevent a successful US invasion of Cuba; instead, Khrushchev made veiled threats about the security of West Berlin.

35 This plagued Khrushchev through the years of 1960–62, as he was to make clear in his memoirs:

> one thought kept hammering away at my brain: what will happen if we lose Cuba? I knew it would be a terrible blow to Marxism–Leninism. It would gravely diminish our stature throughout the world, but especially in Latin America. If Cuba fell, other Latin American countries would reject us, claiming that for all our might the Soviet Union hadn't been able to do anything for Cuba except to make empty protests to the UN. We had to think up some way of confronting America with more than words.

Quoted in A. Gribkov and W. Smith, *Operation Anadyr: US and Soviet Generals Recount the Cuban Missile Crisis* (Chicago: Edition Q, 1994), p. 11.

36 Soviet policy, however, persisted in its aim to ensure the 'institutionalization of the Cuban revolution', not only to secure it from overthrow, as occurred in Algeria, Ghana and Egypt, which led to a consequent expelling of Soviet influence, but also to facilitate the political and institutional incorporation of Cuba into the Soviet bloc. It is no coincidence in this respect that Cuban membership of the CMEA in 1972 was soon followed by further changes in the institutional set of Cuban politics

manifested in the 1975 (1st) Congress of the Cuban Communist Party. As Lévesque, *USSR*, p. 186, states:

> The fact that the Soviet Union attached so much importance to the congress is a good illustration of the fetishism concerning political structures. Despite its greater flexibility on the issues of the transition to socialism and the strategy of the revolutionary movement, the Soviet Union still wanted to consider itself the most advanced model, if not the only possible model, of socialist society.

This can only be emphasized with the contemporaneous attacks on the Soviet model from Eurocommunism in Western Europe.

37 The consequences of the 'Escalante Affair' did not end in 1962, but continued to pervade Soviet–Cuban relations. Even in 1968, after the formal merging of the 'Movement of the 26th of July' with the PCC in 1965, Castro made a speech to the Central Committee where his condemnation of the Escalante 'micro-faction' was a veiled criticism of the USSR. See Brenner, 'Cuba 1962', pp. 82–3.

38 Lévesque, *USSR*, p. 130.

39 The Cubans were very concerned about American hostility and the possibility of a military attack, based on US diplomatic initiatives at the OAS (particularly after Cuba's January 1962 expulsion from the organization), the tightening of the economic embargo, pressures and calls for an invasion from members of the US Congress and the assessments of the American press. See P. Brenner, 'Cuba and the Missile Crisis', *Journal of Latin American Studies*, 22 (February 1990), pp. 117–21.

40 This was, in effect, what happened in the early 1970s with the combination of the political defeat of US military power in south-east Asia paralleled by the USSR reaching a degree of parity with the United States in its strategic nuclear weapons that provided the basis for détente. Thus, it was only after the United States was confronted with a genuine strategic military challenge combined with the domestic political problems, economic as well as political, of deploying military power in the way that it had done in the past, that the possibilities of 'peaceful coexistence' could be realized.

41 Recently published documentary evidence has proved inconclusive as to Soviet and Cuban motives for the installation of nuclear missiles in Cuba in 1962 (see *Cold War International History Project Bulletin*, 1 (spring 1992) and 8–9 (winter 1996–97); J. Blight, B. Allyn *et al.*, *Cuba on the Brink: Castro, the Missile Crisis, and the Soviet Collapse* (New York: Pantheon Books, 1993); and Gribkov, *Operation Anadyr*). Evidence supports two major arguments that the placing of nuclear missiles in Cuba was to defend the revolution and/or strengthen the international position of the USSR vis-à-vis the United States. The argument put forward here stresses the overlapping internal–external linkages within and between the USSR and Cuba, but also stresses the *form* of the political relationship between Moscow and Havana, and, because of the way that each state was socially constituted, the importance of military power both in domestic politics and, for the USSR, its ability to determine the internal and external political direction of the Cuban revolution.

42 Lévesque, *USSR*, p. 40; see also Pavlov, *Soviet–Cuban Alliance*, p. 33.

43 See V. Zubok, '"Dismayed by the Actions of the Soviet Union": Mikoyan's Talks with Fidel Castro and the Cuban Leadership, November 1962', *Cold War International History Project Bulletin*, 5 (spring 1995), pp. 59, 89–109, 159.

44 However, this was consistent with previous Soviet policy. As Pavlov, *Soviet–Cuban Alliance*, p. 59, makes clear, the lack of a clear and unambiguous public Soviet commitment to Cuba reflected a wider Soviet hesitancy to commit itself in its relations with allied regimes, 'to come to the rescue of these regimes in case of aggression'.

45 According to C. Blasier's *The Giant's Rival: The USSR and Latin America* (Pittsburgh, PA: University of Pittsburgh Press, 1983), p. 100, calculations, Soviet economic aid to Cuba between 1961 and 1979 amounted to approximately US$16.7 billion, and military aid in the same period to US$3.8 billion. In addition to these figures, Cuban debt to the USSR between 1961 and 1979 amounted to US$5.7 billion. Duncan's figures state that Soviet aid to Cuba by 1982 was running at approximately US$11 million a day. See W. Duncan, *The Soviet Union and Cuba: Interests and Influence* (New York: Praeger, 1985), p. 1.

46 Duncan, *Soviet Union and Cuba*, pp. 93–4, gives the figure of a US$1.5 billion deficit in Soviet trade with Latin America during the early 1970s. By 1981 the USSR exported goods worth US$178 million to the region and imported goods worth about US$2.5 billion. Blasier, *Giant's Rival*, pp. 54–5; Miller, *Soviet Relations*, pp. 15–18.

47 For an analysis of the history of Vietnamese communism and the Vietnamese revolution see P. Rousset, 'The Peculiarities of Vietnamese Communism', in T. Ali (ed.), *The Stalinist Legacy: Its Impact on Twentieth Century World Politics* (Boulder, CO: Lynne Rienner, 1984), pp. 321–44; Duiker, *Communist Road to Power*; Kolko, *Vietnam*.

48 Zhai, 'Beijing and the Vietnam Conflict', p. 237.

49 See A. Cameron, 'The Soviet Union and Vietnam: The Origins of Involvement', in W. Duncan (ed.), *Soviet Policy in Developing Countries* (Waltham, MA: Ginn-Blaisdell, 1970), p. 170.

50 O. A. Westad, 'Mao on Sino-Soviet Relations', pp. 157, 164–9.

51 The Geneva Agreement was supported by the communist powers in large part because the Chinese, especially after the burden of their involvement in Korea and direct military conflict with the United States, were not only concerned to focus on domestic economic issues like the first five-year plan and the 'liberation' of Taiwan, but also feared US military and possibly nuclear intervention. See C. Jian, 'China and the First Indo-China War, 1950–54', *China Quarterly*, 133 (March 1993), pp. 85–110.

52 I. Gaiduk, 'Soviet Policy towards US Participation in the Vietnam War', *History*, 81, 261 (January 1996), pp. 44–5 supports this view:

Two events played a decisive role in the reversal of Soviet policy towards the Vietnamese conflict: one, the escalation of US involvement in the war, signalled to Gromyko by Rusk in Washington in 1964; and two, information from Moscow's embassy in Hanoi that the Vietnamese were planning to escalate the military conflict in the south.

53 The Soviets were still angry at what they saw as not only Chinese irresponsibility but also betrayal over their attitude towards the Cuban missile crisis. This was the first time, during one of the most dangerous confrontations of the Cold War, that China not only failed to support the USSR, but also publicly condemned it. See M. Prozumenschikov, 'The Sino-Indian Conflict, the Cuban Missile Crisis and the Sino-Soviet Split, October 1962: New Evidence from the Russian Archives', *Cold War International History Project Bulletin*, 8–9 (winter 1996–97), pp. 251–7.

54 I. Gaiduk, 'The Vietnam War and Soviet–American Relations, 1964–73: New Evidence', *Cold War International History Project Bulletin*, 6–7 (winter 1995–96), pp. 232, 250–8.

55 Fraternal assistance was essential for economic reconstruction in North Vietnam. Aid from China and the USSR was particularly important in this respect. Ken Post's *Revolution*, I, figures focus on the July 1955 agreement, which saw the USSR

promise US$150 million and China US$325 million. K. Post, *Revolution, Socialism and Nationalism in Viet Nam*, V, *Winning the War and Losing the Peace* (Aldershot: Dartmouth Publishing Co., 1994). On p. 332 he also makes the claim, with some justification, that aid from the socialist camp, particularly in the period 1965–75, in economic and military terms effectively paid for North Vietnam's industrialization. From a longer-term perspective, Soviet aid to Vietnam amounted to 20 per cent of total Soviet aid to the Third World between 1965 and 1975, and towards the final stages of the war, in August 1973, the USSR forgave North Vietnam earlier credit deliveries totalling over US$1 billion, and between 1974 and 1975 provided more aid worth over US$600 million. See R. Thakur and C. Thayer, *Soviet Relations with India and Vietnam* (London: Macmillan, 1992), pp. 193–4; S. Morris, 'The Soviet-Chinese-Vietnamese Triangle in the 1970s: The View from Moscow', *Cold War International History Project Working Papers*, 25 (April 1999), p. 20; Tai Sung An, *The Vietnam War* (London: Associated University Press, 1998), pp. 268–9.

56 That influence had reached a high point by August 1964, with Le Duan, a leading figure in the Vietnamese leadership, telling the Chinese:

> The support from China is indispensable, it is indeed related to the fate of our motherland ... The Soviet revisionists want to use us as a bargaining chip, and this has been very clear.

C. Jian, 'Personal–Historical puzzles About China and the Vietnam War', in O. A. Westad and C. Jian *et al.* (eds), '77 Conversations Between Chinese and Foreign Leaders on the Wars in Indochina', *Cold War International History Project Working Papers*, 22 (May 1998), p. 28. During this meeting a bilateral treaty of military cooperation was signed which provided for the introduction of thousands of Chinese troops into Vietnam. See Gaiduk, 'Vietnam War', p. 250.

57 The Vietnamese and Soviets disagreed on a number of important issues throughout the 1960s and beyond. Thus, a meeting in Moscow in early 1964 between the CPSU leadership and a delegation from North Vietnam disagreed over policy towards national liberation, with the Soviets continuing to be hesitant about publicly endorsing the NLF. However, the Vietnamese did not have to rely solely on Moscow. They turned to Beijing and quickly signed a bilateral treaty that provided for increased military support from China. With the fall of Khrushchev, the new Soviet leadership, concerned at Sino-Vietnamese closeness, agreed to closer relations with Hanoi, symbolized by the opening of an NLF mission in Moscow and the beginnings of increased aid. See Gaiduk, 'Vietnam War', pp. 250–1.

58 As suggested by I. Gaiduk, *The Soviet Union and the Vietnam War* (Chicago: Ivan R. Dee, 1996), and D. Papp, *Vietnam: The View from Moscow, Peking, Washington* (Jefferson, NC: McFarland, 1981).

59 Thus the Soviets were kept in the dark by their Vietnamese allies about the impending 1972 spring offensive after the latter asked for and received more Soviet military equipment. See Morris, 'Soviet–Chinese-Vietnamese Triangle', p. 19.

60 I. Gaiduk, 'Developing an Alliance: The Soviet Union and Vietnam, 1954–75', in P. Lowe (ed.), *The Vietnam War* (Basingstoke: Macmillan, 1998), p. 139.

61 Thus, as Gaiduk, 'Developing an Alliance', pp. 143–4, shows, in 1966–67 Moscow agreed to supply military equipment worth 500 million roubles (equivalent to US$550.5 million, according to Gaiduk's calculations) to reach an upper limit of 1 billion roubles for the whole period since 1953. In fact the Soviets ended up exceeding this limit, with military aid amounting to 1.1 billion roubles since 1953. Moreover, by 1968, overall Soviet assistance grew to over 50 per cent of all socialist

aid to North Vietnam, and was worth more than US$500 million, compared with US$370 million in 1964. See also Gaiduk, 'Vietnam War', and Gaiduk, 'Soviet Policy'.

62 Gaiduk, *Soviet Union*, pp. 40–58.

63 Ibid.

64 See C. Jian, 'China's Involvement in the Vietnam War, 1964–69', *China Quarterly*, 142 (June 1995), pp. 356–87.

65 Ibid.

66 Thakur, *Soviet Relations with India and Vietnam*, pp. 117–22.

67 In 1968 over two-thirds of all Soviet assistance to North Vietnam consisted of military aid. See Gaiduk, 'Developing an Alliance', p. 144.

68 Either by means of the use of nuclear weapons and/or the invasion of the North. See Zhai, 'Beijing and the Vietnam Conflict', p. 237.

69 R. Smith, *An International History of the Vietnam War*, I, *Revolutions Versus Containment, 1955–1961* (London: Macmillan, 1983), p. 124.

70 This was not the only consideration for the USSR. As Antoni Carlo, 'Structural Causes of Soviet Coexistence Policy', in E. Jahn (ed.), *Soviet Foreign Policy: Its Social and Economic Conditions* (London: Allison & Busby, 1978), p. 66, has argued (though in a rather determinist fashion), from the mid-1950s wider Soviet international relations were premised to a large degree on the Soviets being able to secure material concessions or aid from the West with which to help sustain economic growth within the Soviet Union.

71 Smith, *International History*, I, p. 125 (emphasis added).

72 See R. Smith, *An International History of the Vietnam War*, III, *The Making of a Limited War, 1965–66* (London: Macmillan, 1990), p. 90. See also Post, *Revolution*, V, p. 12.

73 Sung An, *Vietnam War*, p. 404 (n. 41).

74 See K. Post, *Revolution*, II, *Viet Nam Divided* (Aldershot: Dartmouth Publishing, 1989), pp. 332–4. The problem of external but fraternal interference in the internal politics of Vietnam was to be mirrored in the political relations between the Vietnam and the wider Indo-Chinese revolution, notably the tensions that emerged between Vietnam and Cambodia and Laos after the 1975 seizure of power. While Vietnam was concerned that the 'Asian revolution' of the CCP should be limited, it was not so careful to confine its own direct political involvement in the Indo-Chinese revolution to itself.

75 As Ralph Smith, *An International History of the Vietnam War*, II, *The Struggle for South-East Asia, 1961–1965* (London: Macmillan, 1985), p. 354, notes, Soviet strategy differed from China's in the sense that Vietnam was identified as being worthy of political–military support, even if it meant jeopardizing Soviet–US détente, because, like Cuba, it was viable as a 'socialist' state and a revolution that could provide the basis of a regional alternative to US power and local allies through direct Soviet international relations with a number of either non-communist or non-aligned states in the region. This followed the main features of the Soviet policy of 'peaceful coexistence' in that it limited Soviet policy to supporting *a* revolution rather than revolution per se, when in many instances (as in Latin America) at that particular conjuncture social revolution was not a viable political option for the whole region. This was particularly the case for Indonesia (on which the Soviets and Chinese were in accord, despite Beijing's rhetoric). Because of the nature of the United Front and the sympathy of the Indonesian leader, Sukarno, for the PKI (Indonesian Communist Party), there existed the possibility of engineering a 'progressive' politics in the economically, politically, and strategically important Indonesia without a social revolution that would have

led to a massive reduction of US power in the region. This was the wider Soviet goal, which, partly because of Soviet strategy (but more particularly Chinese strategy, because of the close links of the PKI and Sukarno with Beijing), collapsed in 1965 with a military coup and the destruction of the PKI.

76 Papp, *Vietnam*, p. 207, suggests the figures of approximately US$1 billion per year for Soviet involvement and as high as US$30 billion per year for the United States.

77 But without a formal public declaration that this was a military alliance. The Soviets did not intervene in support of Vietnam in the Sino-Vietnamese war of the late 1970s.

7

The International Relations of the United States in the Cold War

Since the international relations of the United States rested on internal social and political arrangements quite different from those of the USSR, they thus took a different form. American international relations saw the *interaction* of, on the one hand, the constituent elements of the capitalist social relationship between the formal and coercive relations of the state manifested in diplomatic authority and military power, and, on the other, the socioeconomic relations of the capitalist market of production and exchange through private 'economic' agents and 'privatized' social relations. Therefore, whereas the Soviet Union was confined to a politics *directly* associated with the political power of the organs of the Party-state and a physical–material presence, the United States, because of its capitalist nature, was constituted by political activity and outcomes determined not only by state power but also by private capitalist economic power. Because of this, the United States could have a political presence in other states without the political–legal trappings. The relatively autonomous sphere of a capitalist market and a wider civil society reflected non-state and transnational sources of power, which meant that the consolidation and expansion of capitalist economic relations in the market could ensure international political expansion without formal and direct political control.

The International Relations of the United States and Social Revolution

This chapter will attempt to highlight the specific nature of American international relations in the Cold War, and the way in which the United States related to the Cuban and Vietnamese revolutions. It will focus on the role of the different forms of American capitalist power – economic, political, legal and military – in American attempts to contain and overthrow the Cuban revolution and to intervene against the Vietnamese revolution. The argument is that the American capitalist form of international relations rested on a political contradiction that derived from the capitalist social relation itself, in the sense of the way in which capitalist social relations originally penetrated a particular society, consolidated, then expanded and were, ultimately, contested and overthrown. The contradiction rested on how capitalist social relations were generated from a class-based antagonism, and how this conflict was conditioned by the uneven incorporation of these states and societies into the international system.

The projection of American capitalist power in the Cold War, in both its 'commodity' and military form, deeply influenced the reproduction of developing capitalist states in both Cuba and Vietnam. Their contestation and overthrow posed a fundamental question about the nature of international capitalism, and how the United States could relate to revolution, and the problems that such a form of politics posed for the realization of American objectives.

With the overthrow of capitalist social relations through the abolition of the private political sphere of capitalist production and civil society, the United States was limited to a politics and international relations that could only affect Cuba or Vietnam, directly, via the revolutionary state. Because of this limitation on American power the United States was forced to base its international relations on sources of politics that could best contest revolutionary politics, yet in so doing problematized the wider reproduction of capitalist social relations by exposing the international and political nature of capitalist social relations. Revolutions, then, because they rested on a rupture in the international capitalist order and the construction of alternative forms of politics, obviously questioned the pre-existing form of capitalist international relations, making it incumbent on the United States to posit an alternative form of capitalist social relations (and politics/international relations) to both contain and overcome revolutions.

This was what happened with American responses towards the Cuban revolution and the Vietnamese revolution/war. American responses to these revolutions reflected a concern to reconfigure capitalist social relations internally within the revolution and more widely in the region, be it south-east Asia or Latin America. In pursuit of these objectives the United States sought to contain and/or overthrow the revolution and address those issues that it saw as being problematic. With respect to Vietnam the problem derived from the colonial nature of the state, and the necessity of ensuring either a French withdrawal and/or the earnest construction of the basis of a formally–politically independent capitalist state tied to an US-led security system. This was not limited to Vietnam, but included the whole colonial edifice in the region: the replacement of formal-colonial capitalism with American capitalism based on independent states. However, unlike in Cuba, the situation in South Vietnam was compounded by the wider strategic situation, particularly the concern to contain Chinese and Soviet communist power in south-east Asia. US policy towards the region as a whole after 1949 centred on preventing an expansion of Soviet or Chinese-backed regimes in the area. South Vietnam, like South Korea, was to be a frontier in south-east Asia for the containment of communism that had already expanded in China, North Korea and North Vietnam and where communist influence remained a threat in Laos, Cambodia, Indonesia, Malaysia and the Philippines. Because of the coupling of the political (and the military) with the economic in China and the DRV, the undermining and possible collapse of South Vietnam was a concern that was as much military–strategic as it was economic. In this sense the 'communist threat' was rightly seen as political and military in that not only would the successful expansion of communism in the region have eliminated the possibility of constructing a liberal-capitalist order based on something other than a coercive politics confined to the state, but also the international relations that followed from such revolutionary transformations would inevitably provoke military tensions through efforts to 'export' revolution.

In Cuba and Latin America the problem that confronted the United States was more profound, for a number of reasons that had to do with Cuba's geographical proximity to the United States, its close historical political–economic ties with the United States, and the potential for the spread of the Cuban revolution to other parts of the region. This being so, because of the pre-revolutionary US–Cuban relationship, the early period of the Cuban revolution provided a situation whereby the United States could influence developments inside Cuba without direct political intervention, because it could command a wide variety of non-state resources, cultural, political and economic. However, with the onset of major structural social transformation in Cuba by the middle of 1960, the United States lost its ability to intervene in Cuban internal affairs through private and non-state capitalist socioeconomic relations. Instead, it had to confront (i.e. overthrow) the Cuban revolutionary state in order to influence Cuban internal politics effectively. Yet it was the explicit politicization of society and economy in Cuba after January 1959 by the United States that helped propel the revolution to its communist conclusion. By attempting to influence, indeed, thwart the prospects of radical socioeconomic transformation in Cuba, by using economic means, the United States exposed the myth of a liberal alternative. Simply put, the options that confronted the Cuban people after the revolution were American-backed reforms that would have left the capitalist socioeconomic edifice more or less intact, or radical changes that would fundamentally redraw the balance of democratic power between post-independence Cuba and the United States. There was no law-based negotiated compromise of a 'middle way'; this had been proved by the fact that the existing sociopolitical order had been engulfed in crisis and overthrown. For the democratic wishes of the Cuban people to be realized required a frontal assault on the institutions and forces that had always opposed those wishes. Thus, the social antagonisms within Cuba that had been present since independence were finally out in the open for all to see. With the failure to prevent a revolutionary social transformation, American objectives could only be realized through the prerequisite of a reconstitution (i.e. overthrow of the revolution) of the prerevolutionary Cuban form of politics. American international relations thus attempted to force such a change, but because of the form of external pressure (the economic embargo) and the problems associated with other (military) forms of influence, American pressure was frustrated.

Revolutions also sparked American attempts to redraw local–regional political and economic realities to consolidate the power and stability of surrounding states, and prevent the spread of the political contestation of the wider existing political order. However, in so doing, American inter-national relations were forced to focus not purely on the expansion and growth of American capital, but rather on the consolidation of state power in these regions, through the 'Alliance for Progress' in Latin America and SEATO in south-east Asia. Thus, American international capitalist rela-tions, concerned with state building and the elimination of revolutionary threats, came to rest on the projection of the varied articulations of American capitalist power. However, because of the form of politics on which social revolutions were based, US responses were forced to focus on the limiting and/or removal from political power of the revolution, which could not be achieved by the 'battering ram' of commodities alone, but instead rested on applications of military power. It is this tension and limitation within American international relations towards the social revolutions of Cuba and Vietnam that the following sections will try to explore.

Cuba

US relations with Cuba were formative, pre- and post-revolution. With a substantial if not dominant presence within the Cuban social formation in 1959,[1] the United States had good reason to be concerned with developments, but also, because of its political and economic presence, it was confident that it had instruments and relationships in place to ensure that its interests were not threatened. The Americans confronted a situation in Cuba in 1959, which, though far from 'clear-cut' in terms of the political direction of the new government, was a cause for concern because a political change had occurred in Cuba without the direct support or influence of the United States. The new leadership[2] was in no way tied to the United States, politically, culturally, economically or militarily.

Previously, and this was something of a pathology of the Cuban polity, politics and governmental change had borne the mark of US interest and sometimes direct sanction.[3] However, this notwithstanding, because of the nature of the Cuban social formation the United States was going to be determinate, in one way or another, for post-revolutionary developments in Cuba, particularly because of the continued structural economic links that persisted, despite the severing of the formal political link.[4] These came in the form of the annual sugar quota, which reflected many commentators' description of Cuba as a 'monoculture economy', and extensive American investments in public utilities, infrastructure, banking, oil, property, tourism and manufacturing. Indeed, the Cuban economy was de facto a part of American capitalism.[5]

Because of the nature of the political change ushered in by the events of early January 1959, many of the traditional levers of American influence were not operational. The lack of American influence at the time was reflected in the rapid departure of Earl Smith, the anti-Castro US ambassador. He was replaced in March 1959 by Philip Bonsal, who had the reputation of being more 'tolerant' of 'nationalist attitudes' in Latin America.[6] However, despite the disintegration of the only cohesive institution of Cuban politics, the army, and the political initiative resting with a guerrilla army, the United States, because of its economic presence within Cuba, had a major source of political influence with which to both promote its interests and secure political influence and/or concessions from the new government. For the initial period,[7] then, US relations with and political influence on the Cuban revolution were to be through the 'economic' relations of American capitalist power on the island, which offered a potential means with which to alter the political direction of the revolution through a combination of pressures and inducements.

The context of US policy towards Cuba after 1959 is important in considering US reactions towards Cuba and also the wider political economy of the region. US policy in the region had undergone a degree of change in the mid-1950s. This came about through a recognition that the US had a direct role to play in terms of the economic development of the region, with the accompanying recognition, after lobbying by a number of Latin American leaders, of the region's long-term problems of economic development. This 'policy initiative' rested on going beyond military links and relying on the military to maintain social order and if necessary US interests, to increasingly using economic aid to assist development projects in the region.[8] The Cuban revolution obviously highlighted the issues of economic development in the region, the best means with which to ensure capitalist economic development, and the safeguarding of US interests. The traditional vehicle – the traditional political elite backed by the local military – was not an option, and in many respects this was recognized as part of the problem by elements within the US leadership.[9]

The Cuban capitalist state had until the 1959 revolution reflected a semblance of 'bourgeois democracy', but in reality rested on the coercive instruments of the state, particularly the army, which the revolution had successfully smashed. Moreover, the state was also tied to the United States. Despite the abrogation of the Platt Amendment in 1934, the US state provided the international and political guarantee for Cuba and Cuban capital, but this had been weakened, if not completely cut, through the revolution.[10] American capital, then, in early 1959 faced a potentially serious political threat to its continued existence in Cuba. However, from the other side of the Florida Strait the continued presence of American capital on the island was to provide the possible means with which to achieve a full and complete restoration of bourgeois legality and political order, which would have not only protected American capital but ended the temporary hiatus of Cuban politics and led to the return to a form of bourgeois political order on the island.

The private 'economic leverage' was supported by the offer of constructive engagement suggested by the new ambassador, Bonsal. Indeed, until the full-scale expropriations of American property which took place after October 1960, US policy, through its ambassador, sought to engage Castro in negotiations and compromises that would ensure structural reform of the Cuban economy, but *with* American support. In this sense, the United States did *not* in the early months of the revolution respond with a belligerent or hostile public position. Rather the initial American response was to attempt to engage with the new government. It was only when it had later become clear that the objectives of the Cuban leadership were hostile to the United States that Washington adopted a much more coercive and hostile policy towards Cuba.

One of the important areas in this respect was agriculture. This was significant for a number of reasons. One was the place of agriculture in American objectives of the capitalist modernization of Latin America that were to be the cornerstone of the later 'Alliance for Progress'. Another was the heavy American investment, direct and indirect, in sectors of Cuban agriculture, from tobacco to sugar and ranches. Thus, the issue of agriculture highlighted the goal of modernizing the Cuban economy and the role in it of American agro-capital. But it also related to what were conflictual class relations in Cuba, particularly involving the rural poor and the rural proletariat, who had provided one of the major sources of support for the revolution. The United States, then, publicly endorsed the goals of agrarian reform, but was concerned to ensure that reform did not lead to expropriations and socialization. As Cole Blasier comments on Bonsal's talks with the revolutionary leadership:

> Bonsal was less concerned about the impact of the application of the Agrarian Law on US interests than damages inflicted on those interests in the *absence of legal authority*. There was a concern about the numerous acts of arbitrary despoilment that victimized Americans in Cuba at the hands of INRA [Instituto Nacional Reforma de la Agraria].[11]

The United States favoured reform, but focused on productivity rather than ownership and class relations, and in doing so, consciously or not, sought to limit the revolutionary nature of the changes in agriculture. Blasier rightly focuses on the legal aspect, but fails fully to 'politicize' how the legal protection for American property, within Cuba, *by* the Cuban state was an example of the political form of the capitalist social relation. This was also the case with respect to wider economic relations, and the subsequent clash because of Cuba's attempts to secure economic and thus political autonomy through developing economic links with the Soviet bloc after February 1960, and also in terms of the internal social transformation, which rested on the socialization of the separate sphere of capitalist production.

Corresponding with the changes in US policy towards Latin America in the mid-1950s already mentioned, US economic power was to be used to ensure that economic development was realized in the region, ensuring, it was hoped, domestic social peace, stability, and a spur to democratization,[12] and an increase in Latin American–US links. This being the case, the United States almost immediately sought to use its economic presence within Cuba to facilitate political relations with the new regime and thus ensure its continued 'allegiance' to the OAS system.[13] The visit to the United States by a Castro-led delegation in April 1959 before the implementation of the first piece of major social transformation (the Agrarian Reform Law of May 1959) provided the first of many opportunities through which the United States sought to determine the long-term political outcome of the revolution through the economic relations.

Although Castro was clear that his delegation's visit was not to solicit economic assistance from the United States, American and International Monetary Fund (IMF) officials did raise the issue with members of the Cuban delegation. The United States, then, through its offers of engagement sought to limit and orient the revolution towards specific goals that rested on what were perceived as 'mutual' economic interests.[14] There has been much discussion of the early days of revolutionary Cuba's relations with the United States. For example, Blasier makes the well-justified claim that

> US responses to the seizures of US property in Cuba were politically most significant during Castro's first year in office, that is before the sharp deterioration set in with events beginning in early 1960. In the first few months particularly, the US responses to Castro's policies affecting US property were potentially significant indicators for the prospects for later collaboration between the two governments.[15]

However, what this really shows is the conflict between the complete unravelling of capitalist social relations in Cuba and attempts by the US state using economic issues to help ensure the protection of American capital in Cuba, and thus the continued capitalist nature of Cuba. Although US policy was not initially limited to the 'economic sphere' alone, economic cooperation was seen as the best means of preserving Cuba as a capitalist state and thus the American presence, and not breaking the OAS line on non-intervention.

The negotiations that took place in mid-1959 and continued on and off until the severing of economic ties by Cuba in late 1960 revolved around the American commitment to provide a loan to Cuba, and what Cuba had to do (or not do) to secure it. The economic situation in Cuba at this juncture was difficult to say the least. Castro had inherited falling economic growth and high levels of unemployment, coupled with heavy debt owed to the US.[16] According to American officials, because of these persistent economic problems Castro faced a critical choice:

> Castro could 'limp along for a few months', the American officials admitted, 'but a day of decision is coming'. They predicted that the point would be reached in October–November 1959. Castro would then have to make up his mind about coming to terms with the US for a loan ... if ... Castro is to get large-scale aid for his ... problems, he will have to agree to a stabilization program ... this would chiefly involve credit restraint and a balanced budget.[17]

This seems to suggest that American offers of aid were tactical devices that had been used before, as in the case when US officials had similarly used the 'carrot' of economic aid to try to limit the possibility of radical social transformation in Argentina in December 1958–January 1959.[18] The international relations of the United States towards Cuba, then, in the early period of the revolution highlighted the international nature of the capitalist social form. In particular it showed the international political nature of the economic presence within Cuba, and how capitalist states have the ability to influence in 'economic' ways the politics of other states, including those going through a period of revolutionary transformation. Moreover, revolutions bring out the tension between the spheres of formal politics and economics within states, and expose the contradictions and class nature of the economic relations and how they are co-defined by the state.

With Cuba not willing to enter into formal negotiations with the United States on economic aid, alongside the assumption that even if they had, negotiations would quickly have foundered, the United States turned to pursue a more coercive 'economic' strategy to influence the revolution. This was centred on the annual sugar quota. If anything represented the structural capitalist dependence of Cuba on the US it was this relationship. Cuba had a guaranteed but limited export market for its principal product, which facilitated a stunted and distorted form of economic development and provided a useful economic lever for the United States to apply at will. The subject of the future of the sugar quota had come up in discussions between the two countries after January 1959.[19] What was most striking in the case of the sugar quota was how the political leadership of the US state initiated and organized the drive to use this as an instrument with which to try to pressure Cuba. It was the US administration that forced through the necessary changes to the sugar quota legislation that allowed Eisenhower to unilaterally abrogate the quota in July 1960.[20] However, because of the nature of the US–Cuban 'sugar relationship', the cutting of the quota only served to consolidate the revolution, particularly when the Soviets offered to purchase the surplus. The severing of the 'sugar link' undermined capitalist social relations, because it unilaterally withdrew the political support that had always been fundamental to the agreement. Without that political link (through the economic agreement of the annual quota), the Americans obviously sought to discipline Cuba economically by removing a substantial portion of needed hard currency, but in politically using the 'sugar weapon' had exposed its political nature and impact on Cuban politics.

With the accelerating process of contention and conflict in the US–Cuban relationship, because of the increasing moves towards expropriations of private property in Cuba that began to sever the political link between private property and economic relations, it was becoming clear that the capitalist presence (and thus, the American presence, 'political and economic') was about to be completely removed. This being the case, the ability of the United States to determine political developments in Cuba was becoming seriously circumscribed. The economic form of its international relations was losing its ability to influence the politics of Cuba, because the new Cuban revolutionary state was politically limiting its autonomy by displacing the 'relative autonomy of the economy' through direct political control. Because of this, the US state took it upon itself to orchestrate international relations through American capital in order to put pressure on the Cuban regime. This manifested itself in the removal of key and technical personnel, the non-delivery of spare parts and, ultimately, the complete obstruction of and non-acquiescence to Cuban government demands.[21] This was most marked in the US oil companies in Cuba by their refusal to refine Soviet crude oil in June 1960. Again, in the same way that the cutting of the sugar quota politicized the economic relationship, this economic but also political act also brought to the surface the contradiction of international capitalism that was resolved with the socialization of the oil companies. By October 1960 Cuba had ceased to be a predominantly capitalist state. The distinction between the spheres of production–distribution and the state had been removed with the direct control of the economy and the removal of the American political–economic presence.

Thus far I have focused on the economic nature of American international capitalist relations. However, even in the early stages, indeed, prior to Castro's seizure of power, the formal organs of US political power were seeking ways to intervene against and/or limit the power of Castro. This ultimately manifested itself in the US-organized debacle at Playa Girón in April 1961, with the defeat of the exiles' invasion. The background to the Bay of Pigs invasion obviously lies in the faltering attempts by the United States to secure, politically or economically, a political presence on the island with which to check the revolution. The military option, in terms of a direct United States invasion, was highly problematic in the context of regional politics. Because of this the United States sought, alongside the 'economic' levers, to use legal and political means[22] to isolate Castro and pressure him into compliance with 'hemisphere politics', and then to contain the revolution. The 'legal option' was combined with continued economic pressure and the provision of a more coercive option.[23] The US sought to expand the 'Cuban problem' from being a purely American concern to being one of the region as a whole, by attempting to include the OAS and the wider international system in the conflict with Cuba. Through securing OAS support the United States would have found it much easier not only to isolate, and thus contain and pressure the revolution, but also to increase the autonomy of its own political–coercive options in dealing with Cuba.

The OAS, however, failed to provide the expected platform for American attempts to discipline Cuba. Although the OAS after 1959 was far from sympathetic towards Cuba, the traditional concerns of all Latin American states, radical, moderate, and conservative alike, regarding an over-mighty American presence and influence, was enough to undermine American attempts at hemispheric unity of action. Indeed, the United States was continually frustrated in its attempts, beginning with the August 1960 OAS declaration of San José that failed to condemn Cuba outright on the basis of international communist influence in the region. Even the successful vote at the OAS conference at Punta del Este in January 1962 to expel Cuba from the organization was not unanimous.[24] What changed the OAS response was the evidence of growing Soviet influence in Cuba and, in particular, military involvement in mid- to late 1962. With this evidence the United States was able to secure unanimous OAS support to take action to quarantine the island in October.[25] The international legal setting, then, though successful in isolating and condemning Cuba and thus providing the basis for its long-term containment, because of the pervasive power of American capitalist international relations recognized by other states in Latin America, failed to provide the United States with a legal and thus political platform from which militarily to overthrow the revolution. International law and the American attempts to foster a multilateral response to Cuba, came up against the contradictions of wider US–Latin American relations. The legal sanctions served to discipline Cuba, but also to defend it, by reducing, because of the other regional political interests, the freedom of political manoeuvre for the United States.[26]

The limitations of legal sanction reduced the autonomy of the United States, which was left to sponsor and organize an exile-led invasion. The invasion plans and organization were begun in late 1959, although the final decision to authorize it was not taken until early 1961.[27] The failure of the invasion reflected the limitations of the political aspect of American international relations. Because of the limitations on the projection of US military power in the Western hemisphere, which derived from the legal–political relationship with the OAS, for the United States to have intervened militarily would have been illegal, and would have jeopardized wider international relations. The invasion failed not only because of its bad organization and planning and the lack of coordination between the relevant agencies of the US state, but because it did not have direct US military support. That support was constrained through US commitment to the legal and political system of the OAS. This obviously offered political and economic benefits in terms of American capitalist power in the region, but it also limited the legal sanction for military power, because of the wider political interests in the region. To have committed military power would have clearly and politically exposed the lie of political–legal equality in the region. There was formal political equality, which was vested in the OAS Charter, but in reality there was US political power, but not in an obvious 'political' form. Political power did not necessarily come from the barrel of a gun, but from the wider and deeper social relations of American capital that dominated the region, but were immune from legal and political sanction. Direct military intervention would have scuppered this.

Thus far I have mainly focused on the form of the international relations of the American response to the Cuban revolution in terms of US–Cuban relations. I should like to close the discussion by looking at the wider international relations of the formal and direct political relations of the state and the informal political relations of economic production and exchange in Latin America that were encapsulated in the 'Alliance for Progress', and at developments in the relationship between the political and economic forms in US foreign economic policy. The events in Cuba raised a number of broader issues other than purely US relations with Cuba. The broader picture mainly concerned the role of democracy in American foreign policy, and how this related to economic change and development; the role of military power as the best means with which to protect American interests; and the role of the state as a social relation of capital in American economic relations with Latin America. As Morley correctly argues, the Cuban expropriations were not simply a function of the size of the American economic stake in Cuba. Rather, the cluster of economic relations between the two countries was part of a larger set of forces that could infect the whole continent.[28]

I shall look at the role of the US state in terms of its relations with capitalist economic expansion. After the Cuban expropriations of American capital, the US government sought to set up an international legal framework whereby the state was directly responsible for the international protection of US foreign investments.[29] This was a consequence of developments that had been simmering within the Eisenhower administration, and were given political impetus by the concern of another 'Cuba' occurring in Latin America. The development of the Inter-American Development Bank (IDB) and, more importantly, the Investment Guarantee Programme (IGP)[30] highlighted US government concerns not only to protect American property in Latin America, but also to encourage American private investment in the region to consolidate capitalism and facilitate economic growth. As von Neumann Whitman suggests, American private investment tended to prioritize domestic over foreign investments, partly because of the risk involved in foreign investments.[31] Thus the US government intervened directly to ensure the security of investments and strengthen economic links with the rest of Latin America through trade and investment.

These policy developments were not limited to Latin America but applied to the Third World as a whole.[32] However, while their regional focus was with the aim of boosting capitalist economic development, it was also aiming to protect American private investments by directly involving the state in the economic relations between American capital and a number of Latin American states. As Blasier recognizes, with the IGP

> the US government formally became a party to expropriation controversies and itself a potential claimant under the provisions of inter-government agreements ... the Chilean expropriations [in 1971–3] ... show how the IGP intimately links US public and private interests, raising fiscal and political complications for the US government.[33]

The IGP and the other forms of economic assistance, both directly to Latin America and, indirectly, through encouraging American private investment, highlighted the interaction between the relations of capitalist economic exchange and the direct–coercive sanction of the state that displays the relative autonomy of American capital, and where the capitalist state deploys particular strategies with which politically to direct economic investment and politicize its relations. Although these developments could not, physically, stop expropriations of American capital in Latin America, they did obstruct it by legal means, and thus, politically, reflected a direct US intervention in the social relations of many states.

Through these political initiatives the United States sought to utilize the 'unity in the separation of politics and economics within the capitalist social relation' to provide direct American legal-political protection to capital in Latin America, which reflected an expansion of the international political capacity of American capitalism and a more obvious and direct, but legal, presence in Latin America. This was not always enough to stop expropriations of American property, but it did limit the capacity of many Latin American states to be fully politically independent. The political power of states that entered into these legal regimes was limited. To exercise full domestic 'economic' sovereignty, states had to break legally binding agreements and risk incurring the more direct political wrath of the United States.

In terms of more direct political interference in American economic investment that sought to discipline states that expropriated or penalized American capital, the 1962 Hickenlooper Amendment is defining of the 'separation but unity' in the capitalist form of international social relations. This legislation bound the American state to seek full and speedy compensation from expropriating governments. It also included clauses under which bilateral aid would be cancelled immediately.[34] The deterrent effect of the legislation was meant to ensure that governments would refrain from intervening in the operations of American capital under the immediate threat of the involvement of the American state. The preemptive nature of the policy was an obvious and direct political intervention in the economic sphere of capitalist social relations. This was a response to the failure of political intervention through economic relations that had characterized the initial American response to the Cuban revolution.

The importance of these political initiatives lay in their impact not only on American foreign investment and the direct capitalist political interference on Latin American states, but also on the programme of the 'Alliance for Progress'.[35] The Alliance was launched in August 1961,[36] reflecting the anti-Cuban and supposedly capitalist modernization credentials of the new Kennedy administration. In some respects the Alliance charter reflected a 'progressive liberal' response to the Cuban revolution, in that it recognized some of the major economic problems of Latin America which implicitly were present in Cuba and contributed to the revolution. These were encapsulated in the Alliance's advocacy of democratization and land-reform. However, what characterized the history of the Alliance, and the impact it had on Latin America, were a set of contradictions that centred on the politics and political consequences of economic reform, and how democratization would affect the political economy of American capitalist relations with the region.

As Morley suggests, many of the governments that signed the Charter were deeply opposed to many of its stated aims. This and the limited political intervention that was proposed to ensure the realization of political and economic reform was further compounded by the need for American private capital to spearhead capitalist modernization. Indeed, much of what followed did not result in any marked economic improvement in the region, but rather an expansion of export drives for American capital through tied loans and so forth.[37] The major form of political intervention in the region was epitomized by President Lyndon Johnson's invasion of the Dominican Republic in 1965 to quash a leftist rebellion, which reflected the augmented role of US military power in the region. US counter-insurgency policy was the principal political intervention in Latin America under the auspices of the Alliance. This rested on forging even closer links with local militaries, which served to undermine any hopes of democratization in the region.[38] US counter-insurgency policy involved training of local militaries and the provision of equipment.[39] It reflected the political concern with the consequences of economic and land reform, and also the Cuban-inspired increase in guerrilla activity throughout the continent.

The Alliance, then, although channelling over US$20 billion to Latin America by the end of the decade,[40] failed to engineer structural reform and substantial democratization. What it did do, however, was to encourage the militarization of much of Latin America,[41] and through counter-insurgency programmes helped contain a number of insurgencies. The military form of American international relations served to consolidate and deepen the links between capitalist states, which, throughout the 1960s, increasingly undermined the autonomy of economic relations, and led to its contention politically. By pursuing a more coercive and militarized form of capitalist international relations the United States exposed many Latin American states not only to a more visible politicization of the economy and production/class relations, but also to a closer identification with the United States.

Vietnam

There has been much historical and theoretical reflection on the United States' involvement in Vietnam. Much of this work has focused on the reasons for American intervention, the nature of the war, and why America 'lost'. Obviously, in a section of this length, I cannot hope to do justice to this literature and to the many questions and issues that it has raised. Instead, I shall address those issues that relate to the specifically capitalist nature of the international relations of the United States in Vietnam. In doing so I hope to bring out the tensions and problems of this form of international relations, and the nature of its impact on the Vietnamese war and revolution. This being the case, many of the issues that the wider historical and theoretical literature raises will, tangentially, be addressed.

United States intervention in Vietnam began soon after the end of the Pacific War. It rested on a number of issues that, with the spectre of the Cold War in Asia, came into conflict with each other. The principal American goal was to encourage decolonization and the building of a new political and economic edifice resting on the twin foundations of further incorporation into the world economy to facilitate capitalist moderniz- ation and links with local political leaderships through military–security relations. With the collapse of Nationalist China in 1949 the main pole of US strategy was the postwar reconstruction of Japan[42] to provide the basis for a new American-inspired capitalist regional entity. The United States, then, sought to restructure the international relations of Asia through trade and economic assistance, and regional security through the projec- tion of military power, and this was to be achieved by the transformation of local political forms from colonial 'states' to formally independent states.

The essence of US policy was concerned with facilitating a change in the form of political rule. Through this new ruling classes would emerge, based on different social and political constituencies, and, with the removal of the colonial edifice, 'independent' relations with the United States and the wider capitalist world economy would be realized. Vietnam came to be paradigmatic of this project and the problems associated with it. The problems for US policy rested on the intertwining of a number of war- and Cold War-related issues that the United States confronted in south-east Asia. The prominent ones were: the emergence of nationalist liberation movements – some of which were communist-led or -dominated, as in Indonesia, the Philippines and Malaysia; the expansion of international communism after 1945 in North Korea, North Vietnam and, most importantly, China; and finally the continued presence of colonial military and political structures.

It was the combination of these factors that provided the main 'external' limitations on the realization of American goals. With respect to Vietnam, the whole American project was problematized by the return of French colonial power after the Japanese surrender and the 'August revolution'. Because of initial French intentions and, more importantly, the impor- tance of France to American concerns in Europe,[43] US policy towards Vietnam was fractured along a divide that was to be, ultimately, impossible to bridge.

US relations with Vietnam began with its support for the French re- occupation and the subsequent war against the Viet Minh.[44] The problem for the United States was that a consolidated French presence, although it guaranteed a Western and capitalist presence in Indo-China, prevented the United States from directly influencing events there. Instead, the Americans, particularly after the 1949 Chinese revolution, were concerned to prevent a Viet Minh victory that would have had serious repercussions for the rest of south-east Asia. The immediate communist threat, then, forced the United States to aid the French in the war.[45] This immediate concern, the containment of international communism, came at the cost of the American objective of facilitating a new form of politics in Indo-China. Because of the French presence and US support, the Americans were, in effect, preventing the emergence of an autonomous national capitalist politics in Vietnam, and instead contributing to a weakening of the anti-communist *national* political order.[46] As Lee puts it,

> The underlying contradiction between, on the one hand, the US attempts to foster an indigenous Western-orientated power grouping in Vietnam and, on the other hand, its need to control and shape the political, economic, and military development of that state ... The irony of the American containment strategy for Vietnam was that it required an increased formal presence to achieve it.[47]

Because of the political limitations incurred through supporting France, the US was confined to an international relations that was not able to determine events in Vietnam. The long-term goal of a capitalist political and economic transformation of Vietnam was seen as being conditional on weakening, if not completely destroying, Viet Minh–communist power. However, such a policy limited American influence to supporting the French colonial form of politics, despite American demands over the need for decolonization and the building of a local nationalist leadership. The lack of an American political presence in Vietnam, in either the 'economic' or 'political' form, served to reduce American flexibility.[48]

The conjuncture of US involvement in Vietnam between 1945 and 1954 highlighted, in one aspect, the problem of formalizing American postwar international relations within a socio-historical context created by a *different* and continuing form of capitalist presence. Although the Americans did not want to see a French defeat in Vietnam, it was only with the political defeat formalized at Geneva in 1954 and the creation of a political entity south of the 17th parallel that the United States could begin to determine events there.[49] The estrangement between the American position and that of France was evident in the Geneva talks, notably with the refusal of the Americans to participate in the closing negotiations and be a party to the stipulations over unification elections in 1956. This reflected the interwoven concerns of the internal political nature of Vietnam and the wider US strategic anxieties in south-east Asia.

This derived from the acute concern at the nature of communist international expansion, where the strategic–military situation was imbued

with the political and economic. Communism was constituted by the unification of political authority and socioeconomic production through the
coercive–militarized institutions of the Party-state. Its expansion, then,
was premised on the elimination of alternative sources of politics that
offered the possibility of a sphere of relative autonomy from the state.
Because of communism's directly political challenge to existing political
authority, a challenge that went beyond existing legal parameters, borders
and traditional political institutions (i.e. it sought the overthrow and transformation of the whole sociopolitical order), capitalist modernization and
'state building' necessitated robust internal and external military security.
And the only way in which communism could be contained was through
strategic containment. It was this problem that was internal and external
to South Vietnam that dominated US policy.

The evidence for this came from the Korean War, which had a major
influence on US policy towards the region. In September 1954 SEATO was
formed, thus making an explicit US military commitment to the region.
Moreover, US policy after the French withdrawal from Indo-China sought
to equip the armed forces of South Vietnam for a conventional military
invasion from the North, the anticipated 'Korean scenario'. Finally, the
early period of US involvement in Vietnam, *before* the commitment of
combat troops in 1965, saw 78 per cent of US assistance go to South
Vietnam's military budget.[50]

The evacuation of French power from Vietnam[51] came on the agreement
to a cessation of the war and an end to Viet Minh military activities south
of the 17th parallel. The temporary end of hostilities and the French
political and military disengagement from Vietnam produced a political
vacuum that the Americans were quick to fill. Indeed, as Kahin notes:

> Rather than working through the French to support the Bao Dai
> regime, which claimed authority over all Vietnam, the US took on
> the mission of establishing a separate non-communist state in the
> southern ... zone prescribed by the Geneva agreements.[52]

This development reflected the American concern, as suggested above, to
facilitate, itself, the construction of a new post-colonial political order
based on capitalist social relations. However, this intervention also highlighted the major structural problems that confronted US policy in
South Vietnam. Because of the nature of the French colonial state, South
Vietnam was without a cohesive political leadership or a class structure
that could provide the foundations for a stable and effective 'independent'
state. Thus, the Americans took it upon themselves to act as an almost
surrogate form of political authority in South Vietnam by supporting one
of the many contending political factions (that led by Ngo Dinh Diem) to
secure political supremacy as the basis for the construction of a southern

state. Initially this rested on securing Diem's military supremacy, internally and also externally, through the September 1954 Manila Pact (establishing SEATO).[53] Once Diem was militarily secure (from other non-communist factions) the US set about a policy of state building in South Vietnam.

It was this project, the construction of an 'independent' state assisted by capitalist modernization and US military protection that the US had tried to facilitate through the French, that was to be the principal objective of American international relations with Vietnam after 1954. The American commitment to this end, economically and militarily, was mammoth and unprecedented in the Third World. Douglas Dacy has calculated that between 1953 and 1961 this amounted to US$1.545 billion in economic assistance and US$0.572 billion in military assistance, and between 1962 and 1974 US$5.770 billion in economic assistance and US$15.566 billion in military assistance.[54]

US policy, in identifying Vietnam as being politically important, should not be considered, however, in isolation from the region (and the Cold War) as a whole. As Ralph Smith has argued, it is important to locate US policy towards Vietnam within a broader international context, particularly regarding some of what came to be crucial US decisions. He identifies the situation in Indonesia between 1958 and 1965 as being of critical concern to the United States; it affected US policy not only towards Indonesia, but also towards Vietnam.[55] US policy here, as in Laos and Cambodia, was conditioned by the dominance of a revolutionary– nationalist leadership. Despite the communist sympathies of Sukarno, the Indonesian leader, and his links with the Chinese, because of the power of the military and other non-communist factions in Indonesia, despite anti-Western rhetoric, the US maintained a political and economic link with Indonesia which was rewarded after 1965 with the military coup that toppled Sukarno and led to the decimation of the PKI.

Vietnam was important in this respect because it provided a major opening through which to intervene in the region and it could act as a beacon of stability in an otherwise unstable and volatile region susceptible to communist subversion. As Smith notes:

> the purpose of military intervention in Indo-China was therefore not *merely* to prevent the total collapse of other 'dominoes' at a later stage, but also to ensure sufficient stability in Indonesia and Malaysia in the short term as well as the longer term to allow investment and economic growth ... [56]

The American commitment to Vietnam was not, then, limited to Vietnam itself, but was rather to the whole of south-east Asia, and to the wider goals of further incorporating the region, under Japanese leadership, into the US-led order, rules and discipline of the capitalist world economy.

What was the nature of American international relations towards Vietnam? I have mentioned the US military and economic commitment to Vietnam, but in what ways was American influence determinate on South Vietnam? And how did the constitution of American international relations contribute to, and detract from, the goal of state building in South Vietnam? In short, how did American capitalist form of international relations work itself out in South Vietnam ?

American international relations with Vietnam as a French colonial state were initially manifested in an explicitly political form, largely because of the absence of any American economic presence in Indo-China. Because of the nature of French colonial rule, the only significant capitalist class was that of the French, and because of this French capital was tied to the colonial regime, its guarantor. The Indo-Chinese social formation was, then, characterized by the structural linkage between the political authority of the colonial state and economic ownership and production. Although this was not all-pervasive,[57] it was enough to ensure French political dominance. The configuration of the Indo-Chinese social formation was such that there were no channels of non-French-dominated local or international influence. Instead, the United States had to work with and through the French colonial state.[58]

American international relations, even after the French political withdrawal, still confronted the structural problem of not only the lack of a state and a set of working political–legal institutions, but also the lack of a coherent and organized national capitalist class. Vietnam was, then, a 'non-political' entity, that consisted of an extremely weak and fragmented political order, despite the formal leadership pretensions of the former emperor Bao Dai, who was entrusted with national leadership by the French, and an uneven and poorly developed economy, that faced disintegration and civil war in late 1954. This was obviously recognized by the United States and explains their non-acceptance of the unification clauses of the Geneva Agreement. It seemed quite evident to them (and probably to the Viet Minh too) that without some form of external intervention the southern zone would either dissolve into civil conflict between the contending political factions, or be quickly subsumed, politically or militarily, into the North.

The Americans quickly sought to construct a viable political entity in the South by extending military support[59] to the Diem faction[60] and providing economic assistance.[61] The US intervention in support of the Diem faction quickly turned into a form of quasi-stewardship of South Vietnam. With the de facto emergence of a southern state, the south soon received legal and diplomatic recognition as a 'formally independent' state that had independently solicited from the United States aid and assistance with which to facilitate economic development and military security.

This situation provided the fundamental political contradiction of American international relations with Vietnam. Though South Vietnam was not a colony, and with American sensitivity to avoid the development of colonial-type relationships, the United States–South Vietnamese relationship was undermined by the necessity of quasi-colonial forms of relations. This is not to suggest that the RV was a colony – it was not – nor that it was politically autonomous from the United States,[62] but rather that the relationship swung between these two poles, whereby the RV was politically and judicially autonomous, but that politics was effectively imbued and anchored in US dollars and military intervention. One could consider the politics of South Vietnam as reflecting the presence of two contradictory political forms, one represented by the RV state and the other, the international expression of the American capitalist state. What characterized this relationship was a blurring of the political boundaries that reflected the tensions between American capitalist power and the weak, but *not* absolutely dependent political edifice of RV. We should be clear about this, because, despite the American capitalist presence, this was not sufficient to undermine completely the 'political autonomy' of the RV state.

This problem of the presence of two political forms in South Vietnam, something largely absent from the North, with, at times, contradictory objectives, at least in the sense of how to reach certain agreed objectives, was also compounded by the shifting nature of American involvement. This stemmed from the differing agendas within the US leadership where there were those who favoured a strengthening of the coercive power of the RV state, epitomized by the Eisenhower presidency, and those who preferred greater democratization and decentralization of political power within South Vietnam, associated with the Kennedy presidency.[63] This was evident in the attempts by the United States to press the Vietnamese leadership and, in particular, Diem, to carry out political and economic reforms. Although Diem agreed to carry out a number of American-sponsored reforms he either backtracked on these commitments or, when they were finally implemented after American threats, they were largely cosmetic, making little difference to the decentralization of political power currently centred on the clique around Diem or the opening up of the economy with land reform.[64] With these reforms stalled, the United States threatened in November 1961 to withhold military aid if they were not quickly implemented. However, Diem responded by vowing to turn to France for supplies or to Taiwan for alternative military advisers. Diem also used his influence in the local press to whip up anti-American feeling.[65] Although Diem did back down by promising to implement reforms, before there was any evidence of this, the US returned to supplying the full-scale military support wanted by the US general in charge of operations in South Vietnam, Maxwell Taylor. And with these further commitments the US lost leverage over Diem in the following months, and promised reforms, such as rural credit programmes, public works to reduce unemployment, increased taxes on imported luxury goods, public health programmes and, most importantly, land reform, were delayed or abandoned. The latter was eventually carried out after March 1962, but because of its incomplete and corrupt implementation it merely served further to alienate and antagonize many peasants.[66] Thus, through Diem onwards, with respect to a number of questions from land reform to democratization and taxation, and the efficiency of the RV state apparatus, the RV political form maintained a degree of separateness from American power.

The presence of two political forms, however, served to undermine the overall political viability of the South. Although it was not run by Washington it could not survive without the American capitalist political and economic presence. The RV state was, then, parasitic on the American economic support, though it vied for overall political supremacy with the political and military support of the United States. Despite American economic aid,[67] the lack of a cohesive local national capitalist class undermined the potential of the South Vietnamese state to be consolidated and anchored within a wider social constituency than the squabbling factions within the political and military elite.

The state and economy remained structurally tied to the American presence. This was a result partly of US policy, particularly the operations of the Commercial Import Programme (CIP), but also of the anti-democratic and corrupt nature of the RV state. The CIP served to ensure that the middle class would remain either loyal or at least passive towards the state, through the provision of consumer goods and improved living standards.[68] The CIP provision of dollars effectively financed the bulk of state spending (which was concentrated on paying civil servants, police and soldiers), but because this programme went 'through' the state, it resulted in a swelling of the state and a corrupt and overbearing inflated direct political involvement in the local economy. This was through the state's control of licensing the importing of American goods. The state, in effect, reduced the autonomous sphere of local private capital, and was facilitated in this by the channelling of aid through the state by the United States.

The South Vietnamese *urban* economy was characterized by the lack of an autonomous, self-reproducing capitalist class,[69] and was instead a form of economics that rested on the direct presence of the RV state in the economy, through its control of import licences and distribution of American aid. But although the state was 'dominant' in political–legal terms, this was only the case because of continuing American support. American economic support, then, was not concerned with the private economy as such, but rather the state.[70] US economic aid, along with increasing military support after 1965, was aimed at consolidating the South Vietnamese state as a viable political form, *not* the development of a private-capitalist economy. This would emerge only with a viable and independent RV state.

The problem in this strategy was that it served to 'swell' the state, but did not facilitate a *South Vietnamese* capitalist political-economy. Instead the emergence of a state, although attached through its presence in the local economy, was not paralleled by a relatively autonomous South Vietnamese economy.[71] Indeed, there was no significant alternative local politics except that involving the NLF. The RV state sought to destroy or incorporate any alternative sources of politics, be they derived from a religious (Buddhist), ethnic, local, and/or economic source. Thus, the ethnic Chinese community that dominated petty-commodity trade and much of the local importing was confined to urban ghettos and politically disenfranchised.[72] Following this, although the state commanded a presence in social relations, it was detached from the 'politics' of society, in the sense that it was undemocratic, authoritarian, corrupt and insulated from wider South Vietnamese society.

American capitalist international relations prioritized the political form in South Vietnam, and ended up distorting capitalist development despite the provisions of the CIP and the amount of money invested in South Vietnam. Instead, South Vietnam was defined by a set of social relations characterized by widescale petty-commodity trading dependent on the state, and a stunted capitalist sector. The state was inflated but not necessarily strengthened. With the increasing intensity of the military conflict, which reached a peak by 1968, the RV state was increasingly reduced to an appendage of the US military machine. But in terms of the effective projection of US military power, the United States was limited not only by the external constraints of possible Soviet and Chinese retaliation and/or intervention, but also the problem of contending with the, at times, rival political form of the RV state. In one sense, then, because of the form of American intervention in South Vietnam, economic support helped support and sustain the political form (rather than cultivating capitalist modernization and a developed capitalist class) of the RV state, but in doing so problematized the politics of the war. By helping to sustain a degree of autonomy for the RV state the Americans, in effect, made it more difficult to prosecute the war.[73]

The contradiction in American international relations that were identified in the nature of its capitalist presence in South Vietnam extended to the place of the military conflict in the struggle in South Vietnam. Because of the nature and dominance of the state, particularly as it manifested itself in the military struggle with the NLF/DRV, the conduct of the war was insulated from the transformation in rural social relations through land reform. Although the Americans called for reform, they were not able to ensure this change because of the rival political claims of the RV state and its social constituency. Thus, the war against the guerrillas was abstracted from the social content of the war. The killing of guerrillas was the killing of guerrillas rather than social revolutionaries who were instrumental in the social transformation of Vietnamese rural social relations. However, despite the failure to offer a genuine social alternative to the communist forces, the sheer scale and intensity of US military power did manage to destroy the social and military infrastructure of the revolutionaries, which was enough to transform the final years of the war and revolution.[74] The US projection of capitalist military power, as a technical formula, detached from social content nearly 'won' the Vietnam War by decimating the South Vietnamese peasantry. Through slaughter or forced migration, the countryside was almost devoid of people. In this sense the nature of American capitalist power was fully apparent, with the unleashing of technical–military power as an attempted solution to the social and political crisis in Vietnam. The logic of this military abstraction was that South Vietnam would remain non-communist, but that South Vietnam would not have a viable rural population or economy.

The unbalanced nature of US intervention, owing to the obstructive behaviour of the local political leadership, meant that military policy became removed from a viable political strategy and an end in itself. Thus, testifying to a congressional committee in January 1966 the US Defence Secretary Robert McNamara supported air attacks because in

> forcing villagers 'to move where they will be safe from attacks ... regardless of their attitude towards the Government of [South] Vietnam' ... not only disrupted Viet Cong guerrillas' activities but also threatened 'a major deterioration of their economic base ... it has been our task all along to root out the Viet Cong infrastructure and establish a Government presence.'[75]

Rather than instituting social and political reform the United States decided to destroy the countryside to the extent that by 1970 US bombing had destroyed about half the crops in the South and about 12 million hectares of forests and hills, and because of this South Vietnam had become a net importer of rice after having been a major exporter.[76]

The form of American capitalist international relations towards South Vietnam reflected the tensions between the economic and political support as projected internationally into a social formation like South Vietnam. This was compounded by the lack of a mature and/or indigenous capitalist presence with which to secure a non-state form of politics. The United States, from the beginning of its relationship with South Vietnam, was limited to, above all else, creating and then securing a state. Once achieved however, American international relations had to work through the political form to determine not only the politics, but also the economics of South Vietnam. By not being able to undermine the South Vietnamese state, the United States was locked in a framework of its own making for supporting the South Vietnamese state, although that state, to a degree, obstructed autonomous capitalist development and burdened the war effort. The only area of 'political autonomy' was in the military sphere, with the United States between 1965 and the late 1960s directing and dominating the war. However, because of the limited political nature of the military effort and because of the contentions with the South Vietnamese state over wider political goals (e.g. land reform, peasant migration etc.), the military effort was reduced to an abstracted technical solution that served to destroy the rural economy and destroy the peasantry, directly or through forced urban migration.

Conclusions

The international relations of the United States with the Cuban and Vietnamese revolutions were concerned with limiting and then destroying the revolution in Cuba, and preventing revolution in South Vietnam. Because of the nature of American capitalist international relations with respect to the Cuban revolution, the United States attempted to facilitate political change through the institution of capitalist private property and economic relations. Although the success of this policy obviously related to the political situation within Cuba and the unity and strength of the revolutionary leadership, it was also related to the political nature of the American economic presence in Cuba. This became quite apparent with the abrogation of the sugar quota and other politically directed acts from Washington that exposed the political nature of the American economic presence. However, what was important in this regard was the fact that the United States actually had a political presence within Cuba with which to influence the revolution, despite having no formal political influence. With the complete expropriation of capitalist property in Cuba after 1960, the US lost its political lever from within, and was forced to adopt a policy of externally influencing Cuban developments through more obviously 'political' sanctions. The 'economic' expropriations exposed the political nature of 'economic relations', and also laid bare the economic necessity of capitalist production and social relations having recourse to legal and political protection. Without a legal–political structure with which to protect it in Cuba, the United States had to resort to an alternative currency based on directly political and military power.

The situation in South Vietnam was different, because at the outset of US intervention there was no cohesive or national political form there. The project of constructing a viable state preoccupied the United States, and became the focus of political and economic aid. This was obviously underlined with the eruption of a full-scale insurgency after 1960. The South Vietnamese state was the object of US policy by means of both military protection and economic assistance. However, with the concentration on making South Vietnam politically viable, local socioeconomic relations were reduced to an appendage of the South Vietnamese state, which only served to undermine its long-term viability. With the increase in the insurgency and the scope of social revolution in the South, the United States, because it competed, politically, with the South Vietnamese state, was unable to institute economic reform, and instead detached its military policy from the wider social relations of the war. American international relations with Vietnam reflected the contradictions of the political limitations of economic relations, as a form of international relations divorced from American political power, and the problems of applying military power abstracted from the wider social context of Vietnam. The consequence was the successful physical destruction of the NLF's rural infrastructure, yet this also served to destroy the basis for an alternative capitalist rural South Vietnam, thus further weakening the South Vietnamese state and ensuring that once US military power had been removed it would quickly fall to the superior political strength of its communist rival.

NOTES

1 Leland Johnson, 'US Business Interests in Cuba and the Rise of Castro', *World Politics*, 17, 3 (April 1965), p. 441, calculates that the 'book value' of American enterprises in Cuba at the time of the revolution was over three times the value of those in the rest of Latin America.

2 This was despite the presence of some 'moderates' like Manuel Urrtia and José Miró Cardona, drawn from the traditional 'democratic' Cuban political classes in the first post-Batista government.

3 This was certainly the case in the first Batista coup in 1933–34. Moreover, its baptism as an independent sovereign state in 1901 was presided over by the United States, which also wrote much of the constitution and included a clause, the Platt Amendment, that legalized US military intervention in Cuba if and when Cuban independence was threatened. See Pérez, *Cuba and the United States*, for a history of the American impact on Cuba.

4 One of the main links between the United States and Cuba was the military one. The United States obviously recognized the institutional and political power of the army in Cuba, an institution that seemed to offer the best hope of maintaining some kind of social order and defence of private property. However, under the leadership of Batista the army terrorized the population and failed effectively to counter the guerrilla threat. With the failure of the 'summer offensive' of 1958 the United States administration embargoed military aid to Batista after coming under congressional pressure, and also as a means to press Batista, or other senior elements within the army, to pursue an alternative strategy against the guerrillas. The end of military aid, did not, however, completely sever US military links with Cuba. These remained through the military assistance programme representatives tied to the US embassy. See M. Morley, *Imperial State and Revolution: The United States and Cuba, 1952–1986* (Cambridge: Cambridge University Press, 1987), pp. 58–65; and W. Smith, *The Closest of Enemies: A Personal and Diplomatic Account of US–Cuban Relations Since 1957* (New York: W. W. Norton, 1987), p. 17.

5 See the section on the Cuban Revolution in Chapter 5.

6 See R. Welch, *Response to Revolution: The United States and the Cuban Revolution, 1959–1961* (Chapel Hill: University of North Carolina Press, 1985), p. 29.

7 We could date this period from January 1959 (when the US recognized the new government) until early to mid-1960, when the United States began to consider alternative means of influencing political developments in Cuba. It did not, however, ever stop using its economic power in one way or another against revolutionary Cuba.

8 See R. Carr, 'The Cold War in Latin America', in J. Plank (ed.), *Cuba and the United States: Long-Range Perspectives* (Washington, DC: Brookings Institution, 1967), pp. 168–9; B. Kaufman, *Trade and Aid: Eisenhower's Foreign Economic Policy, 1953–1961* (Baltimore, MD: Johns Hopkins University Press, 1982); Morley, *Imperial State*, pp. 44–6.

9 Kennedy's 1961 'Alliance for Progress', initiated at the March 1961 OAS conference at Punta del Este, reflected these concerns over economic development and democratization. The 'Alliance' was obviously a response to the revolution, though it could be seen as a more public continuation of developments that had begun under the previous Eisenhower administration. See Carr, 'Cold War', pp. 168–70; Morley, *Imperial State*, p. 116.

10 This was also the case in the period immediately before Castro's seizure of power. It reflected a major contradiction in US policy towards Cuba based on the dominant economic influence and lack of a cohesive autonomous Cuban bourgeoisie and the limitations imposed on the political–institutional order through military dominance. Thus, as Morley, *Imperial State*, p. 70 comments:

> the advanced state of disarray and demobilization within the Cuban armed forces following the failure of the summer 1958 offensive against the guerrillas and Washington's lack of any significant internal political or social base of support sharply limited the US government's room for manoeuvre.

11 C. Blasier, *Hovering Giant: US Responses to Revolutionary Change in Latin America* (Pittsburgh: University of Pittsburgh Press, 1976), p. 90 (emphasis added). See also Morley, *Imperial State*, p. 83.

12 For an extended discussion of the role of democratization in US foreign policy towards Latin America, see A. Lowenthal (ed.), *Exporting Democracy. The United States and Latin America: Themes and Issues* (Baltimore, MD: Johns Hopkins University Press, 1991).

13 The 'OAS system' was heavily imbued with American political and economic influence. It rested on an assumption that the states of the Western hemisphere were bound to organize themselves in a way that promoted 'free trade' and did not permit what were identified as 'foreign ways/ideologies' to develop in the region. This obviously meant socialism, and with the US response towards Guatemala in 1954 it was clear that the US would use the OAS as a vehicle to ensure the exclusion of radical forms of politics in the region. It had used the OAS to isolate Guatemala, which helped legitimize the CIA-inspired coup that overthrew the Arbenz regime. However, one of the pillars of the OAS system which was enshrined in a number of postwar treaties and realized in Roosevelt's 'Good Neighbour Policy' was that of non-intervention. US relations with the states of Latin America in the postwar period were based on the outlawing of direct (i.e. military) interventions in the internal affairs of any member of the OAS. This obviously limited US policy options, but it came with an agreement by the ruling classes of Latin America that they themselves would be against any 'foreign ideologies' or interventions.

14 This is an important point and deals directly both with criticisms of American

responses to the Cuban revolution and with debates about the nature of the revolution. Regarding the former, the point is that had Cuba accepted the offers of cooperation from the United States in terms of economic modernization and aid, this would have been on the basis of an acceptance of the capitalist social form and the politics that flowed from that. This would have inevitably (even with all the best intentions of the 'progressives' in the US administration and capitalist class) led to a structural limiting, politically and legally, in what the revolution could have achieved. Thus, cooperation also meant the acceptance, ultimately, of a continued American capitalist presence in Cuba. The latter relates directly to this and suggests that the revolution did indeed come to rest on forms of class mobilization and conflict. The rejection of the American offers (not all of which were obviously disciplining) shows that, even in the first year of the revolution, Castro was concerned to limit if not crush American capital.

15 Blasier, *Hovering Giant*, p. 90.
16 This economic situation and the impact it had on the Cuban poor and working class underlined the concern of Castro to ensure that his government would be anchored in a social (class) constituency that would most benefit from revolutionary changes, and most importantly provide a means of social mobilization against American hostility. The class nature of the Cuban revolution, then, was soon apparent, particularly when the economic changes pursued by Castro needed class support and mobilization. For a survey of working-class attitudes pre- and post-revolution see M. Zeitlin, *Revolutionary Politics and the Cuban Working Class* (Princeton, NJ: Princeton University Press, 1967); Mintz, 'Foreword', in *Sugar and Society*, pp. xi–xliv.
17 Quoted in W. A. Williams, *The United States, Cuba, and Castro: An Essay on the Dynamics of Revolution and the Dissolution of Empire* (New York: Monthly Review Press, 1962), pp. 100–1.
18 Ibid., p. 101.
19 Morley, *Imperial State*, p. 83.
20 Ibid., pp. 107–13, for an extended discussion of this.
21 For extended discussions on these developments, see the following: Morley, *Imperial State*, p. 105; Blasier, *Hovering Giant*, p. 191; L. Bender, *The Politics of Hostility: Castro's Revolution and United States Policy* (Hato Rey, Puerto Rico: Inter-American University Press, 1975), pp. 13–31; E. Baklanoff, *Expropriation of US Investments in Cuba, Mexico, and Chile* (New York: Praeger, 1975), pp. 118–19; Johnson, 'United States Business Interests', pp. 440–59.
22 These are typical of capitalist forms of international relations. Although they were not limited purely to capitalist states, the Soviet Union and Cuba both argued for the international legal norm of non-intervention. However, international law and legal sanctions are quintessentially capitalist in the following sense. They rest on the 'bourgeois' separation of the spheres of politics and economics whereby the legal norm is anchored in the realm of the state as a subject and object of law. Because of this states appear to be subject to international law as entities separate from their internal social and political constitution. For example, Cuban actions in expropriating foreign property after 1959 were deemed by the United States to be illegal and in breach of international law and the OAS system. However, these actions were concerned with domestic politics within Cuba, in particular the exercise of Cuban 'popular sovereignty' over the Cuban economy. In formal terms these acts should *not* have been a concern of international law, since they were matters concerning domestic jurisdiction. What this tends to highlight is that specific types of domestic policies can and do have international consequences, especially when that policy infringes the rights attaching to private property,

primarily because capital is a transnational social relation. Thus, although international law tends to focus on the external relations between states, and rests on the norm of non-intervention as the basis of sovereignty, the presence of capitalist social relations necessarily limits domestic sovereignty because of the international nature of capital. International law rests on the separation of the domestic from the external legal realms. Although the separation of internal and external legal is clearly the case in the outlawing of direct political involvement in the domestic affairs of a sovereign state, it tends to overlook the less direct, but nevertheless political consequences of the presence of private property relations of capitalist production. In this sense, then, one could also argue that the explicit separation of domestic and international in international law is paralleled by a less explicit, but nevertheless significant separation of politics from economics because whereas politics is assumed to be confined to the state, capitalist economic relations are not confined to the territory or authority of the state, but are transnational in essence. And because of this certain types of domestic political behaviour will be subject to international legal challenge, as they were in Cuba by the United States.

23 Indeed, US Vice-President Richard Nixon was quite clear early on, on the necessity of a military option to deal with the Cuban revolution. Nixon, after meeting Castro in April 1959, suggested using the military option to remove Castro using armed Cuban exiles. See Bender, *Politics of Hostility*, p. 17.

24 The Americans were more successful in the July 1964 meeting of the OAS in Washington, which established sanctions against Cuba on the basis of Venezuelan claims of Cuban intervention in its internal affairs. See Bender, *Politics of Hostility*, p. 27; Dinerstein, *Making of a Missile Crisis*, p. 161.

25 Blight, *Cuba on the Brink*, pp. 144–5.

26 As Dinerstein, *Making of a Missile Crisis*, pp. 97–8, suggests: by organizing the OAS as an instrument of the Cold War against international communism, the US was concerned not to undermine it by breaking the conditions of its charter, as an invasion would have done.

27 Blasier, *Hovering Giant*, p. 191.

28 *Imperial State*, p. 114.

29 The US state had, prior to the Cuban revolution, set up a number of bodies to protect and/or encourage private investment in Latin America, as in the case of the International Finance Corporation set up in 1954 to encourage and 'support private enterprises in underdeveloped countries'. See R. Wagner, *United States Policy Toward Latin America: A Study in Domestic and International Politics* (Stanford, CA: Stanford University Press, 1970), pp. 130–4. However, the establishment of such forms of state involvement in the international economy were not free from controversy and problems, even within the United States, with sections of the state questioning the public–state infringement on the private–capitalist sphere. See B. Mattocks, *The Establishment of the International Financial Corporation and United States Policy* (New York: Praeger, 1957). The issue was resolved because of the political necessity for the United States, pressured by Latin American governments, to assist in the development of the region, something which American capital, alone, seemed hesitant to do.

30 The IGP was established after the Cuban revolution as a political response to the concerns of American capital for the security of its investments in the rest of Latin America, and the risks associated with future investments. It provided public funds (financial guarantees) for US overseas investment where the state would compensate US companies whose property had been expropriated without compensation by a foreign government. For an extended discussion of the sanctioning of coercive legal and political measures to protect American property invested

overseas, see C. Lipson, *Standing Guard: Protecting Foreign Capital in the Nineteenth and Twentieth Centuries* (Berkeley: University of California Press, 1985).

31 M. von Neumann Whitman, *Government Risk-Sharing in Foreign Investment* (Princeton, NJ: Princeton University Press, 1965), p. 10.

32 Another reason for promoting more aggressive American 'economic' penetration of the Third World was the concern to respond to growing Soviet initiatives. See W. Duncan (ed.), *Soviet Policy in Developing Countries* (Waltham, MA: Ginn-Blaisdell, 1970). M. Wilkins, *The Maturing Multinational Enterprise: American Business Abroad from 1914 to 1970* (Cambridge, MA: Harvard University Press, 1974), pp. 328–31, gives the figures:

> by 1963 the US had bilateral treaties (with clauses protecting private property) with 41 different countries ... US government guarantees became particularly important and popular for US business after the ... Cuban revolution.

33 Blasier, *Hovering Giant*, p. 98. Blasier also states:

> Since 1959 the US has signed agreements providing for investment guarantees with most Latin American governments. By June 1971 US$5.6 billion of guarantees had been issued in Latin America, nearly US$2.6 billion of which covered expropriation risks. About one-sixth of the nearly US$16 billion of US investment in the region was then covered by expropriation insurance.

See also Baklanoff, *Expropriation of US Investments*, p. 143, on the problems that the Allende government in Chile posed for the US government's foreign investment insurance programme.

34 See Lipson, *Standing Guard*, pp. 200–26, for discussion of this piece of legislation. Lipson makes it clear that the Hickenlooper Amendment was written as a response to Cuban communism.

35 The Hickenlooper Amendment contradicted many of the provisions of the Alliance. As Lipson, *Standing Guard*, pp. 210–12 highlights, the United Fruit Company in Honduras, in response to a 1962 government land reform, used the provisions of 'Hickenlooper' to force the government to back down.

36 R. Packenham, *Liberal America and the Third World: Political Development Ideas in Foreign Aid and Social Science* (Princeton, NJ: Princeton University Press, 1973), p. 217.

37 Morley, *Imperial State*, p. 127.

38 See M. Klare and C. Amson, 'Exporting Repression: US Support for Authoritarianism in Latin America', in R. Fagen (ed.), *Capitalism and the State in US–Latin American Relations* (Stanford, CA: Stanford University Press, 1979), p. 143.

39 Ibid., p. 148.

40 T. Smith, ' The Alliance for Progress: The 1960s', in A. Lowenthal (ed.), *Exporting Democracy. The United States and Latin America: Themes and Issues* (Baltimore, MD: Johns Hopkins University Press, 1991), p. 72.

41 See Wagner, *United States Policy*, p. 181 on the military coups that followed the Alliance.

42 See A. Iriye, *The Cold War in Asia: A Historical Introduction* (Englewood, NJ: Prentice-Hall, 1974); S. Lee, *Outpost of Empire: Korea, Vietnam, and the Origins of the Cold War in Asia, 1949–1954* (Montreal: McGill-Queen's University Press, 1995).

43 The formation and content of US policy towards Vietnam after 1945 rested on the tensions within the emerging 'Atlantic Alliance' and the Cold War. Because of local

French preponderance the US was committed to working with French colonial power. However, it soon became apparent that US long-term goals clashed with those of the French. The problem for the Americans was that their ability to influence developments in French Indo-China were complicated, to say the least, by the perceived necessity of French cooperation with the United States in Europe to meet the Soviet threat. This problem was finally 'resolved' (unsatisfactorily) by the 1954 Geneva Agreement that secured a French withdrawal from Indo-China. For extended discussions of this see G. Kahin, *Intervention: How America Became Involved in Vietnam* (New York: Alfred A. Knopf, 1986), p. 3, pp. 54–5; W. Duiker, *US Containment Policy and the Conflict in Indo-China* (Stanford, CA: Stanford University Press, 1994), pp. 2, 43; L. Gardner, *Approaching Vietnam: From World War Two Through Dienbienphu, 1941–1954* (New York: W.W. Norton, 1988), p. 14; Lee, *Outposts of Empire*, pp. 15–28, *passim*.

44 As Kahin, *Intervention*, p. 8, notes: 'Within two months of the Japanese surrender, American ships … were carrying French forces to Vietnam.'

45 As I have already mentioned, US policy was not only determined by events in Asia. France was just as important to America's concerns in Europe, more so up until 1949. In terms of American aid to the French in Indo-China, this was substantial. The United States, in effect, especially after 1950, financed the war. Kahin, *Intervention*, pp. 36–8, notes the importance of the 'Lisbon Programme' launched in early 1952, which provided an initial US$200 million for purchases of war matériel, another US$500 million in 1952–53, and US$785 million in 1953–54. This was accompanied by the Mutual Defence Assistance Programme (MDAP), which provided 532,847 tons of military equipment, valued at US$334.7 million, between June 1950 and December 1952. By 1954 the United States was financing over 78 per cent of the French war effort. J. Montgomery, *The Politics of Foreign Aid: American Experience in Southeast Asia* (New York: Frederick A. Praeger, 1962), p. 22, suggests that over 60 per cent of the US$3.5 billion of American aid to French Indo-China in 1950–54 went on military aid.

46 As Lee, *Outposts of Empire* (p. 28), comments:

> The US wanted the French to work towards an informal empire in Vietnam, but American strategy was dictated to a large degree by the French colonial presence and by the inability of Bao Dai to attract popular support.

47 Ibid., p. 115.

48 The limitations of US policy were also shown in the inability of the United States to mobilize international (Western) support for military escalation in the region in support of Vietnam. The American attempts through 'United Action' to internationalize the war in Vietnam, thus allowing a more substantial projection of military power but legitimized by Anglo-French involvement (similar to the international coalition gathered to 'defend' Korea), failed. See Kahin, *Intervention*, pp. 44–8; Duiker, *US Containment Policy*, pp. 163–70.

49 By 1952 the United States was bearing approximately one-third of the cost of the war yet was unable to determine its overall direction. The United States, however, sought a more direct involvement in the war, through providing air power support at Dien Bien Phu and/or committing troops not under French command, and the offer in 1954 of training and equipping local anti-communist forces. See G. Herring, *America's Longest War: The United States and Vietnam, 1950–1975* (New York: John Wiley, 1979), pp. 10–21.

50 See D. Borer, Superpowers *Defeated: Vietnam and Afghanistan Compared* (London: Frank Cass, 1999), pp. 58–60, 95–7.

51 Within months of the Geneva Agreement South Vietnam had severed economic
    and financial links with the French. See Smith, *International History*, I, p. 25.
52 *Intervention*, p. 66.
53 This form of American intervention to secure an 'independent' Vietnam, internally
    and externally, set a precedent, particularly in terms of the military form of that
    intervention. As Gardner, *Approaching Vietnam*, pp. 353–4, has remarked: 'having
    accepted a measure of responsibility for changing the Vietnamese government –
    one may dispute the degree – it was impossible to disengage'.
54 D. Dacy, *Foreign Aid, War and Economic Development: South Vietnam, 1955–1975*
    (Cambridge: Cambridge University Press, 1986), p. 245.
55 *International History*, I, p. 113.
56 Smith, *International History*, II, pp. 142, 203:

> in so far as South Vietnam represented a diplomatic rather than a purely military
> problem, it could not be divorced from the problems of Laos, Cambodia, and
> of Indonesia's confrontation with Malaysia ... during the next year or so the
> various conflicts of the region would become more closely intertwined, creating
> a far more complex situation than that envisaged by the 'domino theory' of the
> 1950s. Any US decision to negotiate military withdrawal from South Vietnam
> depended to some extent on the solution of those other problems.

57 French capitalist penetration was inconsistent, varied and centred on specific areas.
    Much of the rest of the land was a rural-based economy that although affected by
    commodity circulation and capitalist social relations was not characterized by the
    same kind of class and political relations as elsewhere. This being the case, the
    principal local class forces were not open to external relations. All political relations
    were mediated through the French colonial state, but the imprint of French rule
    was not consistently the same throughout Indo-China. See Murray, *Development
    of Capitalism*, and Wiegersma, *Vietnam*.
58 Indeed, as Porter, *Vietnam*, p. 6, has argued, the French presence transformed social
    relations not only in terms of the subordinate classes, but also with the political
    decapitation of the traditional indigenous ruling class. The landlord class became
    dependent on the colonial state for its own social and material reproduction, which
    provided a *dis*incentive for politically challenging French authority.
59 As Kahin, *Intervention*, p. 71, states:

> The US quickly displaced France's political and military presence in the area,
> taking over as paymaster to Vietnamese civil servants and soldiers who had
> collaborated with the French, providing American training and advisers to the
> previously French officered army.

> Post, *Revolution*, I, p. 225, notes that both Diem and the United States recognized
> the importance of military superiority in the South, which was facilitated by the
> setting up of the Military Assistance Advisory Group (MAAG) in 1955.

60 Diem secured himself politically in the South with a dubious referendum victory
    in 1956.
61 Kahin, *Intervention*, p. 85:

> 87% of the initial US grant to Diem of US$327.4 million in 1955 was channelled
> through the CIP [Commercial Import Programme], and thereafter, from 1955
> ... 1961 Washington provided Diem's government with a total of US$1,447
> million in economic grant aid ... mainly through the CIP.

62 The United States had a role in nearly all the changes in government, through

military coups after 1954 in South Vietnam. The removal of Diem in November 1963 has received the most attention, but either through acquiescence or encouragement, the United States acted to undermine politically some South Vietnamese leaders by seeking to ensure that the political leadership in the south was compatible with Washington's political–military goals. See Kahin, *Intervention*, pp. 132–3, 183–205, 294–5, 300–5 for more on US involvement in the many coups in South Vietnam.

63 See D. Macdonald, *Adventures in Chaos: American Intervention for Reform in the Third World* (London: Harvard University Press, 1992), pp. 58–9.

64 Ibid., pp. 188–92.

65 Ibid., p. 209.

66 Ibid., pp. 209–18.

67 A provocative but sympathetic critique of US policy in South Vietnam that focused on American aid provision and highlights the 'stagnatory' effects of US policy with respect to the development of the local economy is Dacy, *Foreign Aid*.

68 See Montgomery, *Politics of Foreign Aid*, p. 87.

69 See Post, *Revolution*, II, pp. 4–5; idem, *Revolution, Socialism and Nationalism in Vietnam*, IV, *The Failure of Counter-Insurgency in the South* (Aldershot: Dartmouth Publishing Co., 1990), p. 46.

70 Without the construction and consolidation of a state form in Vietnam, the operation of a capitalist economy was to be problematic. This obviously related to the ability of the state to protect property through legal sanction and force. But it also related to the consolidation of a specific type of capitalist politics that rested on a specific form of state and its relationship to society. Without the securing of a political order in South Vietnam, the further penetration of capitalist production relations would have foundered on continued political contestation that included a contesting of a commodity-based economy.

71 Indeed, as Montgomery, *Politics of Foreign Aid*, p. 88, comments:

America's long-range plan for encouraging large-scale private expansion … was hampered by a … combination of political considerations and administrative rigidities, both American and Vietnamese. Capital goods costing over US$½ million could not be imported under the CIP without special permission from Washington … A more basic problem arose out of the disagreement about the proper form of ownership for new enterprises: the US permitted capital equipment to be imported under the CIP only for privately owned and operated enterprises, while for its part the Vietnamese government was unwilling to permit any basic industries to be controlled by French or Chinese, and demanded the right to majority stock in all important enterprises. This conflict of principles seriously weakened the CIP as a device for building up the industrial sector.

72 The ethnic Chinese participated with the Vietnamese in the CIP, however, as Post, *Revolution*, IV, p. 348, suggests: although CIP did facilitate the emergence of a local capitalist class, it was one

which was not involved very heavily in production activities and was highly dependent on state patronage in the form of CIP licences and contracts; in return, payments were made to senior bureaucrats, politicians and army officers.

73 This is not to suggest that the United States' intervention in Vietnam would have been assisted by an even weaker state to the point where the American presence was, in effect, the state. This problem underlines the contradiction of US policy that I mentioned earlier. The counter-factual ideal would have been the presence

of a stronger local capitalist state, which could secure more than the depth of legitimacy, independent of external support, than South Vietnam. Because this was not the case the American effort was constrained by the necessity of maintaining the legal-political jurisdiction of South Vietnam.

74 By 1967 the United States had dropped more ordinance in Vietnam than it had in all theatres in the Second World War. The 25,000 tonnes of bombs dropped on North Vietnam in 1965 rose to 226,000 tonnes in 1967. See Borer, *Superpowers Defeated*, p. 157.

75 N. Vinh Long, 'South Vietnam', in P. Lowe (ed.), *The Vietnam War* (Basingstoke: Macmillan, 1998), p. 75.

76 Ibid., pp. 81–2.

8

Conclusion: Understanding the Cold War and Its End

This book has sought to provide an alternative understanding of the Cold War based on a reconceptualization of existing theoretical categories through an engagement with history and sociology. This chapter will be devoted to bringing out and summarizing the main arguments presented at length in the preceding chapters. As well as outlining the main contributions of the book, the final section of this chapter will explicitly relate what has been said in the preceding chapters to the end of the Cold War.

The book began with the premise that the dominant understanding(s) of the Cold War within the discipline of IR have not addressed its historical and sociological uniqueness in international history. This largely derived from the understating of the significance of the Bolshevik Revolution's impact on international relations in the initial period after 1917, and how the form of state created by the Revolution helped determine events after 1945 in Europe and beyond. This marked an essential continuity in Soviet international relations, with the initial hostility towards the Bolsheviks continuing throughout the 1920s and 1930s, and crystallizing in the Second World War, and then after 1945 the conflict between the social forms of capitalism and communism continued until the collapse of Soviet communism in 1989–91.

The continuity in Soviet international relations and the militarized international responses to it, and to social revolution more generally, suggest that the Cold War was not about 'traditional' great-power conflict. Rather, the Cold War was a conflict founded upon the internal configuration of revolutionary states, which meant that not only did that domestic constitution reduce the possibility of a political accommodation with capitalist states, but also that these types of state expanded in such a way that could only be contained through a militarized response. The source and dynamic of the Cold War, then, derived from the outcomes of revolutionary sociopolitical transformation that began in 1917 with the Bolshevik Revolution and continued up until the 1980s.

Furthermore, and this concerns the discussion of the end of the Cold War, we cannot collapse the Cold War into US–Soviet conflict alone. Although the strategic conflict between the United States and the Soviet Union was the most intense and the most dangerous of the Cold War, not only was this bilateral relationship mediated via social conflict within and between other states, but the dynamic of the Cold War emerged, as did the Bolshevik Revolution and the Soviet state, out of the contradictions and conflicts within the development and expansion of capitalist modernity. The Cold War was about the construction of states through social revolution that overthrew the domestic ruling regime and contested the international capitalist order. This was the reason why it was a global conflict. It was not reducible to a state, but rather was the spread of a distinct form of politics that emerged out of the conflicts within capitalist modernity. And rather than seeing the end of the Cold War as being about the collapse of the Soviet bloc in Eastern Europe, we should see it as one of a series of ends, based on the political defeats of the communist–revolutionary challenge that began in 1917, to the international capitalist order. Thus, the importance of 1989 was that it signalled the final end of a distinct type of politics of contestation, which had been contained or defeated earlier in other parts of the world.

The historical sociology of the Cold War that I have outlined in this book consisted of the three elements discussed in Part I, the politics of the state, the nature and role of military power, and how social revolution was a unique political response to capitalist expansion. The conceptual discussion was then related to the histories of social revolution in Cuba and Vietnam as reflective of the shifting international dynamic of the Cold War and the different responses of the United States and the USSR.

Politics and the State

The argument presented in the preceding chapters was that the state needs to be seen in sociological terms as a modern form of politics that emerged alongside the development of capitalism. In this sense the modern state is defined by its unique social characteristics based on the way it relates to society. With respect to the Cold War, the defining distinction in the nature of the major states involved in it was that between capitalist states like the United States and the states of Western Europe, and those states based on the overthrow of capitalism and the construction of alternative forms of politics exemplified by the USSR and other revolutionary states.

What followed from this sociological assumption was that not only was the domestic politics of the superpowers determined by the relationship between the formal rule of the state with the realm of socioeconomic production, but also that this domestic organization of social relations determined the *form* of and their respective relationships with the international system. Whereas the United States was a capitalist state, defined by the interaction between the sphere of formal political authority located in the institutions and agents of the state and the sphere of capitalist civil society, the USSR was configured by an absence of this relationship, in that private and non-state sources of power had been eliminated. The social constitution of each superpower rested on different social structures, relations and different patterns of political authority. Within the United States there was a differentiation (though not static and not always clear) between the sphere of public and coercive power, the state, and the power relations in the realm of private capitalist production and exchange, which meant that politics and power were not reducible to the state and its coercive organs. Whereas in the USSR power was centralized and monopolized in the coercive–militarized apparatus of the Party-state.

The political consequences of the differences in each superpower's internal social and political order went beyond the domestic, in the sense that because of the centralization of political power in the Party-state, the USSR could only relate to other states and the international system in one way, through the Party-state. Thus Soviet international politics was confined to a politics of the state and its coercive organs, rather than recognizing a distinction between formal political relations and private economic relations that characterized the international relations of capitalist states. The Soviet Union did not have economic or cultural relations with other states, because these 'separate' spheres of social activity did not exist. Rather, all relations, domestic and international, political and economic, were reducible to the all-encompassing power of the Party-state.

The significance of the social constitution of the superpowers, and of the USSR in particular, was related not only to the form of each state's international relations, but also to the way in which such a form was conditioned by the ideological orientation and international objectives of each state, and how they could achieve them. Thus, whereas the United States could pursue political *and* economic objectives through formal state-to-state relations and also through international economic relations derived from its capitalist nature, the Soviet Union could only secure its objectives in an explicitly political way. Moreover, while the international politics of the USSR was confined to the organs and relations of the Party-state, such that political expansion could only come through the direct and coercive expansion of the Soviet state, American capitalist expansion was not reducible to the state. Because of the relative autonomy of private capitalist relations and the economic logic of competition and accumulation, the outcomes of American international relations were not attributable solely to the agency of the US state, but also to the diffuse agency of capitalist economic production and exchange. The clearest example of this was to be found in the division of Europe after 1945 and the way in which each superpower sought to achieve its political, economic and military objectives: through direct political–military occupation in the case of the USSR, as opposed to indirect and largely economic structures in the case of the United States.

Military Power as a Currency of Politics

The crucial distinction that the postwar division of Europe highlighted in each superpower's international relations as derived from each state's respective domestic politics was found in the nature and role of its military power. How military power was determinant for the international relations of the Cold War related to the role it played in the realization and reproduction of American capitalism and Soviet communism.

It was not only the fact that politics was reduced to the institutions and agents of the Party-state in the USSR, but also that Soviet politics was much more directly coercive and militarized. Coercive and military power played a much greater role in the domestic politics of revolutionary states such as the Soviet Union because of the domestic and international problems that they confronted. In the case of the domestic problems, the socioeconomic objectives of the Soviet revolutionary regime required a forced and rapid development of the economy that entailed state-directed coercion of large sections of the population. Although such direct coercion, exemplified by the Stalin period, did not continue with the same intensity throughout the USSR's entire existence, because social and economic problems and conflicts were always political, and directly challenged the authority of the Party-state, the USSR continued to rely on coercion and military power to maintain communist power within the USSR and in the wider Soviet bloc and the international communist movement.

In the case of the latter, the USSR had to confront, at its birth, international sponsored counter-revolution. Thus, military power was essential for its survival. However, the role of military power went beyond this, in that Soviet international expansion rested on the destruction of all alternative sources of politics that might challenge communist authority. This required not only a communist presence but also a Soviet military presence as in Eastern Europe after 1945. Because of the coercive and militarized edge that tended to characterize Soviet expansion, then, it was always likely to provoke a Western militarized response, because the only way in which the USSR could be contained was through the threat of greater military force.

Because of the limitation of Soviet international politics to the external projection of military power, the USSR was much more sensitive to geopolitical discipline than the United States. This was not only because of the strategic-nuclear advantage that the United States had over the USSR for most of the Cold War, but because Soviet international expansion was *contingent* either on a geopolitical space that permitted it to project its military power without the risk of provoking a direct conflict with the United States, as it did in the 1970s after the American defeat in IndoChina, or on expansion through its political and military support of revolutionary states that had seized power through the violent overthrow

of the state. However, Soviet military power was not just a means of securing revolutionary states and deterring an escalation in US military hostility
towards such states, but was also the principal means by which to incorporate these states into the discipline and order of the Soviet bloc, thus not
only securing Soviet strategic advantage over the United States, but also
reducing possible fissures and fractures within the communist movement
as exemplified by the Sino-Soviet split.

This contrasted with the role of military power in the politics of the
advanced capitalist states. After 1945, for the first time, inter-capitalist
relations were largely free from military conflict; furthermore, international capitalist consolidation and expansion in Europe and the Third
World did not (always) require the systematic use of coercive–militarized
relations. Moreover, whereas the Soviet bloc was held together through the
coercive–military power of the Party-state and the Red Army, the Western
alliance was held together by a wider and more diffuse set of relations
based on international capitalist exchange and shared liberal democratic
values that did not have to rely on force in the same way as the Soviet bloc.
However, what determined the role of military power in American international relations was not only the domestic nature of American politics,
but the nature of the political challenge to American power. Because of
the proliferation of challenges after 1945 in the Third World, and because
most of those challenges derived from revolutionary and communist
movements dedicated to the overthrow of capitalism, the United States
used force, since this was the only means by which it could contain and
defeat such challenges. Thus it was not the case that the United States was
more pacific in its international relations than the USSR, but whether or
not political challenges to American international order could be contained within the structures of capitalist states. When such challenges
sought the overthrow of the state, the US response, more often than not,
was military intervention.

Capitalism and Revolutionary Social Transformation

Military power was the defining feature of the Cold War, largely because
of the domestic nature of the Soviet Union and the form of its international relations, and because of this, the way in which it provoked
Western military responses. Such responses, however, were not confined to
the USSR, as the Cold War did not see direct conflict between the superpowers, but between the United States, and other capitalist states, and
other revolutionary–communist states. Thus, the third theoretical issue in
our understanding of the Cold War relates to why and how it came to dominate world politics and go beyond the superpower bilateral relationship.

The dynamic of the Cold War was social revolution, the convulsions that erupted mainly after 1945 in the Third World, where forms of developing capitalist states were overthrown and the states reconstituted in ways similar to the USSR. Social Revolution was a product of the uneven expansion of international capitalism and, in particular, the manner in which a number of states were incorporated into the capitalist world economy, and the contradictions and tensions that followed from the imperialist legacy. Just as the USSR abolished non-state (capitalist) sources of political power, so did the social revolutions in China, Korea, Cuba, Vietnam and elsewhere. And, despite the differences between revolutionary states, all were also constituted by a politics characterized by coercive and militarized relations. Although this varied from state to state, it was the combination of the abolition of the sphere of private capitalist socio-economic relations alongside the aggressive pursuit of the 'export' of revolution that led to hostile and militarized responses from Western capitalist states.

Thus, the dynamic of the Cold War from 1917 onwards was located in the level of the political contestation, within states, of the international capitalist order. Whereas the advanced capitalist states (after two world wars) were able successfully to manage the tensions and conflicts within capitalism through a mixture of democratic reform and economic growth, many developing capitalist states were riven by conflicts that could not be contained within the existing form of the state. One outcome of this was social revolution, which entailed not only the overthrow of the domestic social and political regime, but also a wider challenge to the international order.

It was not, however, only the local challenge of social revolution that fuelled the Cold War, but the fact that social revolution provided the USSR with its only means of international expansion other than direct military occupation. Therefore local Cold Wars became incorporated into the global–strategic Cold War, as US–Soviet hostility was mediated through their responses to social revolution.

The Ends of the Cold War

The historical developments within capitalist modernity that saw the contestation of capitalism and its overthrow in social revolution provided the international and social dynamic of the Cold War. The events in the Soviet bloc in 1989–91 were part of this dynamic, as they clearly reflected the internal contradictions and problems within communist–revolutionary states. However, although one would be right in suggesting that the Soviet bloc was facing major political and economic problems by the late 1980s, these problems do not in themselves explain the collapse of communist power. Rather, the collapse came with the emergence of alternative sources of politics and power that challenged the supremacy of the Party-state. Whereas in the past these forms of alternative politics had been quashed, they were allowed to flourish with the acquiescence of the Soviet leader Gorbachev.

The ending of the Brezhnev Doctrine effectively reduced the political power of the local Party-state by undermining the coercive basis of its authority based on Soviet political and military power. With this opening, alternative currencies, within society at large and also within communist parties, emerged to challenge the existing configuration of political order with an alternative (Western-derived) conception of politics. However, what is important in these developments was that just as revolutionary social transformation (imposed by the USSR after 1945) had abolished the distinction between public and private, political and economic, so the changes initiated by Gorbachev and manifested in Eastern Europe in 1989 served to renegotiate those boundaries. Not only this, the relationship between the domestic and international was also reconstituted.

Because of the justified hostility to the authoritarian–coercive nature of the existing form of politics, the focus of people's concern was to remove the obvious political authoritarianism of Party-state rule. However, this internal political goal was infused with the renegotiation of the relationship between the domestic and international. The subsequent redefinition of politics, then, saw the removal of Party-state power over the economy, and alongside this the opening of this newly 'liberated' private sphere to the international. This came not only in the importing of capital and commodities from the West, but also in terms of travel and the lifting of other restrictions on the freedom of the individual.

The result was that the foundations were laid for the penetration by capitalist social relations of the Soviet bloc. This is not to suggest that it was an even and determined process. There were great variations between different countries. But the institutional and organizational foundations were laid for the separation of the spheres of political rule and social–material production. With the removal of Soviet military power and the coercive apparatus, the state, because it had become so alienated from wider society, was left detached and without *active* support. This made it easier for alternative currencies of politics to emerge and grow, particularly when the internal political vacuum had been pierced by the influx of Western capitalist influence.

The situation within the USSR itself was slightly different. Gorbachev's internal programme of *reforming* the relationship between the Party-state and the economy was also premised on renegotiating the international position of the USSR. This, for Gorbachev, was an admission that the USSR's international relations could not facilitate continued material development. Gorbachev's reforms highlighted the linkage between the internal politics of the USSR and its international relations. The change in one realm could not be achieved without change in the other.

Because of the nature of the USSR's international relations, a new political dispensation, not based on a coercive–military politics, rested on the need to redefine the relationship between Party-state and society within the USSR. Without this the USSR would not have been able to offer an alternative form of international relations. Gorbachev recognized, then, the need for a reconstitution of the currency of Soviet politics. Thus, the transformation of Soviet international relations required, indeed, was *determined* by, a change in the USSR's internal constitution. However, the ability to achieve this depended not only on positive internal changes, but also on the transformation of the content of those relations, without which there was little likelihood that his hope of demilitarizing Soviet international relations could be realized. This amounted to a public commitment to assure the United States that the USSR would not try to expand its international influence through supporting revolution and thus challenging American power. With this, the ideological and political link that had defined Soviet foreign policy since 1917 was finally broken. The USSR committed itself to instituting conventional international relations with all states rather than to seeking to prioritize unique relations with specific kinds of state based on the communist revolutionary challenge to capitalism.

The severing of the link between the USSR and international social revolution effectively terminated the possibility of the USSR continuing to offer an international political alternative to Western capitalism. This was an indication of the magnitude of the internal material cost to the USSR to which the link had contributed in the Cold War, particularly when that link was at its most pronounced in political–military relations. However, it went beyond this to include the wider contestation of the American capitalist-led international order. The Cold War finally ended in 1989 with the USSR closing the department of the Party-state dedicated to fostering links with international revolutionary movements. However, this focus on the events of 1989, important though they were, needs to be related to wider international and historical developments.

Although the superpower relationship at times conditioned the Cold War, the dynamic of the Cold War actually lay in the politics of the contestation of the postwar international order, particularly the conscious attempts by specific forms of communist and revolutionary political agency to challenge the international capitalist order and reconstitute alternative forms of politics. If this proposal is accepted as valid, then, although the Cold War may finally have ended in 1989, these events should not be seen in isolation from the 'ends' in terms of the failure or containment of revolutionary and socialist alternatives to capitalism that were found in other parts of the world. Such ends were directly tied up with the conduct of the United States and the USSR, particularly after the Second World War in Western Europe, where the revolutionary left found itself within a social and historical conjuncture favourable to radical social transformation. It was principally the actions of the United States in Western Europe, where it used its political and economic presence to support local non-communist forces, that had a major impact on subsequent developments there. In this sense, the hopes of radical social and political transformation in Western Europe were to be lost by 1947–8, with the isolation of communists and other radicals, and was not helped by Soviet actions in the east. The internal 'revolutionary' challenge to the capitalist order in Western Europe had been either incorporated into the institutions of the status quo or effectively marginalized. In effect the Cold War within Europe was over, with the internal political defeat of the radical left.

However, this was not the case elsewhere. With decolonization and the transformation of political structures throughout the world, political power was contested and with this the relationship between political power and the economy. These challenges were not temporally or geographically confined, but reflected the power of class-based movements, and the forces of the status quo usually supported by the United States. The Cold War continued from one 'theatre of conflict' to another, in one area being decided by force of arms, in another by democratic procedure. Whereas the Cold War ended in Western Europe by the late 1940s and in Eastern Europe by the late 1980s, it ended in Chile in 1973, in Indonesia in 1965, and in China in 1977. It depended on the local strengths of the revolutionary left and the existing state opposing it. Whereas for most of the post-1917 period the international revolutionary left could look to secure some guidance and support from the USSR, with the transformation of the USSR under Gorbachev the legacy of 1917 was finally laid to rest.

The 'ends' of the Cold War defy a single temporal and geographical position. Yet the collapse of the Soviet bloc was a monumental conclusion to the failure of the revolutionary left to foster an alternative internal and international politics. Although the Cold War in Latin America, southern Africa and south-east Asia was about the *local* political conflicts that were generalized as challenges to the local and international capitalist order, their long-term strength and viability was partly conditional on securing degrees of economic and military support from the USSR. With the collapse of the politics of the USSR, not only did the USSR withdraw from contesting international politics itself, but the local manifestations of that politics, in terms of ideology, organization and strategy, disintegrated. Thus, although international revolution was *not* reducible to either the policy or the form of the Soviet state, it *was* reducible to the actuality of its international existence and the social and political relations that it instituted. Without the Soviet bloc, as a material, social, political and military presence, there was no international alternative to capitalism.

Bibliography

Alperovitz, G., *Cold War Essays* (Garden City, NJ: Anchor Books, 1970).

An, Tai Sung, *The Vietnam War* (London: Associated University Press, 1998).

Anderson, P., 'Trostky's Interpretation of Stalinism', *New Left Review*, 139 (1983).

——, *The Tragedy of American Diplomacy*, 2nd edn (New York: Dell Publishing, 1972).

—— (ed.), *From Colony to Empire: Essays in the History of American Foreign Relations* (New York: John Wiley, 1972).

Armstrong, D. *Revolution and World Order: The Revolutionary State in International Society* (Oxford: Clarendon Press, 1993).

Armstrong, P., Glyn, A. and Harrison, J., *Capitalism since 1945* (Oxford: Basil Blackwell, 1991).

Baklanoff, E., *Expropriation of US Investments in Cuba, Mexico, and Chile* (New York: Praeger, 1975).

Baran, P. and Sweezy, P., *Monopoly Capital: An Essay on the American Economic and Social Order* (Harmondsworth: Penguin, 1968).

Barnet, R., *Intervention and Revolution: The United States in the Third World* (New York: New American Library, 1972).

Bender, L., *The Politics of Hostility: Castro's Revolution and United States Policy* (Hato Rey, Puerto Rico: Inter-American University Press, 1975).

Bettelheim, C., *Class Struggles in the USSR*, I: *First Period, 1917–1923* (Hassocks: Harvester Press, 1977).

——, *Class Struggles in the USSR*, II: *Second Period, 1923–1930* (Hassocks: Harvester Press, 1978).

Binns, P. and Gonzales, M., 'Cuba, Castro and Socialism', *International Socialism*, 2, 8 (spring 1980).

Binns, P., Cliff, T. and Harman, C. *Russia: From Workers' State to State Capitalism* (London: Bookmarks, 1987).

Black, C. and Thornton, T. (eds), *Communism and Revolution: The Strategic Uses of Political Violence* (Princeton, NJ: Princeton University Press, 1971).

Blackburn, R., 'Prologue to the Cuban Revolution', *New Left Review*, 21 (October 1963).

——, 'Class Forces in the Cuban Revolution: A Reply to Peter Binns and Mike Gonzales', *International Socialism*, 2, 9 (summer 1980).

Blasier, C., *Hovering Giant: US Responses to Revolutionary Change in Latin America* (Pittsburgh, PA: University of Pittsburgh Press, 1976).

——, *The Giant's Rival: The USSR and Latin America* (Pittsburgh, PA: University of Pittsburgh Press, 1983).

Blight, J., Allyn, B. and Welch D. *Cuba on the Brink: Castro, the Missile Crisis, and the Soviet Collapse* (New York: Pantheon Books, 1993).

Borer, D., *Superpowers Defeated: Vietnam and Afghanistan Compared* (London: Frank Cass, 1999).

Brenner, P., 'Cuba and the Missile Crisis', *Journal of Latin American Studies*, 22, 1, (February 1990).

Brenner, P. and Blight, J., 'Cuba 1962. The Crisis and Cuban–Soviet Relations: Fidel Castro's 1968 Speech', *Cold War International History Project Bulletin*, 5 (spring 1995).

Brett, E. A., *The World Economy since the War: The Politics of Uneven Development* (Basingstoke: Macmillan, 1985).

Brewer, A., *Marxist Theories of Imperialism* (London: Routledge, 1990).

Bromley, S., *Rethinking Middle East Politics: State Formation and Development* (Cambridge: Polity Press, 1994).

Bull, H., *The Anarchical Society: A Study of Order in World Politics* (London: Macmillan, 1977).

——, 'The Revolt Against the West', in H. Bull and A. Watson (eds), *The Expansion of International Society* (Oxford: Clarendon Press, 1985).

Bull, H. and Watson, A. (eds), *The Expansion of International Society* (Oxford: Clarendon Press, 1985).

Cameron, A., 'The Soviet Union and Vietnam: The Origins of Involvement', in W. Duncan (ed.), *Soviet Policy in Developing Countries* (Waltham, MA: Ginn-Blaisdell, 1970).

Cammack, P., 'Bringing the State Back In?', *British Journal of Political Science*, 19, 2 (April 1989).

Carlo, A., 'Structural Causes of the Soviet Coexistence Policy', in E. Jahn (ed.), *Soviet Foreign Policy: Its Economic and Social Conditions* (London: Allison & Busby, 1978).

Carr, E. H., *The October Revolution: Before and After* (New York: Alfred A. Knopf, 1969).

——, *The Russian Revolution From Lenin to Stalin (1917–1929)* (Basingstoke: Macmillan, 1979).

Carr, R., 'The Cold War in Latin America', in J. Plank (ed.), *Cuba and the United States: Long Range Perspectives* (Washington, DC: The Brookings Institution, 1967).

Checkel, J., *Ideas and Political Change: Soviet/Russian Behaviour and the End of the Cold War* (New Haven, CT: Yale University Press, 1997).

Cliff, T., *State Capitalism in Russia Today* (London: Bookmarks, 1988).

Cliff, T. and Harman, C., *Russia: Workers' State to State Capitalism* (London: Bookmarks, 1987).

Corrigan, P., Ramsay, H. and Sayer, D. *Socialist Construction and Marxist Theory: Bolshevism and Its Critique* (London: Macmillan, 1978).

——, 'The State as a Relation of Production', in P. Corrigan (ed.), *Capitalism, State Formation and Marxist Theory* (London: Quartet Books, 1980).

Cox, M., 'Western Capitalism and the Cold War System', in M. Shaw (ed.), *War, State and Society* (London: Macmillan, 1984).

——, 'From Détente to the "New Cold War": The Crisis of the Cold War System', *Millennium: Journal of International Studies*, 15, 3 (winter 1984).

——, 'The Cold War in the Age of Capitalist Decline', *Critique*, 17 (1986).

——, 'The Soviet-American Conflict in the Third World', in P. Shearman and P. Williams (eds), *The Superpowers, Central America and the Middle East* (London: Brassey's, 1988).

——, 'Whatever Happened to the "Second" Cold War? Soviet–American Relations, 1980–88', *Review of International Studies*, 16, 2 (April 1990).

——, 'From Truman Doctrine to the Second Cold War. Superpower Détente: The Rise and Fall of the Cold War', *Journal of Peace Research*, 27, 1 (February 1990).

——, 'The Revolutionary Betrayed: *The New Left Review* and Leon Trotsky', in M. Cox and H. Ticktin (eds), *The Ideas of Leon Trotsky* (London: Porcupine Press, 1995).

Cox, R., *Production, Power, and World Order. Social Forces in the Making of History* (New York: Columbia University Press, 1987).

Crockatt, R., *The Fifty Years War: The United States and the Soviet Union in World Politics, 1941–1991* (London: Routledge, 1995).

Dacy, D., *Foreign Aid, War, and Economic Development: South Vietnam, 1955–1975* (Cambridge: Cambridge University Press, 1986).

Davis, M., 'Nuclear Imperialism and Extended Deterrence', in *New Left Review* (ed.), *Exterminism and Cold War* (London: New Left Books, 1982).

Deudney, D. and Ikenberry, G. John, 'Soviet Reform and the End of the Cold War: Explaining Large Scale Historical Change', *Review of International Studies*, 17, 3 (1991).

——, 'The International Sources of Soviet Change', *International Security*, 16, 3 (winter 1991–92).

Deutscher, I., *The Great Contest: Russia and the West* (London: Oxford University Press, 1960).

——, *Ironies of History: Essays on Contemporary Communism* (London: Oxford University Press, 1966).

——, *The Unfinished Revolution, Russia 1917–1967* (London: Oxford University Press, 1967).

——, *Russia, China, and the West*, ed. Fred Halliday (Harmondsworth: Penguin Books, 1970).

——, *Marxism, Wars and Revolutions: Essays From Four Decades* (London: Verso, 1984).

——, *Stalin: A Political Biography* (London: Penguin, 1988).

Dibb, P., *The Soviet Union: Incomplete Superpower* (Basingstoke: Macmillan, 1986).

Dinerstein, H., *The Making of a Missile Crisis: October 1962* (Baltimore, MD: Johns Hopkins University Press, 1976).

Doyle, M., 'Liberalism and World Politics', *American Political Science Review*, 80, 4 (December, 1986).

Duiker, W., 'The Red Soviets of Nghe-Tinh: An Early Communist Rebellion in Vietnam', *Journal of Southeast Asian Studies*, 4, 2 (September 1973).

——, *US Containment Policy and the Conflict in Indochina* (Stanford, CA: Stanford University Press, 1994).

——, *The Communist Road to Power in Vietnam*, 2nd edn (Boulder, CO: Westview Press, 1996).

Duncan, W., *The Soviet Union and Cuba: Interests and Influence* (New York: Praeger, 1985).

Duncan, W. (ed.), *Soviet Policy in Developing Countries* (Waltham, MA: Ginn-Blaisdell, 1970).

Ellsberg, D., 'Introduction: Call to Mutiny', in E. P. Thompson and D. Smith (eds), *Protest and Survive* (New York: Monthly Review Press, 1981).

Farber, S., *Revolution and Reaction in Cuba, 1933–1960: A Political Sociology from Machado to Castro* (Middletown, CT: Wesleyan University Press, 1976).

Feinberg, R., *The Intemperate Zone: The Third World Challenge to US Foreign Policy* (New York: W. W. Norton, 1983).

Fowkes, B., *The Rise and Fall of Communism in Eastern Europe* (New York: St Martin's Press, 1993).

Fursenko, A. and Naftali, T., *'One Hell of a Gamble': Khrushchev, Castro, Kennedy and the Cuban Missile Crisis, 1958–1964* (London: John Murray, 1997).

Gaddis, J. L., *Strategies of Containment: A Critical Appraisal of Postwar American National Security Policy* (New York: Oxford University Press, 1982).

——, 'The Emerging Post-Revisionist Synthesis on the Origins of the Cold War', *Diplomatic History*, 7, 3 (summer 1983).

——, *The Long Peace: Enquiries into the History of the Cold War* (New York: Oxford University Press, 1987).

——, 'International Relations Theory and the End of the Cold War,' *International Security*, 17, 3 (winter 1992).

——, *The United States and the End of the Cold War: Implications, Reconsiderations, Provocations* (New York: Oxford University Press, 1992).

——, 'The Cold War, the Long Peace, and the Future', in M. Hogan (ed.), *The End of the Cold War: Its Meaning and Implications* (Cambridge: Cambridge University Press, 1992).

——, *We Now Know: Rethinking Cold War History* (Oxford: Clarendon Press, 1997).

Gaiduk, I., 'The Vietnam War and Soviet–American Relations, 1964–73: New Evidence', *Cold War International History Project Bulletin*, 6–7 (winter 1995–96).

——, *The Soviet Union and the Vietnam War* (Chicago: Ivan R. Dee, 1996).

——, 'Soviet Policy Towards US Participation in the Vietnam War', *History*, 81, 261 (January 1996).

——, 'Developing an Alliance: The Soviet Union and Vietnam: 1954–75', in P. Lowe (ed.), *The Vietnam War* (Basingstoke: Macmillan, 1998).

Gardner, L., *Approaching Vietnam: From World War Two Through Dienbienphu, 1941–1954* (New York: W. W. Norton, 1988).

Garthoff, R., 'Why Did the Cold War Arise and Why Did it End?' in M. Hogan (ed.), *The End of the Cold War: Its Meaning and Implications* (Cambridge: Cambridge University Press, 1992).

——, *The Great Transition: American–Soviet Relations and the End of the Cold War* (Washington, DC: Brookings Institution, 1994).

Gidwitz, B., 'Labour Unrest in the Soviet Union', *Problems of Communism*, 31, 6 (November–December 1982).

Gribkov, A. and Smith, W., *Operation Anadyr. US and Soviet Generals Recount the Cuban Missile Crisis* (Chicago: Edition Q, 1994).

Halliday, F., *The Making of the Second Cold War*, 2nd edn (London: Verso, 1986).

——, *From Kabul to Managua: Soviet–American Relations in the 1980s* (New York: Pantheon Books, 1989).

——, 'Revolution in the Third World: 1945 and After', in E. E. Rice (ed.), *Revolution and Counter-Revolution* (Oxford: Basil Blackwell, 1991).

——, *Rethinking International Relations* (Basingstoke: Macmillan, 1994).

——, 'Interpreting the Cold War: Neither Geostrategy nor Internalism', *Contention*, 14, 1 (fall 1994).

——, *Revolution and World Politics: The Rise and Fall of the Sixth Great Power* (London: Macmillan, 1999).

Harman, C. *Class Struggles in Eastern Europe, 1945–83* (London: Bookmarks, 1988).

Herring, G., *America's Longest War: The United States and Vietnam, 1950–1975* (New York: John Wiley, 1979).

Hershberg, J., 'New Evidence on the Cuban Missile Crisis: More Documents from the Russian Archives', *Cold War International History Project Bulletin,* 8–9 (winter 1996–97).

Hobsbawm, E., *Age of Extremes: The Short Twentieth Century 1914–1991* (London: Michael Joseph, 1994).

Hogan, M., *The Marshall Plan: America, Britain and the Reconstruction of Western Europe, 1947–1952* (Cambridge: Cambridge University Press, 1987).

Holloway, D., 'War, Militarism and the Soviet State', in E. P. Thompson and D. Smith (eds), *Protest and Survive* (Harmondsworth: Penguin Books, 1980).

——, *The Soviet Union and the Arms Race*, 2nd edn (New Haven, CT: Yale University Press, 1984).

Holloway, J. and Picciotto, S. (eds), *State and Capital: A Marxist Debate* (London: Edward Arnold, 1978).

Horowitz, D., *From Yalta to Vietnam: American Foreign Policy in the Cold War* (Harmondsworth: Penguin, 1967).

——, *Imperialism and Revolution* (London: Allen Lane, 1969).

Horowitz, D. (ed.), *Containment and Revolution: Western Policy Towards Social Revolution, 1917 to Vietnam* (London: Anthony Blond, 1967).

——, *Corporations and the Cold War* (New York: Monthly Review Press, 1969).

Hough, J., *The Struggle for the Third World: Soviet Debates and American Options* (Washington, DC: Brookings Institution, 1985).

Huntington, S., *Political Order in Changing Societies* (New Haven, CT: Yale University Press, 1968).

Iriye, A., *The Cold War in Asia: A Historical Introduction* (Englewood, NJ: Prentice-Hall, 1974).

Jervis, R., *Perception and Misperception in International Politics* (Princeton, NJ: Princeton University Press, 1976).

Jian, C., 'China and the First Indo-China War, 1950–54', *China Quarterly*, 133 (March 1993).

——, 'China's Involvement in the Vietnam War, 1964–69', *China Quarterly*, 142 (June 1995).

——, 'Personal–Historical puzzles About China and the Vietnam War', in O. A. Westad, C. Jian, S. Tønnesson, N. Vu Tung and J. Hershberg (eds), *77 Conversations Between Chinese and Foreign Leaders on the Wars in Indochina*, Cold War International History Project Working Papers 22 (May 1998).

Johnson, L., 'United States Business Interests in Cuba and the Rise of Castro', *World Politics*, 17, 3 (April 1965).

Jones, C., 'Soviet Allies in Europe: The Warsaw Pact', in R. Menon and D. Nelson (eds), *Limits to Soviet Power* (Lexington, MA: Lexington Books, 1989).

Kahin, G., *Intervention: How America Became Involved in Vietnam* (New York: Alfred A. Knopf, 1986).

Kaldor, M., *The Disintegrating West* (Harmondsworth: Penguin, 1978).

——, 'Warfare and Capitalism', in *New Left Review* (ed.), *Exterminism and Cold War* (London: New Left Books, 1982).

——, *The Baroque Arsenal* (London: André Deutsch, 1983).

——, *The Imaginary War: Understanding the East–West Conflict* (Oxford: Basil Blackwell, 1990).

Kaldor, M., Holden, G. and Falk, R. (eds), *The New Détente: Rethinking East–West Relations* (London: Verso, 1989).

Karol, K. S., *Guerrillas in Power: The Course of the Cuban Revolution* (London: Jonathan Cape, 1971).

Kaufman, B., *Trade and Aid: Eisenhower's Foreign Economic Policy, 1953–1961* (Baltimore: Johns Hopkins University Press, 1982).

Kautsky, J., *Communism and the Politics of Development: Persistent Myths and Changing Behaviour* (New York: John Wiley & Sons, 1968).

Kautsky, J. (ed.), *Political Change in Underdeveloped Countries: Nationalism and Communism* (New York: Robert E. Krieger, 1976).

Kegley, C. Jr (ed.), *The Long Postwar Peace: Contending Explanations and Projections* (New York: HarperCollins, 1991).

Kennan, G., 'X' Article, 'The Sources of Soviet Conduct', *Foreign Affairs*, 25, 4 (July 1947).

——, *Realities of American Foreign Policy* (London: Oxford University Press, 1954).

——, *Russia and the West Under Lenin and Stalin* (Boston, MA: Little, Brown, 1960).

——, *Memoirs, 1950–1963* (London: Hutchinson, 1972).

——, *Soviet Foreign Policy, 1917–1941* (Westport,CT: Greenwood Press, 1978).

——, *The Nuclear Delusion: Soviet–American Relations in the Atomic Age* (New York: Pantheon Books, 1982).

——, *American Diplomacy* (Chicago, IL: University of Chicago Press, 1984).

Kennedy, P., *The Rise and Fall of the Great Powers: Economic Change and Military Conflict from 1500 to 2000* (London: Fontana, 1989).

Kidron, M., *Western Capitalism Since the War*, revised edn (Harmondsworth: Penguin, 1970).

——, *A Permanent Arms Economy* (London: Socialist Workers' Party, 1989).

Kiernan, B., *The United States, Communism and the Emergent World* (Bloomington: Indiana University Press, 1972).

Kim Khánh, H., *Vietnamese Communism, 1925–45* (Ithaca, NY: Cornell University Press, 1982).

Kissinger, H., *Diplomacy* (New York: Simon & Schuster, 1994).

Klare, M. and Amson, C., 'Exporting Repression: US Support for Authoritarianism in Latin America', in R. Fagen (ed.), *Capitalism and the State in US–Latin American Relations* (Stanford,CA: Stanford University Press, 1979).

Kolko, G., *The Roots of American Foreign Policy: An Analysis of Power and Purpose* (Boston, MA: Beacon Press, 1969).

——, *Vietnam: Anatomy of a War, 1940–1975* (London: Allen & Unwin, 1986).

——, *Confronting the Third World: United States Foreign Policy, 1945–1980* (New York: Pantheon Books, 1988).

——, *Century of War: Politics, Conflicts and Society Since 1914* (New York: The New Press, 1994).

Kopstein, J., *The Politics of Economic Decline in East Germany, 1945–1989* (Chapel Hill: University of North Carolina Press, 1997).

Koslowski, R., and Kratochwil, F., 'Understanding Change in International Politics: The Soviet Empire's Demise and the International System', *International Organization*, 48, 2 (spring 1994).

Kramer, M., 'Ideology and the Cold War', *Review of International Studies*, 25, 4 (October 1999).

——, 'The Early Post-Stalin Succession Struggle and Upheavals in East-Central Europe: Internal–External Linkages in Soviet Policy Making', *Journal of Cold War Studies*, 1, 3 (fall 1999).

Kratochwil, F., 'The Embarrassment of Changes: Neo-Realism as the Science of Realpolitik', *Review of International Studies*, 19, 1 (January 1993).

Krippendorff, E., 'Revolutionary Foreign Policy in a Capitalist Environment', in E. Jahn (ed.), *Soviet Foreign Policy: Its Social and Economic Conditions* (London: Allison & Busby, 1978).

LaFeber, W., *America, Russia and the Cold War, 1945–1992*, 7th edn (New York: McGraw-Hill, 1993).

Latham, R., *The Liberal Moment: Modernity, Security, and the Making of the Postwar International Order* (New York: Columbia University Press, 1997).

Lebow, R., 'The Long Peace, the End of the Cold War, and the Failure of Realism', *International Organization*, 48, 2 (spring 1994).

Lebow, R. and Risse-Kappen, T. (eds), *International Relations Theory and the End of the Cold War* (New York: Columbia University Press, 1995).

Lee, S., *Outposts of Empire: Korea, Vietnam, and the Origins of the Cold War in Asia, 1949–1954* (Montreal: McGill-Queen's University Press, 1995).

Lefort, C., *The Political Forms of Modern Society: Bureaucracy, Democracy, Totalitarianism*, edited and introduced by J. Thompson (Oxford: Polity Press, 1986).

Lenin, V. I., Imperialism, *The Highest Stage of Capitalism* (Moscow: Progress Publishers, 1934).

Lévesque, J., *The USSR and the Cuban Revolution: Soviet Ideological and Strategical Perspectives, 1959–77* (New York: Praeger, 1978).

Light, M., *The Soviet Theory of International Relations* (Brighton: Wheatsheaf, 1988).

Lipson, C., *Standing Guard: Protecting Foreign Capital in the Nineteenth and Twentieth Centuries* (Berkeley: University of California Press, 1985).

Long, N. Vinh, 'South Vietnam', in P. Lowe (ed.), *The Vietnam War* (Basingstoke: Macmillan, 1998).

Lowenthal, A. (ed.), *Exporting Democracy: The United States and Latin America: Themes and Issues* (Baltimore, MD: Johns Hopkins University Press, 1991).

Lowenthal, R., *Model or Ally. The Communist Powers and the Developing Countries* (New York: Oxford University Press, 1977).

Löwy, M., *The Politics of Combined and Uneven Development: The Theory of Permanent Revolution* (London: Verso, 1981).

Lundestad, G., *'Empire' by Invitation: The United States and European Integration, 1945–1997* (Oxford: Oxford University Press, 1998).

Lynch, A., *The Cold War Is Over – Again* (Boulder, CO: Westview Press, 1992).

Lyons, P., 'New States and International Order', in A. James (ed.), *The Bases of International Order* (Oxford: Oxford University Press, 1973).

Macdonald, D., *Adventures in Chaos: American Intervention for Reform in the Third World* (London: Harvard University Press, 1992).

Maier, C., 'The Politics of Productivity: Foundations of American International Economic Policy after World War Two', *International Organization*, 31, 4 (1977).

——, 'Alliance and Autonomy: European Identity and US Foreign Policy Objectives in the Truman Years', in M. Lacey (ed.), *The Truman Presidency* (Cambridge: Cambridge University Press, 1989).

Mandel, E., *The Meaning of the Second World War* (London: Verso, 1986).

Mann, M., *States, War and Capitalism: Studies in Political Sociology* (Oxford: Basil Blackwell, 1988).

Marx, K., *Capital*, I (Harmondsworth: Penguin Books, 1990 [1867]).

Marx, K. and Engels, F., *Collected Works*, III (London: Lawrence & Wishart, 1975).

Mattocks, B., *The Establishment of the International Financial Corporation and United States Policy* (New York: Praeger, 1957).

Mayer, A., *The Politics and Diplomacy of Peacemaking: Containment and Counterrevolution at Versailles 1918–1919* (London: Weidenfeld & Nicolson, 1968).

J. Mearsheimer, 'Back to the Future: Instability in Europe after the Cold War', *International Security*, 15, 1 (summer 1990).

Melanson, R., *Writing History and Making Policy: The Cold War, Vietnam, and Revisionism*, VI (Lanham, MD: University Press of America, 1983).

Melman, S., *The Permanent War Economy: American Capitalism in Decline* (New York: Simon & Schuster, 1974).

Mikesell, R., *US Private and Government Investment Abroad* (Eugene, OR: University of Oregon Books, 1962).

Miller, N., *Soviet Relations with Latin America* (Cambridge: Cambridge University Press, 1989).

Milliband, R., 'State Power and Class Interests', *New Left Review*, 138 (March–April 1983).

Mintz, S. 'Foreward', in R. Guerra y Sanchez, *Sugar and Society in the Caribbean: An Economic History of Cuban Agriculture* (New Haven, CT: Yale University Press, 1964).

Montgomery, J., *The Politics of Foreign Aid: American Experience in Southeast Asia* (New York: Frederick A. Praeger, 1962).

Moore, B., *The Social Origins of Dictatorship and Development: Lord and Peasant in the Making of the Modern World* (London: Penguin Books, 1967).

Morgenthau, H., *Politics Among Nations: The Struggle for Power and Peace* (New York: Alfred A. Knopf, 1948).

——, *Vietnam and the United States* (Washington: Public Affairs Press, 1965).

Morley, M., *Imperial State and Revolution: The United States and Cuba, 1952–1986* (Cambridge: Cambridge University Press, 1987).

Morris, S., *The Soviet–Chinese–Vietnamese Triangle in the 1970s: The View from Moscow,* Cold War International History Project Working Papers 25 (April 1999).

Murray, M., *The Development of Capitalism in Colonial Indochina* (Los Angeles: University of California Press, 1980).

Nation, R., *Black Earth, Red Star: A History of Soviet Security Policy, 1917–1991* (New York: Columbia University Press, 1992).

Nelson, K., *The Making of Détente: Soviet–American Relations in the Shadow of Vietnam* (Baltimore, MD: Johns Hopkins University Press, 1995).

Nove, A., *An Economic History of the USSR, 1917–1991* (Harmondsworth: Penguin, 1992).

O'Connor, J., 'Cuba: Its Political Economy', in R. Bonachea and N. Valdés (eds), *Cuba in Revolution* (Garden City, NJ: Anchor Books, 1972).

Packenham, R., *Liberal America and the Third World: Political Development Ideas in Foreign Aid and Social Science* (Princeton, NJ: Princeton University Press, 1973).

Papp, D., *Vietnam: The View From Moscow, Peking, Washington* (Jefferson, North Carolina: McFarland, 1981).

Pavlov, Y., *Soviet–Cuban Alliance: 1959–1991* (Miami, FL: North–South Centre Press/University of Miami Press, 1994).

Pérez, L., *Cuba and the United States: Ties of Singular Intimacy* (Athens, GA: University of Georgia Press, 1990).

Pérez-Stable, M., *The Cuban Revolution: Origins, Course and Legacy* (New York: Oxford University Press, 1999).

Petras, J., 'Socialist Revolutions and their Class Components', *New Left Review*, 111 (September–October 1978).

——, *Critical Perspectives on Imperialism and Social Class in the Third World* (New York: Monthly Review Press, 1978).

Petras, J., Morley, M., DeWitt, P. and Havens, A. Eugene (eds), *Class, State and Power in the Third World* (London: Zed Press, 1981).

Plamenatz, J., *German Marxism and Russian Communism* (London: Longman, Green,1954).

Pollard, R., *Economic Security and the Origins of the Cold War: The Strategic Ends of US Foreign Policy, 1945–1950* (New York: Columbia University Press, 1985).

Porter, G., *Vietnam: The Politics of Bureaucratic Socialism* (Ithaca, NY: Cornell University Press, 1993).

Post, K., *Revolution, Socialism and Nationalism in Viet Nam*, I: *An Interrupted Revolution* (Aldershot: Dartmouth, 1989).

——, *Revolution, Socialism and Nationalism in Viet Nam*, II: *Viet Nam Divided* (Aldershot: Dartmouth, 1989).

——, *Revolution, Socialism and Nationalism in Viet Nam*, IV: *The Failure of Counter Insurgency in the South* (Aldershot: Dartmouth, 1990).

——, *Revolution, Socialism and Nationalism in Viet Nam*, V: *Winning the War and Losing the Peace* (Aldershot: Dartmouth, 1994).

Prozumenschikov, M., 'The Sino-Indian Conflict, the Cuban Missile Crisis and the Sino-Soviet Split, October 1962: New Evidence from the Russian Archives', *Cold War International History Project Bulletin*, 8–9 (winter 1996–97).

Risse-Kappen, T., 'Did "Peace Through Strength" End the Cold War?', *International Security*, 16, 1 (Winter, 1991–92).

——, 'Ideas Do Not Float Freely: Transnational Coalitions, Domestic Structures, and the End of the Cold War', *International Organization*, 48, 2 (spring 1994).

Roberts, G., *The Soviet Union in World Politics: Coexistence, Revolution and Cold War, 1945–1991* (London: Routledge, 1999).

Rosenberg, J., *The Empire of Civil Society: A Critique of the Realist Theory of International Relations* (London: Verso, 1994).

Rostow, W. W., *The Stages of Economic Growth: A Non-Communist Manifesto* (Cambridge: Cambridge University Press, 1971).

Rousset, P., 'The Peculiarities of Vietnamese Communism', in T. Ali (ed.), *The Stalinist Legacy: Its Impact on Twentieth Century World Politics* (Boulder, CO: Lynne Reiner, 1984).

Ruffin, P., *Capitalism and Socialism in Cuba: A Study of Dependency, Development and Underdevelopment* (London: Macmillan, 1990).

Ruggie, J. G., 'Multilateralism: The Anatomy of an Institution', in J. G. Ruggie (ed.), *Multilateralism Matters: The Theory and Praxis of an Institutional Form* (New York: Columbia University Press, 1993).

——, *Constructing World Polity: Essays on International Institutionalization* (London: Routledge, 1998).

Rupert, M., *Producing Hegemony: The Politics of Mass Production and American Global Power* (Cambridge: Cambridge University Press, 1995).

Skocpol, T., *States and Social Revolutions: A Comparative Analysis of France, Russia and China* (Cambridge: Cambridge University Press, 1979).

Smith, R., 'Military Expenditure and Capitalism', *Cambridge Journal of Economics*, 1, 1 (1977).

Smith, Ralph, *An International History of the Vietnam War*, I, *Revolution Versus Containment, 1955–61* (London: Macmillan, 1983).

——, *An International History of the Vietnam War*, II, *The Struggle for South-East Asia, 1961–65* (London: Macmillan, 1985).

——, *An International History of the Vietnam War*, III, *The Making of a Limited War, 1965–66* (London: Macmillan, 1990).

Smith, T., 'The Alliance for Progress: The 1960s', in A. Lowenthal (ed.), *Exporting Democracy. The United States and Latin America: Themes and Issues* (Baltimore, MD: Johns Hopkins University Press, 1991).

Smith, W., *The Closest of Enemies: A Personal and Diplomatic Account of US–Cuban Relations Since 1957* (New York: W. W. Norton, 1987).

Suarez, A., *Cuba: Castroism and Communism, 1959–1966* (Cambridge, MA: The MIT Press, 1987).

Thakur, R. and Thayer, C., *Soviet Relations with India and Vietnam* (London: Macmillan, 1992).

Thomas, H., *Cuba or the Pursuit of Freedom* (London: Eyre & Spottiswoode, 1971).

Ticktin, H. *The Origins of the Crisis in the USSR: Essays on the Political Economy of a Disintegrating System* (Armonk, NY: M. E. Shape, 1992).

Tilly, C., *Coercion, Capital, and European States, AD 990–1990* (Oxford: Basil Blackwell, 1990).

Trotsky, L., *The Permanent Revolution and Results and Prospects* (London: New Park Publications, 1962).

Ulam, A., *Expansion and Coexistence: Soviet Foreign Policy, 1917–73*, 2nd edn (New York: Holt, Rinehart & Winston, 1974).

Valkeneir, E., *The Soviet Union and the Third World: An Economic Bind* (New York: Praeger, 1983).

Vance, T. *et al.*, *The Permanent War Economy* (Berkeley, CA: Independent Socialist Press, 1970).

Vincent, R. J., 'Order in International Politics', in J. Miller and R. J. Vincent (eds), *Order and Violence: Hedley Bull and International Relations* (Oxford: Clarendon Press, 1990).

Wagner, R., *United States Policy Toward Latin America: A Study in Domestic and International Politics* (Stanford, CA: Stanford University Press, 1970).

Waltz, K., *Man, the State, and War: A Theoretical Analysis* (New York: Columbia University Press, 1959).

——, *Theory of International Politics* (Reading, MA: Addison-Wesley, 1979).

——, 'Realist Thought and Neo-Realist Theory', in C. Kegley Jr (ed.), *Controversies in International Relations Theory. Realism and the Neoliberal Challenge* (New York: St Martin's Press, 1995).

Watnick, M., 'The Appeal of Communism to the Peoples of the Underdeveloped Areas', in S. M. Lipset and R. Bendix (eds), *Class, Status and Power: Social Stratifications in Comparative Perspective*, 2nd edn (London: Routledge & Kegan Paul, 1967).

Welch, R., *Response to Revolution: The United States and the Cuban Revolution, 1959–1961* (Chapel Hill: University of North Carolina Press, 1985).

Wendt, A., *Social Theory of International Politics* (Cambridge: Cambridge University Press, 1999).

Westad, O. A., 'Mao on Sino-Soviet Relations: Conversations with the Soviet Ambassador', *Cold War International Project Bulletin*, 6–7 (winter 1995–96).

Westad, O. A. (ed.), *Brothers in Arms: The Rise and Fall of the Sino-Soviet Alliance, 1945–63* (Stanford, CA: Stanford University Press, 1998).

Westad, O. A. and Jian, C. (eds), *77 Conversations Between Chinese and Foreign Leaders on the Wars in Indochina*, Cold War International History Project Working Papers 22 (May 1998).

White, G., Murray, R. and White, C. (eds), *Revolutionary Socialist Development in the Third World* (Brighton: Wheatsheaf Books, 1983).

Whitman, M. von Neumann, *Government Risk-Sharing in Foreign Investment* (Princeton, NJ: Princeton University Press, 1965).

Wiegersma, N., *Vietnam: Peasant Land, Peasant Revolution. Patriarchy and Collectivity in the Rural Economy* (London: Macmillan, 1988).

Wilkins, M., *The Maturing Multinational Enterprise: American Business Abroad from 1914 to 1970* (Cambridge, MA: Harvard University Press, 1974).

Williams, W. A., *The United States, Cuba and Castro: An Essay on the Dynamics of Revolution and Dissolution of Empire* (New York: Monthly Review Press, 1962).

Wohlforth, W., 'Realism and the End of the Cold War', *International Security*, 19, 3 (winter 1994–95).

Wood, D., 'The Long Revolution: Class Relations and Political Conflict in Cuba, 1868–1968', *Science and Society: An Independent Journal of Marxism*, 34, 1 (spring 1970).

Wood, E., *Democracy Against Capitalism: Renewing Historical Materialism* (Cambridge: Cambridge University Press, 1995.

Zeitlin, M., *Revolutionary Politics and the Cuban Working Class* (Princeton, NJ: Princeton University Press, 1967).

Zhai, Q., 'Beijing and the Vietnam Conflict, 1964–65: New Evidence', *Cold War International History Project Bulletin*, 6–7 (winter 1995–96).

Zubok, V., 'Document Two: Khrushchev's Secret Speech on the Berlin Crisis, August 1961', *Cold War International History Project Bulletin*, 1 (spring 1992).

——, '"Dismayed by the Actions of the Soviet Union": Mikoyan's Talks with Fidel Castro and the Cuban Leadership, November 1962', *Cold War International History Project Bulletin*, 5 (spring 1995).

——, 'Khrushchev's Nuclear Promise to Beijing During the 1958 Crisis', *Cold War International History Project Bulletin*, 6–7 (winter 1995–96).

Zubok, Z. and Pleshakov, C., *Inside the Kremlin's Cold War: From Stalin to Khrushchev* (Cambridge, MA: Harvard University Press, 1996).

Index